My friend Lisa Miller-Rich is a pastor-tea
anyone takes a significant word from Scrip
that person has my attention. Joy is one of
our time. Lisa, in a helpful and encouraging way, ------

MW01078227

Dr. J.K. Jones
Pastor of Spiritual Formation, Eastview Christian Church
Normal, IL
Director, Master of Arts degree, Lincoln Christian University
Lincoln, IL

Joy can feel elusive. If you've ever felt your joy flat-lining or if you've thought of joy as being "the emotion when we have everything we desire," buckle your seatbelt and prepare to explore what God says about joy. Dive in; this interactive journey will empower you to own joy that lasts.

Robin Bertram
Founder of Robin Bertram Ministries
Vice President of Christian Women in Media Association
Executive Producer of *Freedom Today* Television
Author, Speaker, and Podcaster with Charisma Podcast Network

This is the book I've been waiting for! In thirty years of ministry, I have found that the pursuit of joy is a common struggle for us all. Lisa Miller-Rich hit it out of the park with this roadmap back to the authentic joy God has for us. *218 Ways to Own Joy* is now my "go to" resource for helping people rediscover joy.

Mark Eiken
Campus Pastor, 12Stone Church
Atlanta, GA

In *218 Ways to Own Joy,* Lisa Miller-Rich challenges us to find joy no matter what by expanding on the various meanings of joy and the many ways it can show up in our lives—big joy, quiet joy, and everything in between. A thoughtfully designed Bible study of a different sort, *218 Ways to Own Joy* can be studied individually, with a friend, or with a group. Each nugget is bite sized and easy to work through at your own pace. *218 Ways to Own Joy* is an excellent tool for anyone desiring to understand and experience the fullness of joy in daily living, regardless of their circumstances.

Angela Howell
Speaker, Coach, and Author of *Finding the Gift: Daily Meditations for Mindfulness*

Open your heart and pour this stuff in! I love the way Lisa incorporates actual biblical stories with laughter and inspiration to help us understand how valuable the precious gift of joy is to our peace, hope, and contentment in life. This book is timely in teaching us how to engrave our hearts with the power of living a joyous life despite our circumstances.

Terri Allen Atwood
Licensed Professional Counselor

In a "happy-driven" world, joy often gets lost in the shuffle of human experience. Thankfully, in *218 Ways to Own Joy,* Lisa has written a readable and helpful resource that takes us on a joy tour through the Scriptures. Reading this book will help you get past fleeting happiness and into the joy God desires.

Mike Baker
Senior Pastor, Eastview Christian Church
Normal, IL

WHAT A BLAST! I laughed, pondered, meditated, prayed, and rejoiced at the revelation of discovering untapped areas of joy! From beginning to end, *218 Ways to Own Joy* stirred my heart and awakened my soul to greater potential for joy. It was not only the momentary ecstasies of joy that thrilled me; it was also the peaceful moments of comfort that reached into my deepest need.

Patty Mason
Founder of Liberty in Christ Ministries
Author of *Finally Free: Breaking the Bonds of Depression without Drugs*

Lisa Miller-Rich's attention to detail with an in-depth look at each mention of joy in the Bible brought to light aspects of joy that I've never considered. It's both encouraging and challenging as she pushes us to go beyond the surface and dig deep into what it's like to truly experience joy.

Sharon Wilharm
Writer/Director of *Summer of '67, Providence, The Good Book*

We all need guides on our spiritual journey. Let Lisa Miller-Rich be your guide through this interactive study of the 218 times the word joy appears in the Bible. With wit and wisdom gained through her own journey of joy, Lisa will help you use this as a guidebook for *your* journey. Grab your Bible, a pen, and take the first steps into a deeper experience of joy.

Rick Champ
Director of North American Partnership with GO Ministries

If you're like me and struggle with a codependent nature, this book is a must! Grounding yourself in joy—the kind that God designed us to have, instead of in other people's happiness or in our circumstances—is a tool all codependents need. I highly recommend this fantastic tool to understand joy, gain joy, keep joy, and regain control of your everyday perspective no matter what life throws at you!

Christy Neal
Author of *Don't Ever Tell*
Speaker and Founder of Choose Different Ministries

Lisa Miller-Rich nails it with "Joy isn't only found in the high, happy places of life." Amen! I've experienced the joy she describes as "spiritual oxygen" when I've been in the valley, screaming at God about my pain. If you want no-matter-what kind of joy, be encouraged by Lisa's inspiring look at the 218 times joy is found in the Bible.

Jack Patterson
Children's Pastor of Operations, Eastview Christian Church
Normal, IL

I knew after reading the first paragraph of *218 Ways to Own Joy* that I would like it. It is rare to read words on a page and hear the writer's voice. Lisa's sense of humor and transparency leap off the page. It is as if you are in a comfy chair exploring and discussing one single joy scripture from the Word of God face to face with Lisa. The appealing layout of the entries helps record what is learned from the scripture and easily share the journey to owning joy with others in a small group or a social media community. Thanks, Lisa, for making the journey to joy so en"joy"able!

Wanda O. Holt
Author of *BROKEN: Finding Purpose from Brokenness*

We all experience crisis. Life is not always easy. Sometimes our lives get complicated and difficult. We're not always going to feel happy, but as a Christ follower, our lives can be filled with *joy*. You're going to love Lisa Miller-Rich's book, *218 Ways to Own Joy*. As she leads you through God's Word about joy, you'll discover practical and hands-on ways to discover and live with joy—every day.

Sue Z. McGray
Regional Director, Christian Women in Media
Speaker and Author of *Becoming Visible: Letting Go of the Things that Hide Your True Beauty*

The distinction between joy and happiness is paramount to knowing true joy and being content outside of situational happiness. This study will help you discover the difference and learn how to live in the joy the Father desires you to have. With its read a little, write a little, think a little, reflect a little, and read some more format, *218 Ways to Own Joy* will make a great study tool for groups, couples, and individuals.

Jason Shepherd
Lead Pastor, Well House Church
Goodlettsville, TN

The key to owning more joy is in understanding what God says about it. Lisa Miller-Rich has written an engaging and accessible tour guide through all 218 places where God speaks about joy in the Bible. Each entry brings you one step closer to owning joy that lasts.

Jeanne Lunde
Discipleship Minister, Crossroads Community Church
Aurora, IL

If you're uncertain about how to differentiate between being happy and having true joy, this book will settle the matter. Lisa Miller-Rich does a masterful job of teaching us how to cultivate the fruit of joy in our lives and maintain it. She challenges us to consistently examine our joy level through the mirror of God's Word. This book is practical, thought-provoking, and very insightful. It's undeniably a great resource for anyone who wants to experience real joy in their lives in every season.

Kathy R. Green
Teacher and Prayer Author of *Pray-ers Bear Fruit: Become a Person of Prayer*

Lisa Miller-Rich takes seekers on an honest, encouraging, and thoughtful pursuit of the true meaning of the word "joy." Join her on this guided tour of all 218 places where God speaks about joy in the Bible. This is a must-read for all who truly want to love life and see good days whatever the circumstances.

Leanne Shelby
Involvement Pastor, Well House Church
Goodlettsville, TN

For those who are seeking to increase their quality of life, this book is an invaluable resource for manifesting genuine joy and a state of well-being. Lisa's *218 Ways to Own Joy* offers you an opportunity to move past circumstantial happiness to sustaining joyfulness. Life doesn't always feel great, and moods can be like a swinging pendulum. Imagine a consistent state of joy. This book empowers you to own God-created joy that could change your life forever.

Lisa Hooks, MA
Counselor and Talk Show Host

Concise, engaging, refreshing, illuminating, creative, challenging, and practical are my chosen words for Lisa Miller-Rich's interactive journey to pure and powerful Godly joy. She helps each one of us take ownership of Spirit-filled joy by choice and to become stewards of our joy through practical life application that will bless others and honor the Father. Discover the truth that joy is in Jesus, and He is enough!

Bob Knapp
She is Safe (SIS), Country Director for Mali
International Ministry Pastor (retired), Eastview Christian Church
Normal, IL

The culture tells us (incessantly!) that what we crave is happiness—and that couldn't be more wrong! What we crave is *joy*—and there is a big difference. Lisa Miller-Rich's beautiful book will explain the difference and why it's so important to us as Christians.

Daren Snow
Lead Pastor, Crossroads Community Church
Aurora, Illinois

Join Lisa Miller-Rich in a scriptural discovery of joy. *218 Ways to Own Joy* is designed to be interactive. Lisa filters the studies through her own life experiences and then invites readers to filter them through theirs. She clearly states her two purposes: life application and the release of joy. I predict this is what you will experience by book's end: pure joy!

Wanda Carver
Author of *Everyday Experiences with God* and *Everyday Experiences with God: The Prayer Journal*

How exciting it is to see this message about joy become available to us. Lisa presents a unique way for all of us to relate to joy in our everyday lives. Even in times of trials, Lisa helps us become more aware of knowing and trusting God. Throughout the pages, she conveys God's message of, "I'M HERE." Breathe deep, read, and be encouraged as you receive joy 218 ways.

Rebecca Klar Lusk
Author of the *IT'S ALL ABOUT* Christian children's books

While the world is struggling with sadness, Lisa Miller-Rich refreshes with *218 Ways to Own Joy*. Her down-to-earth style and insights capture the true spirit of joy. I'd encourage Bible believers to keep this book close as a refreshing daily devotional or small group study.

Crystal McDowell
Blogger and Author of *Seriously God? Spiritual Insights When Life Suddenly Changes*

No matter where you find yourself on your faith journey—searching, new to the faith, or a long-time believer—Lisa Miller-Rich's study will give you fresh insight on finding joy to be "the spiritual oxygen" needed for every circumstance of life. Lisa's format (write the passage, commentary, and respond) is a helpful tool in making the Bible become practical and alive! Having the privilege to minister alongside of Lisa on several occasions, I have found her to be a person with a contagious and evident joy—a worthy example to follow!

Jerry McCorkle
Executive Director, Spread Truth Ministries

I love a good sightseeing trip where I learn something new around every corner. This book is a sightseeing trip through the Bible. As you visit every joy-sighting, you'll expand your understanding and perspective about what joy looks like in everyday life. Buckle up—it's quite a ride!

Jill Savage
Author of 12 books including *Real Moms . . . Real Jesus*

218
Ways to Own

An Interactive Journey
Through all Bible Verses
Containing Joy

LISA MILLER-RICH

Carpenter's Son Publishing

218 Ways to Own Joy

Published by Carpenter's Son Publishing, Franklin, Tennessee

Published in association with Larry Carpenter of Christian Book Services, LLC

www.christianbookservices.com

Edited by Adept Content Solutions

Cover by Suzanne Lawing

Interior Design by Adept Content Solutions

978-1-946889-12-6

To my husband, Art, and my children, Lukas, and Zandra:
I adore being a part of our Fab Four.

To Mom and Pop: It's bizarre that I can't put this book
into your hands.
Thank you for all the wisdom
you deposited in me before you left …
wisdom that my hands put into this book.

Introduction

O nce upon a time—okay, it was 2005—I was nearing the end of my study at God University. God U is what I affectionately label the eight-year season between the time I knew God called me to go into ministry and the time He actually let me pursue it. When the Lord originally made it clear He wanted to use me this way, I tried to make it happen immediately. Now, have you ever seen a tall person straight-arming the forehead of a much shorter person while the shorty tries to move forward? The little one struggles to make progress, but the bigger one prohibits any forward motion. I was that li'l guy trying to get past God at the beginning. I finally quit pushing and settled into listening. Seemingly assured I was done trying to work around Him, the Lord stopped palming me and showed me that my character wasn't ready for ministry. He had refining work to do in me and after only a little arguing, I agreed. At that point, the Dean of My Life began enrolling me in character-refining course after character-refining course.

My syllabus, if you will, was a Bible concordance. A concordance is a reference book in which every occurrence of the principal words in a book is arranged in an alphabetical index. When, through multi-media channels, God would point out a character area in which I was deficient, I'd get out my concordance and look it up. One a day, I would study, pray and journal through every verse in the Bible containing that word. For eight years, I studied the Bible through the lenses of these topics, and the Word of God changed me from the inside out. While I was in the midst of it, I had no idea how long I would be enrolled in God U. Every once in a while, I'd say to God, "Hey, I thought You wanted to use me in ministry! It's been two … four … six … eight years! Did I miss something?" One time, the Holy Spirit shot back, "I gave Moses forty years of wandering. You want some of that?" Me: "No Sir. I'll just be down here studying. You let me know when it's 'go' time."

It turns out, joy was the last "course" I took at God U before the Lord allowed me to begin publicly studying for ministry. The insights I learned through my years in God U not only taught me to live my personal life with joy through all its wonderful highs and valleys, it also prepared me to lead with joy in the ups and downs of ministry settings.

"What is the definition of joy?"

"How do you distinguish joy from happiness and peace?"
I'm convinced that one definition cannot capture God-created joy. Joy has multiple windows and it is multi-faceted. Here's why I think this is important to understand. If you look up "joy" in Merriam-Webster's dictionary, you read, "Joy: The emotion evoked by well-being, success, or good fortune or by the prospect of possessing what one desires." If this is the true definition, then we Christians are falling short a lot of the time from living up to the command in God's Word that says, "Rejoice in the Lord, always. I will say it again: Rejoice!" (Philippians 4:4). If joy only means the emotion we have when everything is super-dee-duper, we will mistakenly think we're failing to live in *joy always* on the days we're not feeling it. Follow any human being around for a

day, and his or her life will testify that it's not realistic to "rejoice always" if this is all that joy means.

That's the problem with a worldly definition of a Godly invention. Rather than bringing us closer to understanding joy, a singular definition actually causes us to feel farther away from it when we cannot connect with the world's definition.

God knew this. That's why the Bible contains the word "joy" 218 times. Each occurrence presents a wider look at joy. When taken collectively, these facets shape a truer understanding of joy and it is a joy we can own. This joy has a no-matter-what quality based in, on, and out of our relationship with God. To own it, we must know what God says about joy so we can access it through all the myriad messes and milestones of our journey.

> Sometimes joy is like the loud, clanging sound of a marching band as the overwhelming emotion of an amazing moment sweeps us along. This joy is delightful, it's real, and it's easy to access.

> Other times, joy is a quiet heartbeat. In our hardest, darkest valleys, it's being able to discern God's presence in the soft, drawing sound of "I'm here." This joy is soothing, it's real, and it's a comfort that a hurting heart can access.

Joy sometimes feels elusive. We want it in abundance, yet it feels a bit beyond our reach when we don't understand how to experience it in the rhythms of our lives. God wouldn't command us to do something that isn't possible. He gave us the fullness of His Word to equip us to live out His command to "Rejoice always." He makes biblically true joy available so we can live victoriously through our wins *and* our losses.

In writing this book, I, of course, brought my life-experience filters to the project. Sometimes, when we've been hurt, it's hard not to be skeptical reading of another person's positive experience with something that caused us pain. On the other hand, it's challenging to read about someone's struggle in an area in which we have only had positive experiences. This isn't a book of doctrine; it's a book that explores a couple hundred ways to experience joy. And, while it's called 218 Ways to Own Joy, God will reveal even more than 218 as you layer your life-filters on top of what He's shown me!

How to Use This Book

The 218 entries containing the word "joy" are listed in canonical order from Genesis to Revelation. (Canonical order is what you see in the index of a Bible. It's the arrangement of the sixty-six books as they were grouped by content.)

Each entry is set up in the following way:

> **Bible verse reference.** I strongly encourage you to read the chapter in the Bible that contains the verse so you have a better idea of the context.

> **Blank lines.** Here, you'll handwrite the verse listed. Writing it gives you the opportunity to put Deuteronomy 17:18 into action, "... write for [your] self a copy of this instruction" (New Living Translation). It's powerful for our pen to make a copy of God's word.

Two paragraphs from me. One paragraph will creatively let you know the context of what's going on around the verse you just wrote. The second paragraph will provide a life application of the verse.

Guiding questions. Based on the life application, I list a couple of questions to get you thinking.

Blank spaces below. I provide space for you to write your reflections on what you've read. You can respond to the questions or journal something the Holy Spirit is teaching you. If you need more space, additional blank pages are at the back of the book.

Tweet. For my Twitter folks, I created a ready-made Tweet that you can post to encourage others.

Two ways you can interact with this project:

In order. Starting with the first entry in Genesis, you can dive in and journey through all 218 entries until you reach the end. If you choose to go through this book from Genesis to Revelation, be prepared for the prophets. Some sections get kind of heavy because the prophets had a weighty call. They had to look at the miserable condition of a people who would not listen to God and be the messengers of "Now, you've done it." For us, this has practical application. If we're to fully experience joy, it's important we understand the many facets of joy we can only experience during challenging times.

Topically. Starting on page 220, you'll find an index of keywords. If you need a quick word of insight or want to explore a specific area of life, look to the index. All entries that speak to your topic of interest are listed under that keyword.

Technical Notes

This book is not a purely exegetical unpacking of each passage, although the smells of exegesis waft through the pages. That note is primarily directed to those who already know what the term "exegesis" means. For those who don't, I could've left that statement out and it would not have impacted your joy. However, for the sake of expanding knowledge, exegesis (ek-se-je-sus) means unpacking a critical explanation or interpretation of a text, particularly a religious text.[1] For a project to do any earthly good, exegetical insights need to point to the practical. Life application and release of joy are the purposes of this work.

In a few cases, a Bible verse contained the word "joy" two or more times. When I encountered those, I wrote an entry for the (a), (b), and (c—if applicable) of each verse. You'll find examples of this in Isaiah 35:10 and Isaiah 51:11. Scriptures like these underscore the beautiful truth that God's word is living and speaks to us in multiple

---

[1]   "Exegesis | Definition of exegesis in English by Oxford Dictionaries." Oxford Dictionaries | English. Accessed September 28, 2017. https://en.oxforddictionaries.com/definition/exegesis"

layers. We can read the same passage and glean different applications with each read.

I worked from the New International Version (NIV) of the Bible. If you prefer a different version, you'll still be able to track with this book easily. In some cases where the NIV translated a word as "joy", your version may use a synonym for it. However, the context will be the same. Why did I choose the NIV, and the 1984 version at that? ("Gasp," say some scholars) Simple: It's my comfort food. If you have reasons why you think I should have used a different version, all I can tell you is this: Write your own book.

Within the NIV translation, some verses will render the word "joy" differently depending on the publication date of the NIV you read. Three examples are: Romans 16:19 is "full of joy" in the 1984 version and "rejoice" in the 2011, Galatians 4:15 is "all your joy" in the 1984 and "blessing" in the 2011, and Philippians 1:26 is "joy" in the 1984 and "boasting" in the 2011.

Do any of these technical considerations dampen or distract me from my joy? Only if I let them. Arguing about technicalities doesn't lead me to joy; therefore, I lay all this out here so it's clear I'm aware of it, then I'm driving on. My mission—and my invitation to you—is to own the joy God offers.

Joy-filled
—— Acknowledgments ——

I read acknowledgments in which people say, "I couldn't have done it without _____." When I think about my husband, I connect with that sentiment to the highest degree. He believed in me as a writer before I would dare call myself one. He watches my walk with Christ and, as the one who views it the most intimately, puts his stamp of authenticity on it. He selflessly provided the resources and life-space necessary to allow me to focus on bringing this project to life. He prayed for me and lifted my chin when the inevitable hiccups to happiness occurred along the way. You wouldn't be holding *218 Ways to Own Joy* in your hands if it weren't for his belief in, trust in, and support of me. I deeply respect him, and I'm grateful for his love and his covering.

To all who prayed for me along the way, thank you. In the marvelous mystery that is prayer, God knit us together to bring this book from a concept to a reality.

Are you ready to own the joy that God has for you? He's ready for you! Turn the page and get ready to be changed. Let's giddyup to the "Glory Up!"

Joy Inventory

As you embark on your journey to owning more joy, take this quick inventory to establish your baseline understanding of joy. You'll do a similar assessment at the end of the project so you can compare your growth.

How would you define joy? _____

_____

_____

_____

Circle the answer that would best describe your current feeling for each statement. Don't overthink it; go with your gut.

1. I don't think too much about joy.
Strongly Agree   *Agree*   *Not Sure*   *Disagree*   *Strongly Disagree*

2. I only feel joy when everything is going well.
Strongly Agree   *Agree*   *Not Sure*   *Disagree*   *Strongly Disagree*

3. Joy is hard to come by.
Strongly Agree   *Agree*   *Not Sure*   *Disagree*   *Strongly Disagree*

4. Joy comes and goes.
Strongly Agree   *Agree*   *Not Sure*   *Disagree*   *Strongly Disagree*

5. I've tried to find joy through many means but I feel overwhelmed, exhausted, and sometimes defeated because I still don't have it.
Strongly Agree   *Agree*   *Not Sure*   *Disagree*   *Strongly Disagree*

6. It isn't that I'm depressed but I'd like to see the world in more colors.
Strongly Agree   *Agree*   *Not Sure*   *Disagree*   *Strongly Disagree*

7. I believe in God but He's not always where I go to find joy.
Strongly Agree   *Agree*   *Not Sure*   *Disagree*   *Strongly Disagree*

8. I'm willing to invest a few minutes each day to investigate joy … but I don't really expect to be changed by this project.
Strongly Agree   *Agree*   *Not Sure*   *Disagree*   *Strongly Disagree*

9. Joy is a choice.
Strongly Agree   *Agree*   *Not Sure*   *Disagree*   *Strongly Disagree*

10. I feel guilty for not walking in joy when I have so many blessings.
Strongly Agree   *Agree*   *Not Sure*   *Disagree*   *Strongly Disagree*

If you haven't already, read the Introduction to discover how to get the most from this project.

Let's explore joy together! Join our Facebook group "218 Ways to Own Joy."

—— Manipulation of Joy ——

Genesis 31:27

_____

_____

_____

_____

"Liar, liar, pants on fire!" It would've been awesome if a sky full of angels harked and heralded this chant above Laban's head. After deceiving Jacob for years (Genesis 29–31), Laban now guilt-trips Jacob for sneaking off. Laban says he would have given Jacob a joyous send off if he'd known he was leaving. Yeah, right: Genesis 28:10–31:55 reveals that Laban didn't want to celebrate Jacob; he was using joy as a weapon in an attempt to swindle him again.

Have you ever felt manipulated? It's especially hard if a family member is the one pulling the strings. We could judge Laban if it weren't so easy for us to relate to him. We, too, can turn our withholding-of-joy weapon on others when they displease us. Maybe we don't brandish it from a holster, but it is every bit as destructive in terms of our relationships. It's in the frozen silences, the steely glances, or the unkind words we fire. But, God offers a more joy-filled way. Our role, as God leads, is to speak the truth in love about consequences for sin if we see someone veering off a path. From there, it's God's role to grant or deny blessings. When we withhold joy and communication, it rarely leads anyone to more joy. Joy is found in allowing others to follow God's direction for their lives, not ours.

Which has hindered your joy more: A time when someone manipulated you by withholding their approval or when you have done it to someone else?

_____

_____

_____

_____

_____

_____

_____

_____

_____

_____

Joy is found in allowing others to follow their path. #joy218ways

—Joy in Great Leadership—

_____
_____
_____
_____
_____
_____

When was the last time a great leader caused you to fall out in joy? In this verse, the Israelites have gathered at the end of a week-long ordination for an offering ceremony as detailed in Leviticus 8 and 9. Those assembled had the opportunity to see God move in a powerful way after their leaders followed the directions God gave. The result? The crowd went wild!

We all have influence as leaders. It may be in our families, churches, civic or community organizations, work groups, teams, or schools. What would it be like if the people we led reacted like the folks in the above verse to our leadership? As a parent, wouldn't it be awesome for our kids to shout for joy and fall face down at the privilege of being led by us? "Clean your room," we say. And, tumbling to the floor in joy, our little blessings holler, "Oh, my powerfully-led parent from God, what a fantastic idea!" We can dare to dream. In all spiritual seriousness, however, exercising our leadership in God-honoring ways helps connect those we lead to the joy of following. God's truth instructs that if we lead, we'd better be praying for how He wants it done. Joy in great leadership is a gift we give when we lead people by obeying God's direction for the group.

Where do you have influence with people? Are you leading them with God's joy-filled direction?

_____
_____
_____
_____
_____
_____
_____

Great leaders give the joy-gift of vision and clarity when their
leadership reflects obedience to God's directives. #joy218ways

Holiday Joy

_____

_____

_____

_____

_____

_____

Does the thought of holiday gatherings fill you with joy or dread? Family dynamics and family history will shape how you answer. From the beginning, the idea of holiday get-togethers was God's. In Deuteronomy 16:1–17, God outlines three annual holidays—known as the Pilgrim Festivals—that He set in motion. I imagine He knew there'd be times when gathering for a holiday would be stressful because in Deuteronomy 16:14, He told the folks to "Be joyful" *samach* on His holidays. That Hebrew verb, *samach*, is stated as though this is a completed action in God's mind. Perhaps it's God saying, "Here's a thought: Don't disrespect my set-apart days. Get in the right frame of mind and be prepared to enjoy your time celebrating Me."

Even if we're fortunate to have family we enjoy, we sometimes elevate the celebration above the celebration-giver. The key to maintaining joy during the holidays is remembering they are supposed to be about God. If we love traditions more than we love Jesus, the holidays will exhaust us. We can easily lose opportunities to worship Him, and we can lose heart when family situations get tough. The days that mark important times in the life of Jesus are the foundation of our Christian faith. True holiday joy can be ours if we'll toss aside burdensome traditions and focus on Him when family stress threatens our joy.

When family situations are difficult, what can you do to focus on the reason for the holiday? Are there any holiday traditions that take the place of worshiping Jesus?

_____

_____

_____

_____

_____

_____

If we love holiday traditions more than we love Jesus, we can easily lose joy when situations get tough. Focus on Him. #joy218ways

—— If This, Then This Joy ——

Judges 9:19

_____
_____
_____

The lure of doing things our way instead of God's is powerful. In Judges 9, a power-hungry Abimelech knew how to convince the non-thinking people of Shechem that he should rule. He persuaded them by telling them what they wanted to hear. In response to their approval, the small detail of seventy brothers in line before him was simply a day's work of having them killed to remove that barrier to his power. As the people rejoiced in their new leader, a voice—the lone surviving brother, Jotham—cried out the challenge in Judges 9:19–20. "If you have thought this through and it's the right, God-honoring thing, then I hope you have joy. If you haven't, then you're going to get burnt." Reading through the rest of Judges 9, we see that over the course of the next few years, their lack of following God led to their destruction. "Thus God repaid the wickedness that Abimelech had done to his father by murdering his seventy brothers. God also made the people of Shechem pay for all their wickedness. The curse of Jotham son of Jerub-Baal came on them." (Judges 9:56–57)

Sometimes the choice that is right in our faces is not the right choice. It could destroy our joy. Stop and pray. Listen to God, think, and obey. God will always lead us toward joy even if we have to struggle to get there.

When have you been tempted to do things your way instead of God's? How does stopping to pray before following the crowd protect your joy?

_____
_____
_____
_____
_____
_____
_____
_____
_____

Tweet

Sometimes the choice right in our face is not the right choice. It could destroy our joy. Stop, pray, listen, obey. #joy218ways

Cause for Joy

_____

_____

_____

_____

_____

It's a party! 1 Chronicles 11 and 12 tell of David assembling his army as he prepared to enter his role as king. Victories had piled up, news of his success had spread, and it was evident that God's hand was on his mission. As the movement led by this dynamic leader grew, people were drawn to support this great cause. Without the benefit of contributing online, they loaded their support on a line of animals and headed to the rally in Hebron. They trusted that God would multiply what they gave to make a kingdom impact.

The diversity in our world is amazing, and the needs of the under-resourced are massive. While there is no shortage of great causes, those leading the efforts often run short on finding people to support them. What is God calling us to support? It may be with our money, or He might call us to be His hands and feet to encourage those in need. When we align with something bigger than ourselves, God can use us to help it succeed. In those moments of uniting with others, we unlock and own a joy that can't be found in isolation.

What great causes exist of which you are aware? Are you growing your joy as you support one of them? If not, ask God to direct you to where He wants you to bring the joy of your time and resources.

_____

_____

_____

_____

_____

_____

Tweet

In those moments we unite with others to further a great cause, we unlock a joy that can't be found in isolation. #joy218ways

——Joy in the Dwelling——

I'll bet when you think about your favorite song, memories and emotions start humming in your brain. The sound of the notes and the lyrics literally call up the sight, smell, and touch moments when the song embedded itself in your story. In 1 Chronicles 16:8–36, David pours his heart into a worship song, and his passion rings through. By verse 27, he is overwhelmed at being in God's dwelling place. So, exactly where does God dwell? Certainly it is in the hearts of all believers (Ephesians 3:17), but He also pours out His Spirit on assemblies—the churches—gathered for His glory.

Churches can be awesome dwelling places. They can also be places that cause hurt and dampen joy. I've been crushed to the point of wanting to give up on church. However, if we've been burned by a church, it was never God that imparted the damage, it was people. When humans don't "human" well, we can't allow that to interfere with our joy-connection to God. The church is God's design and is His delight. He graciously provides the church and invites us to be a part of it. We don't *have* to do church, we *get* to. Looking to God's Word, we see that places where He dwells are filled with splendor, majesty, strength, and joy. Find a church that matches this description, and then sing for joy in His dwelling place!

Has a church ever dampened your joy? If not, thank God for the journey you've enjoyed! If so, can you peel the "human" off the hurt and stay connected to God's joy through His church?

_____

_____

_____

_____

_____

_____

_____

_____

_____

_____

When humans don't "human" well, we can't allow that to
interfere with our joy-connection to God. #joy218ways

Natural Joy

_____
_____
_____

The other day, I listened to a message I gave at a women's conference. I was talking 100 miles per hour with gusts up to 120! I was so excited and passionate about my topic that I swept everyone along on a quick, breezy ride. As a public speaker, I made note for future reference to rein that in but, man, it was fun to bubble over with joy in the moment! That's how I "hear" David's psalm in 1 Chronicles 16:8–36. He is giddy with the joy of bringing the Ark of the Covenant (Exodus 25:10–22) into Jerusalem. He starts praising God and, toward the end, even calls the sea, fields, and trees to get in on the act.

Is it whimsical to think of trees singing? Perhaps it is, if we limit music to human vocals. But, think of the way rustling leaves tickle your ear. Have you been still enough to hear the bass tones of a tree trunk as it danced? No human can sing like that. Creation is full of joy, and it sings to its creator. If you want to hear a cool, off-the-charts example of this, Google[1] the video of "Stars and Whales" by Louie Giglio. It's a sixteen-minute clip that will open your ears to a little more of what God hears. Our joy finds fuller expression when we soak in the symphony of nature's joy.

When was the last time you sat and simply listened to nature? How does nature lead you to experience joy?

_____
_____
_____
_____
_____
_____
_____
_____
_____

Creation is full of joy and sings to its creator. Our joy finds fuller expression when we soak in nature's symphony. #joy218ways

[1] "Stars and Whales by Louie Giglio." Vimeo. 26 September, 2011. Accessed 28 September 2017. https://vimeo.com/54384759.

——— Giving with Joy ———

_____

_____

_____

_____

_____

If you had more money, what would you do with it? David kicked off a massive capital campaign to build God's temple with his in 1 Chronicles 29:1–9. Gold, silver, iron, wood, jewels ... it was his joy to give. How could he so willingly part with his wealth? In verses 14 and 16, he boiled it down to this truth: He was only giving back to God what God had given to him. He modeled the biblical truth of 2 Corinthians 9:7, "Each man should give what he has decided in his heart to give, not reluctantly or under compulsion, for God loves a cheerful giver."

A powerful money trap is to believe that, "When I make more money, I'll start giving. Right now, I need every penny to make it." We may go through seasons where this is true, but sometimes "making it" involves us trying to cover more than just our basic needs. Often, when we make more money, we increase our living, but not our giving. The test of our generosity is not the size of our bank account or the items we own, it's in how joyfully we handle what God has currently entrusted to us. Everything we have belongs to God—it's His stuff (v. 16). There is deep joy when we share what we have with others. We can chase dollars and change or we can be world-changers with our dollars.

What is your motivation for gaining more "stuff"? Where could you place more of your money/resources to bring world-changing joy?

_____

_____

_____

_____

_____

_____

We can chase dollars and change or we can bring joyful
world-change with our dollars. #joy218ways

– Joy in the Politics of God –

1 Chronicles 29:22

_____

_____

_____

_____

_____

As King David affirms his son Solomon, 1 Chronicles 29:21–30 demonstrates the joy people take in seeing one leader hand over power to his successor. But as in many current political climates, this transition didn't come without drama. In 1 Kings 1:1–2:25, another of David's sons, Adonijah, attempted to take the crown. Tracking the full story reads like a modern-day political thriller complete with coups, back-room deals, power brokering, and murders (… and people say the Bible is boring). Adonijah's rebellion fell apart when David outmaneuvered him but his quest for self-declared power ushered in confusion and, ultimately, his destruction.

Politics can be polarizing and joy-sucking if we let it. We worry if our values will be violated through legislation. Our thought life may become consumed with fears about our leaders and how their decisions will affect our families. Unchecked, this can replace our confidence in God. It's not happy-hoping to maintain joy in the face of the political landscape even as we have concerns. Joy strengthens when we elevate the truth of Romans 13:1 over the words of the Constitution: "Let everyone be subject to the governing authorities, for there is no authority except that which God has established. The authorities that exist have been established by God." My daughter said it best when she prayed, "God, sometimes leaders are in place to lead and sometimes they are there for a lesson." In either case, joy comes in knowing God is in control.

Does your confidence in God allow you to have joy in politically uncertain times?

_____

_____

_____

_____

_____

_____

Tweet

Joy strengthens as we elevate the truth of Romans 13:1 over the words of the Constitution. God is the ruler of all kings. #joy218ways

Revival Joy

Gypsy Smith was a nineteenth-century revivalist who conducted evangelistic campaigns in the United States and Great Britain for more than seventy years. When he came to a new town, he'd stop on the outskirts and draw a circle in the dirt. Then he would stand inside that circle and say, "O God, please send a revival to this town, and let it begin inside this circle." In 2 Chronicles 29–30, revival was brewing in Judah. King Hezekiah took stock of his nation and saw a people who had forgotten the God who loved them. With a heart for the Lord and the spirit of a reformer, he pointed the people back to God. Before calling for change, he had to be honest about the practices that were not in alignment with God's ways. The result was a renewal of joy that had lain dormant for years.

A thing in need of revival is something that once had life but, currently, has lost its strength. In our faith-walk, it can be easy to go through the motions. We can "do" church without being changed by encountering the Holy Spirit. At every stage of our lives, we should experience God in awe-inspiring ways. Revival begins inside us with a wake up call. If we are feeling dead in our faith, we need a joy-jolt of revival from the Holy Spirit to experience the fullness of God.

If you feel flat in your relationship with God, pray for the joy of revival. Remember, revival begins in your circle. If you are in a season of great joy in your experience of God, where can you spread that fire?

We need a joy-jolt of revival from the Holy Spirit to
experience the fullness of God. #joy218ways

—The Joy of "What's Next"—

Ezra 3:12

After the destruction of God's temple some fifty years previous, the Israelites have returned from captivity to rebuild it in Jerusalem. Ezra 1–3 unpacks the "who" and "how" of this new reality. It was a time to celebrate but, within the ranks, some were weeping, mourning, and longing for the old temple. The glory of their former house of worship remained huge in their minds and in their hearts. It cast a shadow of sadness and dimmed their joy when they looked at the foundation of the new site.

I remember a time when this was me. We'd moved to a new town and a new church. In the comparison battle between the new church and our former one, the new guy was taking a beating. All I could see was what it wasn't. I longed for the old people, the old ways of worship, and the old interaction I had with the Holy Spirit. A brave—and, I thought, stupid—friend at the new church finally said, "You're never going to find a home here if you keep looking back." I was offended and then convicted. We trade our joy when we constantly look through the rear-view mirror and long for "what was." Joy is found in embracing "what's next."

Do you have any areas in which you long for things to be how they used to be? How can the Holy Spirit guide you to the joy of embracing "what's next?"

Tweet

We trade our joy when we look through the rear-view mirror and long for "what was." Joy is found in embracing "what's next." #joy218ways

11

Sorrow and Joy:
—— Odd Companions ——

Ezra 3:13

_____

_____

_____

They laughed, they cried, they ran the gamut of emotions. With celebration, Zerubbabel's team laid the foundation to rebuild God's temple fifty years after its destruction (Ezra 3:7–13). Among those assembled, however, many remembered not only the glory of the former temple but also the reason it fell. Previously, the Lord had removed His favor from the Jewish people after years of them ignoring His ways. In 586 BC, God allowed the Babylonians to destroy the temple in Jerusalem, slaughter many and take the rest as slaves. Now, fifty years later, even though the Jewish elders were glad to see this new construction and restoration, their hearts grieved recalling how the people's sin had brought the destruction in the first place.

I imagine many of us have been in a similar situation. We're attending a joyous occasion, yet, because of "life," we find we can't connect to the party. Perhaps we trip across triggers that remind us of past hurts or of situations where God's ways were ignored or obliterated. It's powerful to look at the complexity of joy. We can be in the presence of God with joy and gratitude for what He's brought us through, while, at the same time, we have thoughts of sorrow and correction filling our minds. Joy is found in knowing that God is never done with us. As the foundation for our restoration, God will lead us in building new joy from our past sorrow.

From your life experiences, what triggers can cause your joy to dampen? Does it help to know that joy and sorrow can show up in the same moments?

_____

_____

_____

_____

_____

_____

_____

Tweet

We can be in the presence of God with joy and gratitude and, at the same time, be mindful of times of sorrow and correction. #joy218ways

— Crock Pot of Delayed Joy —

_____

_____

_____

_____

"Hope deferred makes the heart sick, but a longing fulfilled is a tree of life" (Proverbs 13:12). God had written a great "longing" on the hearts of the Jewish people: Return from captivity and rebuild the temple (Ezra 1–3). They came in fired up, but soon experienced a delay-of-game interference as opposition met them in Jerusalem (Ezra 4). Fear caused the work to grind to a halt. Finally, in 516 BC—twenty years later—the temple was complete and the people celebrated the fulfillment of their hearts' desire.

When I first heard from God that I was to go into ministry, I got fired up and tried to make it happen immediately. That wasn't God's plan. I experienced a 14-year delay-of-game before I received the joy of serving in ministry. Often, during those waiting years, my "deferred hope" caused me to lose heart. However, I clung to what God had told me even when I couldn't see progress toward it. The day I began ministry, I experienced a joy made deeper because I had waited so long. Delayed joy is crock-pot joy. If we relax into the wait, we'll enjoy the life-smells of preparation. The wait may be outside our control, but finding the joy in the waiting is ours to savor.

Are you waiting for God to fulfill a promise or to move in a certain area of your life? How can you savor joy as you wait?

_____

_____

_____

_____

_____

_____

_____

_____

_____

_____

_____

Delayed joy is crock-pot joy. The timing of fulfillment may be outside our control, but the joy in the waiting is ours to savor. #joy218ways

—— Holiday Freedom Joy ——

Ezra 6:22a

Imagine the Grinch stole Christmas from your family for seventy years. No trees, no gifts, no fa-la-la. Eventually, a Cindy Lou Who-type character shows up. Because of her intervention, his hard shell melts, the oppression stops and you're able to reinstate your faith-holiday. This is the vibe in the first part of Ezra 6:22. The year is 516 BC, and the Israelites are celebrating Passover for the first time since their captivity in 586 BC. While they were in the holiday re-instating mode, they immediately followed Passover with *Chag HaMatzot*, the Festival of Unleavened Bread. After seventy years, they were finally home for the holidays.

It's unlikely that Christmas will be sent packing for seventy years, so what can we learn from this passage? Regardless of which holiday it is, let's not take holiday-joy for granted. Since we have the freedom to celebrate our faith, let's take captive anything that may try to steal our joy (2 Corinthians 10:5). Families, finances, and holiday functions can be so stressful that we trade our joy in exchange for a mess. When anything threatens our joy, it's important to evaluate if it's healthy and God-honoring for us to continue engaging with it. We're free to have holiday-fun; the only way we lose that joy is if we give it away. Remember: We have the freedom to celebrate holidays. May the joy of that freedom guide our holiday plans.

What if your freedom to celebrate was taken from you? How can tapping into this freedom be a source of joy when facing stressful situations?

_____

_____

_____

_____

_____

_____

_____

_____

_____

_____

Tweet

It's easy to lose holiday-joy over families, finances and functions. Remember, we're free to celebrate; let that joy be our guide! #joy218ways

———— Incomplete Joy ————

Ezra 6:22b

_____

_____

_____

_____

Is there something you've been praying about for a long time? The folks in Ezra 3–6 can relate to your wait. The Lord allowed them to start rebuilding the temple in Jerusalem, and they got the foundation laid in 536 BC (Ezra 3). Unfortunately, they hit major opposition and work stopped (Ezra 4). Can you imagine their pain as they walked by that temple foundation day after day for sixteen years? You know people were praying, but nothing was happening. Finally, in 520 BC, the Lord changed the attitude of the person in power over them. That king not only allowed them to build, but also assisted to provide the necessary resources.

I suppose they were just lucky, don't you? Probably, that king got up on the right side of the bed one day and decided to make all their dreams come true. If you read Ezra 5, you'll see luck had nothing to do with it. They had a vision of what would bring them joy, and they didn't give it up. During the long years when the joy of a rebuilt temple was incomplete, they maintained their joy through prayer. As we wait, we never know whom God will use. We never know how God will work. What we do know is that we have the joy of praying to the God who is able.

Of the people you know, who is struggling with incomplete joy? How can you pray as you/they wait for God to answer in His timing?

_____

_____

_____

_____

_____

_____

_____

_____

_____

_____

Tweet

You never know whom God will use. You never know how God will work.
But you do have the joy of knowing the God who is able. #joy218ways

—Don't Condemn My Joy—

Nehemiah 8:10

_____

_____

_____

_____

_____

_____

Let the party begin! The year is 445 BC and after being demolished, the wall of Jerusalem is back in place. So why would Nehemiah tell the people not to grieve as they gathered to commemorate this great day? As part of the celebration, Ezra the priest had read from the Book of Moses—probably the Torah, the five books at the beginning of the Bible. For many, it was the first time they'd heard it. As they compared their lives to the Word of God, they began to weep. They could tell how far they were from God's ways, and it broke their hearts. Nehemiah pointed them to a higher truth than the condemnation they were feeling: God delights in you, now come delight in Him.

Maybe you, like me, have messed up somewhere along the way. When you stopped and looked at your mistakes through the filter of God's Word and His ways, you might connect with the grief the Israelites felt. My hope is that a mature Christian came alongside you and pointed you to a higher truth. Yes, be grieved over your sin. However, God's ways are in place because of His love for us. We should never feel condemned by God's Word … or by God's people. His ways should call us to change out of love for Him and trust that His ways lead to freedom and joy.

Has anyone ever made you feel condemned because of your mistakes? How does the truth that God's ways are in place to draw us to freedom and joy help shed that wrong thinking?

_____

_____

_____

_____

_____

_____

_____

Tweet

We shouldn't feel condemned by God's Word or by His people. His ways lead to joy and life-change out of our love for Him. #joy218ways

Grace-Filled Joy

Nehemiah 8:12

_____

_____

_____

_____

_____

Just two verses earlier (Nehemiah 8:10), the people had come undone at the reflection of their sins in the mirror of God's Word. Nehemiah instructed them to stop weeping and, instead, celebrate the day God had given them. What I love about this section of scripture is the great leadership and the right response of the people. As they chose a joy-filled reaction, they were freed up to be more receptive to God's direction. If they had continued to weep with condemnation, they would've missed the opportunity to serve others and would've missed taking their next step toward God.

I think a stumbling block for many people is that God's grace is too good to be true. We feel like we need to beat ourselves up when we make mistakes. We want to punish ourselves to make atonement. Yes, we need to feel broken so we come to a place of repentance. However, if we keep berating ourselves, the danger is that we may never feel forgiven. God tells us that when we confess, our sins are, to Him, as far as the east is from the west (Psalm 103:12). When we keep bringing the same junk to God, it's as though He says, "What are we talking about?" God's grace is a reason for joy. It frees us up to love God and to love others in response to His goodness.

Is there a mistake for which you cannot forgive yourself? If you have confessed it to God, you are forgiven. Pray for the joy of feeling that forgiveness so you can walk in His grace-filled freedom.

_____

_____

_____

_____

_____

_____

_____

Tweet

God's grace and forgiveness free us to love God and to love others in response to His goodness. God's grace is reason for joy! #joy218ways

——Joy Doesn't Stink——

Nehemiah 8:17

_____

_____

_____

_____

_____

Have you ever stopped to consider if the way you celebrate holidays lines up with how God wants them done? The Israelites apparently hadn't. After hearing God's Word read aloud (Nehemiah 8:13), they discovered they hadn't been observing the Feast of the Tabernacles according to His outline (Leviticus 23:33–44). Now, for the first time in years, the Israelites fully were observing God's design for this holiday. As they aligned their way of commemorating the feast to God's original intent, they connected to a heritage-joy by recalling how God had rescued their people from Egypt. He asked them to make the booths of branches to remember the years their ancestors spent in shelters under His protection and following His lead in the desert.

We can hijack God's plan for His holy days by layering traditions over His original design. If we stink like stress instead of emitting the fragrance of joy during a holiday, we're marching to our own beat. I frequently say, "Show me the verse in the Bible where it says, 'And Jesus was stressed.'" We won't find it because it's not His way. As we clear away layers of holiday traditions, we'll replace the stink of stress with an attractive smelling holy-joy.

What traditions require so much effort you don't have time to focus on God's design for a holiday? What will happen to your joy if you don't do those traditions? How can you make your traditions align with God's original intent for the holiday?

_____

_____

_____

_____

_____

_____

Tweet

If we stink like stress instead of emitting the fragrance of joy during a holiday, we're marching to our own beat. #joy218ways

Broadcast Joy

Nehemiah 12:43

_____
_____
_____
_____
_____

The temple is built (Ezra 3–6), the city walls are up (Nehemiah 1–6), and a spiritual awakening is sweeping the Jewish remnant returned from Babylonian captivity (Nehemiah 8–10). "God had given them great joy." The people have much to celebrate and are aware of the One who's made it possible. Years of waiting melt into memories as tears of joy flow from grateful hearts. The last part of this verse is awesome. "The sound of rejoicing in Jerusalem could be heard far away." They couldn't help but broadcast their joy at being part of God's mighty work.

Given the ways we can communicate in our modern context, we have powerful opportunities to "broadcast" when God moves in our lives. It doesn't have to be in relation to over-the-top answers to prayer, like the rebuilding of a wall. God cares about the small things as well as the big ones. He knows the hairs on our heads and cares about every living thing (Luke 12:6–7). As we become aware that He has moved on our behalf, our response should be to share that joy. It could range from a one-on-one encounter with a friend needing encouragement to a more public forum. Our world needs to hear of the joy-filled ways God is at work in the lives of His people. Shout!

Are you comfortable sharing when "God gives you great joy"? Pray for opportunities to broadcast your God-given joy.

_____
_____
_____
_____
_____
_____
_____
_____

Tweet

Our world needs to hear us broadcast our joy when God works
in our lives. Share when God moves! #joy218ways

Joy of Deliverance

Esther going from "We're all going to die ... seriously" to "Never mind; we've been saved" is an incredible story of bravery in the face of terror (Esther 1–8). Her enemy, Haman, hatched a plot to destroy the Jewish people throughout the kingdom of Xerxes. Not only did God block that scheme on behalf of the Jewish people, He also used Haman's instrument of death against himself (Esther 7). Reading the story of Esther, it's clear how desperately she and her cousin, Mordecai, saw that unless God moved, they were doomed.

I think we can all relate to a time we desperately needed God to deliver us from a situation. Maybe, like Esther, God answered in ways that aligned with what we asked of Him. At other times, however, God chose to deliver us in unexpected ways that may have seemed painful and unfair. Yet, what would have happened if God had answered in the way we asked? What events have happened in our lives since then that give us a glimpse of how God used our pain to work some good? His Word assures us that He sees, hears, and answers our prayers (1 John 5:14–15). It's on us to recognize in what form His deliverance comes. For us, as for the Jews, when we recognize how God delivers, it leads us to times of joy.

Has God delivered you at a critical point in your life? Have you ever been disappointed in the way God delivered you? How can knowing that He delivered you connect you to the joy of His deliverance?

_____

_____

_____

_____

_____

_____

_____

_____

_____

_____

God delivers us from tough situations—sometimes in painful/unexpected ways. Recognizing HOW He delivers leads to times of joy. #joy218ways

Heritage Joy

_____

_____

_____

_____

_____

_____

From 1933–1945, Adolf Hitler carried out plans to destroy the Jewish people. Millions of victims died under his warped ideology of hating people because of their ethnic and religious heritage. This same type of evil faced the Jewish people in the Persian kingdom ruled by King Xerxes during the time of Queen Esther. When God moved to intervene on behalf of the Jews, a different type of ethnic identity sensation swept the country. Now, instead of the Persians viewing the Jews as weak riffraff, their status as God's kids elevated them to a desirable position.

The diversity in our world is tremendous. We, increasingly, have opportunities to be around people who don't share our ethnic heritage. Unfortunately, in our human frailty we allow that to be a dividing factor rather than something to celebrate. However, one power has the ability to destroy all barriers created by human standards. That power is Jesus. Ephesians 2:11–22 describe His power to unify us. Belonging to the family of Christ-followers is our primary heritage. We are children of God. The joy of knowing that should attract people to His power and His invitation to be a part of His family.

Do you consider the joy of your identity as God's son/daughter to be your primary heritage? Do you view all Christ-followers as equal brothers and sisters or are there any groups you struggle to accept?

_____

_____

_____

_____

_____

_____

_____

Tweet

Above ethnic identity, being a Christ-follower is our primary heritage.
All believers share this joy; all are welcome. #joy218ways

Joy of Justice

_____

_____

_____

It seems a bit odd that verse sixteen describes how "they" killed 75,000 people, and then the next day in verse seventeen, "they" chilled and partied. In our modern context, that's quite a jump. However, for the Jews who had faced the threat of annihilation on the thirteenth day of Adar (Esther 3:5–13), this was a celebration of God's salvation. God had delivered them from their enemies by allowing them to defend themselves (Esther 8:8–12).

Maybe our enemies haven't come at us with swords and the intent to kill, but they have stolen areas of our life's joy. It might have come in the form of slander, gossip, adultery, theft, betrayal, or backstabbing. Whatever the method of their madness, the result left sections of our hearts bleeding. When attacked, it's tempting to take matters into our own hands and return fire with fire. Yet, God—if given the space—can deal out justice more powerfully than we could ever imagine. I have literally seen God's justice on my behalf play out in surprising, God-only kinds of ways that left me shaking my head in joy and awe. Stifling my way of dealing with the slight was difficult. While I waited on the God of Justice to move on my behalf, I clung to stories like this one in Esther as my joy and strength.

Have you been wounded to the point of wanting retaliation? How does understanding God's kind of justice help you wait for Him to give you the joy of justice?

_____

_____

_____

_____

_____

_____

_____

_____

_____

Dealing with injustice is difficult. The God of Justice will move on our behalf and give us joy if we wait for Him to work. #joy218ways

Flexing Holiday Joy

Esther 9:18

_____

_____

_____

The Persian capital city of Susa (Shushan) was walled. When it came time for the Jews to defend themselves from extermination, Queen Esther asked the king if the Jews in Susa might be allowed to contend with their attackers for two days instead of the one granted those in the outlying villages (Esther 9:13). The king agreed; therefore, those inside the city walls celebrated the first Purim one day later than those in the villages. The holiday of Purim (PUH-rim) is named after the pur (the lot) that the Jews' enemy, Haman, used when choosing the date on which to kill all the Jews (Esther 3:7, 13). Today, cities that were walled at the time of Joshua (1355–1245 BC) still observe the holiday of Purim one day later than other Jews around the world. Jerusalem is the main city in which this holiday, known as Shushan Purim, is celebrated.

… a holiday that is observed on different days. This got me thinking about the joy-sucking stress that happens when scheduling family get-togethers around the holidays. Some families cling to the importance of the actual date and get offended if anyone bucks that tradition. The important thing is the meaning of the holiday and making time to celebrate it. If we hold traditions as more important than the reason why we gather to celebrate, we can lose our joy when schedules don't align with an actual date. Being flexible allows that joy to flow.

What holiday gathering—if any—brings you the most joy? Are there areas in which you need to be more flexible about how your family celebrates the holidays?

_____

_____

_____

_____

_____

_____

_____

_____

Tweet

Our joy can get sucked away when we love holiday traditions more than we love Jesus. Be flexible about how to celebrate! #joy218ways

——— Joy in Diversity ———

_____

_____

_____

Still today, Orthodox Jewish communities observe the holiday called "Purim" (PUH-rim). It gets its name from the pur (the lot) that Haman used to determine in which month the Jews would be annihilated (Esther 3:7, 13). Purim, today, is a jolly holiday to commemorate God's salvation of the Jews. Happening in March, it's marked by the reading of the Megillah of Esther (scroll of the full story), giving money gifts to at least two poor people, sending gifts of two kinds of food to at least one person, and a feast with great drink. Children get to dress up in costumes ... it's a fun day! (One source told me, "If there were ever a day to 'let loose' and just be Jewish, this is it!")

I wonder: Were you familiar with the modern-day holiday of Purim? I had some friends in Brooklyn who were Orthodox Jews. When I first saw pictures of their kids dressed up for the holiday, it helped open up a dialog between them and myself about their holiday and some of my Christian holiday traditions. When we encounter people from different faiths, joy is found in asking questions and learning rather than out-of-hand judging. If we listen, we'll discover the joy of being allowed into another person's world. It's in those intimate circles, then, that we have the joy of sharing our faith in Christ.

Do you have friends/acquaintances who have beliefs other than Christianity? How much do you know about their traditions? If you don't have any, pray for God to connect you to others.

_____

_____

_____

_____

_____

_____

_____

_____

When we encounter people from different faiths, joy is found in asking questions and learning rather than out-of-hand judging. #joy218ways

—— Joy to the Rescue ——

Esther 9:22a

Purim (PUH-rim) is one of two Jewish festivals not commanded by God in the Mosaic law. (The other one is Hannukah, which commemorates the dedication of the rebuilt Temple in 165 BC by the Maccabees.) Purim sprang up as an expression of spontaneous joy when the Jews were delivered from extermination during the time of Queen Esther. Seeing God's hand move on their behalf through the actions of their leaders turned their sorrow into joy. From that day forward, they remembered and celebrated that date as a day of rescue.

I think back to the significant times when God has moved on my behalf to "give me relief from my enemies." Whatever form the enemy took, when the pressure of their dislike, distrust, or disrespect was lifted, it was a good day in my world. It's challenging to maintain our joy when we're facing difficult people. In times like these, I take strength from David's words as he was readying to battle Goliath. He remembered the other moments in which God had come through for him. "The Lord who rescued me from the paw of the lion and the paw of the bear will rescue me from the hand of this Philistine" (1 Samuel 17:37). He didn't know *how* God was going to handle this new enemy; he just knew *that* God would do it. When our knees are shaking, the joy of knowing God will never leave us gives us strength to keep going.

When has God rescued you in the past? What "enemy" is currently weighing you down? Pray to tap into the strong joy of knowing God will not leave you in this alone.

Tweet

When our knees are shaking, the joy of knowing that God will never leave us strengthens us to keep going. #joy218ways

– Joy in the Least of These –

Esther 9:22b

_____

_____

_____

Mordecai, Queen Esther's cousin, rose up as the leader who plotted the overthrow of the decree originally designed to exterminate the Jews. In celebration of his people's victory, Mordecai wrote down all the events that happened and created an annual holiday of remembrance called Purim (PUH-rim). Today, it is still a Jewish holiday filled with feasting on some of the "best holiday food" (according to a Jewish friend), giving gifts of food (called Mishloach Manot), and giving charity to the poor.

Reading this verse, I'm especially captivated by the last phrase, "gifts to the poor." Thanksgiving baskets and Christmas toys provide plenty of end-of-the-year-holiday outlets for kind-hearted people to help meet needs of those who are struggling. Having worked in this area of ministry for years, I know that most of these families get their needs met during the holidays. What challenges me is to take it to the next level. Jesus said, "The poor you will always have with you, and you can help them anytime you want" (Mark 14:7). He said this to correct those trying to shame the woman who anointed His feet with expensive oil. Yet, His next words, "You will not always have Me," coupled with Matthew 25:40, "Whatever you did for one of the least of these brothers and sisters of mine, you did for Me," gives us a window into Jesus' heart. When we take care of the poor, we own the joy of bringing joy to Jesus. How can we expand this joy past the holidays?

Outside of the holidays, are you regularly helping care for those in your community who are struggling? If so, pray for them now. If not, ask God to direct you to them.

_____

_____

_____

_____

_____

_____

_____

_____

Tweet

When we take care of the poor, we get the joy of
bringing joy to Jesus. #joy218ways

— Anti-joy Points to Joy —

Job 3:7

_____

_____

Job was a faithful and faith-filled man. To our way of thinking, that should have protected him from anything bad happening. However, that's not biblical thinking because, as we know, stuff happens. In this early chapter of the book of Job, Job's reaction to losing his possessions, family, and health was to curse the day he was born. He invoked what I call "anti-joy"—something used to come against naturally occurring joy. No one can blame him; his life circumstances were awful. Yet, let's inspect a joy concept with Job's situation as the backdrop. This isn't to say Job should've "gotten over it"; it's simply for the sake of understanding a truth.

When a baby is born, she generally brings a rush of joy from the moment her tiny face makes an appearance on the stage of her world. This joy is the natural joy that God designed new life to give. By Job asking God to remove the joy associated with his birth, he actually underscores something special: Joy is a natural and expected part of life. Joy isn't something for which we should feel we have to work hard. The interesting truth that gets buried as life piles on disappointment and responsibility is this: Joy is easy to connect with until something blocks it. All we have to do is look at children who are happy and loved. They exude joy until a grumpy grown-up dumps a bucket of life over them. Let's ask the Holy Spirit to help remove any blockages to our joy!

How true do you think the statement is that "Joy is a natural and expected part of life"? Pray for the Holy Spirit to remind you that joy is natural and show you what might be blocking it in your life.

_____

_____

_____

_____

_____

_____

_____

_____

_____

Tweet

Joy is a natural and expected part of life. It's easy to
connect with until something blocks it. #joy218ways

— Joy in Unrelenting Pain —

_____

_____

_____

Job wishes he were dead. He hopes that God will allow him to die because of his great suffering. Yet, in his devastation, he shares that his "joy in unrelenting pain" is that he has not denied his faith but is stubbornly clinging to it. It's almost as if he's saying, "Okay, let's end all of this before I lose my faith."

Even though it's a given in life, our tendency is to try to live lives insulated from suffering. The truth is that anything can and will happen, so how do we maintain joy in the midst of it? When we're in a trial, I think one of the hardest parts is not knowing how long it's going to last. If we knew that our pain would "end" on a set date, we could pace ourselves as we navigated getting there. A powerful question I ask myself when I'm facing a crushing blow is this: After all the billions of people who have lived on the earth, have I finally found the one thing the God of the Universe can't handle? Of course I haven't. Having that settled, I dig to the next layer in dealing with the issue by making the choice to trust God. By faith, I trust He will ultimately bring good and glory from it. Put simply, I'm going to have to go through this pain, so trusting that God is at work maintains my connection to joy during the worst.

Are you currently facing a tough situation? How does trusting that God will handle your issue(s) allow you to tap into joy during painful times?

_____

_____

_____

_____

_____

_____

_____

_____

_____

_____

Suffering is unavoidable. Trusting that God is at work maintains our connection to joy during the worst of it. #joy218ways

Easy Joy

_____

_____

Job's friend, Bildad the Shuhite, is telling Job that if he will get right with God then all his pain will go away and better days are ahead. In chapter 8, Bildad links all that's happened to Job to the fact that there must be some sin or wickedness bringing this calamity upon him. We know this isn't true, and I can only imagine the look on Job's face when Bil-Daddy laid this track on him. I bet Job was like, "I am not picking up what you're putting down."

Bildad represents a common, if erroneous, view of God: If we do what's right, God will bless us and nothing bad will happen. This isn't a promise in the Bible. What God promises is to be with us through good and bad (Deuteronomy 31:6). Yet, we do know there is the kind of "easy joy" that Bildad mentions here. It's the kind we walk in when things are good. It's real and we love it because it's easily accessible. It doesn't require much strength of character or reliance on God to bask in this type of joy, but it certainly brings us closer to Him when we convert this joy to praise and gratitude. Always keeping in mind that our easy joy is a gift from God, our right reaction is to thank Him for it and enjoy it to the fullest!

Were you raised to believe that if you do things right, God will make everything good in your life? What "easy joys" are you currently enjoying? Give God some praise for them!

_____

_____

_____

_____

_____

_____

_____

_____

_____

_____

When God gives us areas of "easy joy," our right reaction is to
thank Him and enjoy them to the fullest! #joy218ways

——Joy of a Silent Friend——

_____

_____

_____

Job's heart is on display to his friend, Bildad. Through chapters 9–10, Job is starting to wallow in self-pity from the intensity and length of his suffering. In part, Job's friends compound his pain because they can't keep their mouths shut in the face of his difficulties. Their intentions are right, but so filled with confidence they have Job's pain figured out, their flapping lips are like arrows to his hurting heart.

When wounded people look at us and ask, "Why is this happening?" we want to have an answer. The honest answer is, "Only God knows." However, when a heart is raw with hurt, it usually doesn't help. While it's true, devastated people sometimes need something more tangible in those moments. What they need is … silence. We can heap tremendous pain on top of their struggle if we attempt to use words to answer what is, at the moment, unanswerable. There are times when the sound of joy is the sound of silent companionship. Mother Teresa said, "We need to find God, and He cannot be found in noise and restlessness. God is the friend of silence. See how nature—the trees, flowers, and grass—grows in silence; see the stars, the moon and the sun, how they move in silence … We need silence to be able to touch souls."[1] Not being alone, but not having to "be on" is a powerful joy-gift we can give those who are struggling to keep going.

Have you ever been wounded by the words of a well-meaning friend when you were hurting? Would it be easy or difficult for you to give the joy-gift of silent companionship to a hurting friend?

_____

_____

_____

_____

_____

_____

_____

When we're hurting, sometimes the sound of joy is the
sound of silent companionship. #joy218ways

_____

[1]   Mother Teresa - 75 quotes | [Page 3]." Great-Quotes.com. Accessed August 15, 2017.
http://www.great-quotes.com/quotes/author/Mother/Teresa/pg/3.

———— Life Line to Joy ————

_____

_____

Reading Job 9–10 is like watching a one-player ping-pong match. First, Job serves God notice that if he's sinned, God should just let him know. In the next breath, he volleys by assuring God and all else who can hear that he hasn't done anything to deserve the catastrophe in his life. By verse 10:20, Job is questioning God and wishing he could die. It's almost as if he's saying, "Hey God: If You could stop focusing Your attention on me, I might be able to catch a minute of joy."

In our quest to know why bad things happen to us, we can guard our joy by keeping one important filter firmly in place: God is good and is always for us. Sometimes our pain comes because our good Father loves us too much to let us waste away in our self-made comfort. At other times, the evil at work in our fallen world is the cause of the devastation in our lives. Picture the bad things in life as a rope in our hands. We could use the rope of our rotten circumstances to beat against God, but it wouldn't move us forward because we're hitting against the source of help. Instead, getting to the end of our rope, we toss it to God and connect to a joy we only experience when we're drowning in sorrow. As we pray and cry out, we encounter the soothing joy of being pulled upward and lovingly sustained.

Have you been mad at God? He can handle all your emotions, so it's freeing to be honest with Him. How does the image of throwing God the end of your rope point you to experiencing the soothing joy of being sustained in your sorrow?

_____

_____

_____

_____

_____

_____

_____

_____

_____

_____

When we're drowning in sorrow, we experience the soothing joy of being pulled upward as we throw the end of our rope to God. #joy218ways

No Joy in FoMO

_____

_____

Imagine that life has sucked the joy out of you. Now envision three of your closest friends coming to "comfort" you by telling you over and over that everything happening is your fault. Deep comfort, huh? In Job 20, Zophar tries to package Job's pain under the heading of "Bad things only happen to bad people." It may make human sense, but it's not a biblical truth because bad things happen to good people, too. Even though Zophar was off in the big picture, he was right in saying that people who thumb their nose at God eventually lose their joy.

In our culture, we see people not living according to God's ways and they seem to have it all. While we work hard, we don't have as many toys or adventures as they do. We can easily get infected with FoMO—Fear of Missing Out—and it can be deadly. The antidote is found in looking to God for our sense of worth, value, and purpose. If we compare our lives to what we perceive other people's are like, our joy will come up short ... but our lives are not only about the short game. Eternity doesn't start when we get to heaven; it started the moment we said "Yes" to God. The "godless", on the other hand, will not share in our eternal joy of being with Him. When FoMO threatens our outlook on life, let's take that thought captive and replace it with this truth: We look to God, not others, for the definition of what brings us joy.

How easily do you get infected with FoMO? How does that affect your joy?

_____

_____

_____

_____

_____

_____

_____

_____

_____

_____

Getting infected with FoMO (Fear of Missing Out) can be deadly to our joy. Looking to God, not others, is the antidote. #joy218ways

Joy in Unexplainable Mystery

Job 33:26

_____
_____
_____
_____

When my grandmother had thoughts about a situation but kept them to herself, she was family-famous for saying, "I never said a word; I never let on." In Job 32–37, Elihu, a young acquaintance of Job, starts his 157-verse speech by essentially saying he'd "never said a word" for as long as he could. He has listened to the debating, but now, he uncorks all he has bottled up. In a nutshell, he's irritated with Job's other friends for trying to convince Job that his suffering is a direct result of his sin. He is equally frustrated with Job for his suggestion that God has acted unjustly toward him. Elihu's argument is that God may use our suffering to refine us.

All the players in the book of Job attempt to speak for God. While it's tempting to give a suffering person an answer to "Why is this happening?" a humble representative of God will operate from the truth that there are mysteries about God we'll never fully understand. By choosing to stubbornly trust that God is good no matter our circumstances, we keep our eyes open for what we can learn through a trial. We don't always know why we suffer, and we can kill our joy in our pursuit of that answer. In the most faith-stretching of ways, joy is found by embracing the mystery that while we may never know 'Why?' we have the comfort of being connected to the One who knows and works all things for good (Romans 8:28).

What trial in your life stretched your faith to a breaking point? How challenging is the idea that embracing the unexplainable mysteries of God leads to joy?

_____
_____
_____
_____
_____
_____
_____

Tweet

We may never know why we suffer. In the most faith-stretching way,
joy is found by embracing the mystery of God's ways. #joy218ways

——— Joy of Perspective ———

Job 38:7

_____

_____

_____

A number of years ago I was driving in the country while it was raining. For a moment, there was a break in the storm and something to the left caught my eye. The sun was beautifully highlighting a funnel cloud that was touching down about ten miles away! It was fascinating to view that power without being in the face of it. In Job 38, poor old Job got a face-full of God speaking to him out of a storm. After all Job's questioning and complaining, after all Job's friends' well-intentioned but somewhat misguided explanations for suffering, God answered. He, now, was the questioner. By asking Job if he had the wisdom and power to create the world, God demonstrated that the events in his life were small compared to the power of the One who gave him life.

When hardships pile up, perspective flies out the window. Right perspective is not about, "There's always someone who has it worse." (I'm pretty sure that never helped anyone.) Instead, it's about cracking our self-created shell of despair by acknowledging our prayers are connecting to the Creator of the world. Practically, it means instead of centering on all that is wrong in our life, we pause for a moment and recall God's power. Feeding our pain by focusing on it will starve our joy. Instead, praising the incredible work of God gives us a break from our pain and resets us for the battle. In our lowest times, this drawing joy is quiet, yet it's loud enough to overpower our fear.

When you struggle, what are some ways you could focus on God's power instead of your pain? How can this perspective help you understand this quiet yet powerful aspect of joy?

_____

_____

_____

_____

_____

_____

_____

_____

_____

Tweet

Feeding our pain by focusing on it starves our joy. Praising God gives
us a break from pain and resets us for the battle. #joy218ways

Joy in Unseeable
Treasure

Psalm 4:7

_____

_____

Psalm 4 opens with David crying out to God for relief in his distress and closes with him resting safely in God's arms. In between, David warns his enemies not to mess with him because he is God's kid (v. 3). In verse 6, those in David's camp look to him for assurance that relief is on the way after the hard season they'd endured. David may not be able to give them the "good" they long for, but he does the better thing of praying a blessing over them. By verse 7, David takes a breath and exhales joy when he compares the unseeable treasures God has deposited in his heart to the earthly possessions his enemies lose their lives pursuing.

Our days are filled with accumulating. We go to work to pay for the stuff we've already bought. We shop to fill our homes with new stuff. We surf the web to find the future stuff we think we can't live without. Stuff, stuff, and more stuff. Yet, the accumulation grind can never give us the security our hearts crave. Our deepest joy is in the unseeable treasures God deposits in our hearts—His love and salvation. Thinking through whether we'd be fine even if we lost all our stuff is a good test of the depth of that joy. When we have God's invisible assurance anchored in our heart, we feel a protective blanket of safety around us that money can't buy.

Have you considered how much of your perception of joy is tied to what you own? How would it change your joy if you lost all your possessions?

_____

_____

_____

_____

_____

_____

_____

_____

_____

Tweet

Thinking through if we'd be fine even if we lost all our stuff is a good test of whether we have the kind of joy that lasts. #joy218ways

-Joy Comes in the Morning-

Psalm 5:11

_____

_____

_____

Must … go … to … sleep. Have you ever gone to bed with something heavy on your mind? What happens when you wake up the next morning? The joy-sucking situation is usually there to greet you with a piping hot cup of gloom. David was having one of those days. His enemies were pressing in, and they were his first thought as he rubbed the sleep from his eyes. However, in Psalm 5, David models a powerful pathway to joy in the way he addressed his mess. Instead of letting his troubles set the tone for his day, he took aim and fired prayer (v. 3). He connected to God, his source of joy, and basically tattled on the ones trying to do him harm.

Whether our day is filled with a heavy load of challenges or a light basket of "to-dos," our best shot at navigating the hours ahead in joy is to dial up in prayer before our feet hit the floor. Put another way: If we don't begin our day in prayer, we're saying in effect we can do the day without God's help and guidance. I love the children's song, "Good morning, God. This is Your day. I am Your child. Show me Your way." With joy, pray your way to a great day!

Is prayer your first thought in the morning? What joy do you think God could unlock as you pray tomorrow morning?

_____

_____

_____

_____

_____

_____

_____

_____

_____

_____

Tweet

Our best shot at navigating the hours in our day with joy is to
dial up in prayer before our feet hit the floor. #joy218ways

—— Joy of Eternal Life ——

Psalm 16:11

_____

_____

_____

Crickets are chirping, stars light the sky, and David is thinking about death (vv. 7–10). His thoughts ramble in a disorganized way, from asking God to keep him safe to considering the differences between those who live for God and those who don't. At one point, he celebrates the fact that God's blessings are better than the best inheritance a human could give (vv. 5–6). Finally, in his nighttime reflection, he lands on the joy that awaits him after death. He has enjoyed his relationship with God during his lifetime, and he is confident that God is not going to allow the grave (Sheol) to cause that to end.

While many things in life are not certain, we know it's inevitable that our earthly life eventually comes to a close. The thought of death can be scary because we have to accept what happens next by faith. Yet, God graciously gives us bright indicators in His Word that what comes next is better than anything we could imagine. In light of David's outlook in Psalm 5, I like what Mitch Albom wrote in _Tuesdays with Morrie_, "Death ends a life, not a relationship."[1] As we continue to deepen our relationship with God on this side of heaven, we have the joy of knowing that death is not all there is. For Christians, death doesn't end the joy of our fellowship with God. Death is simply a beautiful continuation of that relationship in a new setting. His gift of eternal life is our joy.

Does anything scare you about death? How does the idea of seeing death as a continuation of your relationship with God allow you to feel joy at the prospect?

_____

_____

_____

_____

_____

_____

_____

_____

Tweet

Death doesn't end the joy of our relationship with God. It's simply a beautiful continuation of it in a new setting. #joy218ways

---

[1] Albom, Mitch. Tuesdays with Morrie: an Old Man, a Young Man, and Life's Greatest Lesson. New York: Sphere, 2017.

Joy in God's Word
— and Works —

Psalm 19:8

_____

_____

_____

_____

Ellen G. White wrote, "We need no fanciful teaching regarding the personality of God. What God desires us to know of Him is revealed in His Word and His works."[1] This captures the essence of what David communicates in Psalm 19. Leading with his admiration of the heavens and the sun, David listens as the stunning work of creation testifies without words to the glory of God. He continues his adoration of the Lord by proclaiming the beauty, power, and richness of His Word. David's delight in God's Word and His works is infectious.

Throughout Scripture, God reveals Himself to be the Creator and the Law-Giver. Both are life-giving gifts to us. Yet, in our busyness, we can be guilty of blowing by His written revelation and His creation. When we pause to think about the magnificence of the Bible and of nature, it's a bit unbelievable that we would approach them casually or that we would neglect them. Even though we were made to enjoy God's Word and His works, we often think it's a burden to pay attention to one or both. If our joy in His Word and His works isn't vibrant, prayer is the springboard that will release the joy that busyness is blocking. Get busy enjoying His Word and His works!

When was the last time you laid on your back simply to soak in the joy of God's works? Does the thought of spending time in God's Word bring you joy? Spend time thanking God for the gift of both and asking Him to deepen your joy in both.

_____

_____

_____

_____

_____

_____

Tweet

If our joy in God's works and His Word isn't vibrant, prayer is the springboard to release the joy that busyness is blocking. #joy218ways

---

[1] White, Ellen G. "Life Sketches of Ellen G. White." — Ellen G. White Writings. Accessed August 20, 2017. https://m.egwwritings.org/en/book/41.491.

Joy in the Wisdom
of Praying

Psalm 20:5

_____
_____
_____
_____

The smell of battle is in the air. King David is geared up to lead his troops, and the men and horses strain to be off. Before leaving, he wisely pauses and puts himself in front of his people to soak in their prayers over him. It would've been just as easy and, perhaps, more efficient in terms of time to assemble his chariots, arms, and warriors and head out. However, he knows that prayer is the most important battle preparation he can "do." He leads well by acknowledging that victory will be a result of God moving on their behalf.

We face the battles of bills, family stress, work, relationships, unexpected trauma, and disappointments on a regular basis. It's tempting to attack our issues in our own strength. Maybe we throw a prayer or two at the situation but when things heat up, we dive in without talking to God first. We might even think it's not realistic to pause and pray when we get shoved to the battlefront. We take charge and collect names. But, honestly, how does that way work out for us? We might think we've "won," but the trail of battered people and depleted joy left behind is not a victory to celebrate. God invites us to a better way: Pause and pray. The joy that comes from being wise enough to pray is that we'll hear God's words replace ours as we deal with our challenge. That is a victory in the making.

In the face of a "battle," is your default to pause and pray? How would having God's words replace yours lead to more victorious joy?

_____
_____
_____
_____
_____
_____
_____
_____

Tweet

In the face of battle, pause and pray before diving in. Letting God's words replace ours leads to victorious joy. #joy218ways

39

—Joy of Answered Prayer—

_____
_____
_____
_____

Directly linked to Psalm 20, here David thanks God for giving him victory. He's giddy with the joy of seeing how God answered his prayers. David not only remembers to thank God, but his words powerfully demonstrate that he recognizes that God is the source of all the blessings in which he is basking. I can hear his voice ringing with joy in verse 2, "You have granted [me] the desires of [my] heart and have not withheld the request of [my] lips."

Like David, our prayers can be marked by boldness to ask what we desire and filled with humility and trust that God will do what's best (Psalm 21:7). Our joy grows as we have the childlike innocence to bring Him our hopes, the spiritual maturity to be humbly grateful for His answers, and the faith to know He hears and will act in our best interests. When God answers our prayers in the way we hoped and asked, the taste of joy is easy and sweet. Gratitude that our request aligned with His will allows us to savor and enjoy those moments. When we have the giddy joy of seeing our requests answered with a "yes" from the Lord, we should create a spiritual altar of remembrance. Then, during seasons of waiting or adjusting to a "no" from God, we can return to this altar and be reminded that He is always working for our good.

Have you ever asked God for something and received what you asked? If so, how did that strengthen your joy? If not, did it cause you to lose joy or to grow in trust?

_____
_____
_____
_____
_____
_____
_____
_____
_____
_____

When God answers our prayers in the way we hoped and asked, joy tastes easy and sweet. Humbly ask and trust He knows best. #joy218ways

——Joy of God's Presence ——

_____

_____

_____

_____

"Thank You for victory, thank You for answering, thank You for a crown of gold, thank You for…" David is overflowing with gratitude. It's almost as though he is overwhelmed by the many ways God has blessed him. Smack in the center of this thankful-list, David tells God how grateful he is for the gift of being in His presence. "You have made [me] glad with the joy of Your presence" (v. 6). Reading through the story of David's life and the Psalms he wrote, it's evident that David enjoyed a dynamic relationship with God.

What a blessing to know that we, too, can come into God's presence and be glad to be there. Too often, we see spending time with God as something we should do or something we'll get around to doing. So much of our lives is filled with responsibilities that drain us and distractions that numb us. The more we open ourselves to focusing on God, the better we'll navigate our lives with joy. It's a matter of the heart. Perhaps a good question to consider is this: What in the world do we have to do that is better than spending time with God? Our answers will reveal the glaring areas in our lives that hinder us from feeling the joy of His presence.

What in the world do you have to do that's better than spending time with God? Pray for a heart that desires the joy of being in His presence.

_____

_____

_____

_____

_____

_____

_____

_____

_____

_____

Tweet

What do we have to do that's better than spending time with God? Our answers reveal areas blocking the joy of His presence. #joy218ways

41

— God's Got Your Back Joy —

_____
_____
_____
_____

"The ache for home lives in all of us. The safe place where
we can go as we are and not be questioned."
—Maya Angelou[1]

In Psalm 27:4–5, David talks about God allowing him to dwell in the house of the Lord—to be in tight communion with Him. He goes on to say that when trouble comes, he knows he'll be safe by being in God's house (presence). In verse 6, David shouts for joy because of the protection and shelter God gives him. Knowing he is close to God comforts him even as he is aware of the evil swirling around him (vv. 2–3, 5–6).

It's never a matter of _if_ we'll need a divine covering to ward off life's blows when they hit, it's simply a matter of _when_. Life-storms come, and the knowledge that God's got our back becomes our shield of joy. We need a defender to cover us and help us feel safe. God may show up with physical protection or we may feel His protection in the form of a deep peace that passes all understanding. Navigating the messes in life will never be comfortable, but they are doable when we know we're under God's covering. As we stay close to Him in the midst of a trial, we encounter the joy and comfort of knowing we're home.

Do you have the feeling that God has your back when life's blows hit? How can the words in Psalm 27:1 be your shield of joy from the messes of life?

_____
_____
_____
_____
_____
_____
_____

As we stay close to God in the midst of a trial, His
covering becomes our shield of joy. #joy218ways

---

[1] Angelou, Maya. All God's Children Need Traveling Shoes. New York, NY: Random House, 1997.

Joy of Expecting Good Things

Psalm 28:7

_____

_____

_____

_____

In Psalm 28, David begins by crying out to God for help and protection. He then highlights the flaws of the wicked—those who have no interest in God (vv. 3–5). David knows that when he has a need, he takes it to God, The Way-Maker, and cries out for His merciful help (v. 6). Confident that God not only has heard his prayer but also will answer it, David breaks into a song of joy/exaltation in verse 7. He asks for help in one breath and in the next, he is praising God before the answer arrives.

Waiting is hard. It's when we have no idea how long our waiting will last that we lose heart. Waiting is a verb, but what adverb describes our attitude of _how_ we wait? Do we wait impatiently or patiently, angrily or calmly, fearfully or expectantly? We have no control over the verb; we can do nothing to make things happen as we wait on The Way-Maker to bring answers in His timing. But the adverb of attitude is our choice. We have control over _how_ we'll wait. Like David, we can ask what we need in one breath, and in the next we can let the Lord know we trust Him to answer. When we choose to wait expectantly, fully believing that God is at work, the delay of an answer doesn't overshadow the joy of today.

What adverb best describes your attitude when you have to wait? How does waiting expectantly allow you to tap into the joy that's around you today?

_____

_____

_____

_____

_____

_____

_____

Tweet

When we choose to wait expectantly, knowing God is at work, the delay of an answer doesn't overshadow the joy of today. #joy218ways

Joy of Giving Credit
—— Where It's Due ——

_____

_____

_____

"Hey David, how was your day?" If we asked him that when Psalm 30 was on his mind, David would've downloaded how the Lord rescued him from enemies, death, and God's holy anger (vv. 1–5). "Wow, friend. Big day. Anything else?" A bit sheepishly, he'd then confess that he got a little self-reliant for a minute (vv. 6–7). However, David quickly realized that God wasn't going to do His amazing God-moves on his behalf if he didn't follow Him. David shares that when he turned from his pride and admitted he needed God's guidance, the Lord turned his situation around (vv. 8–12).

Having to be strung-out-dependent on God is so uncomfortable that we often try to avoid situations in which we need Him that strongly. It's human nature to gravitate to life-settings in which we can remain in the comfort zone of our skill sets. It's especially dicey to stay dependent on God when we've achieved success in an area. We can, mistakenly, think that our accomplishments are a direct result of us making them happen. Hard work is a factor, but it's important to stay humble. It's a praise offering to God when we acknowledge that our ability to do something well is due to Him giving us the gifts and talents it took to make it happen. We don't lose a thing when we give God His due. In fact, we open new pathways to joy when we marvel at how God has gifted us instead of taking credit for those gifts.

What are your strongest gifts or talents? Do you practice the joy of giving God the credit when those talents are on display?

_____

_____

_____

_____

_____

_____

We open new pathways to joy when we marvel at how God has
gifted us instead of taking credit for those gifts. #joy218ways

---

- Joy of Praise and Worship -

Psalm 33:3

_____

_____

Psalm 147:1 says, "Praise the Lord. How good it is to sing praises to our God, how pleasant and fitting to praise Him!" As a praise exercise, I sometimes write out the alphabet and ascribe a word of praise to God that starts with every letter. X is always a little tricky; I could xylograph a word to cover that detail (look it up). In Psalm 33, the psalmist gets on a roll of praise and covers everything from celebrating God's Word to declaring the beauty of God's works. When you start praising, it can be a long time before you want to stop!

When we're in the zone praising God through music and singing, a two-way street is instantly built between the Lord and us. We give God our praise simply because He's God. We find ourselves singing because our hearts are full, and we're grateful for the outlet musical worship provides. Yet, other times, we may be in a worship setting and find ourselves going through the motions of praise without connecting to the joy of it. If distractions are the issue, we need to pause and pray them away. If a bruised heart is the issue, we can soak in the praise that others are offering and allow ourselves to experience worshiping God in a new, quiet way. Our praise should be "skillful" (from the Hebrew word *yatab* meaning "do well or thoroughly"). Whether we are shouting for joy or silently abiding in His presence, joy is ours when we praise our God with all we have in that moment.

If you are a churchgoer, do you prayerfully clear your mind before you start musical worship or do you just start singing? In what other settings do you experience the joy of praising God with your all?

_____

_____

_____

_____

_____

_____

_____

_____

Tweet

When we're in the zone praising God through music/singing, we build an instant 2-way street of joy. #joy218ways

Joy in Having —— a Protective Daddy ——

Psalm 35:27

_____

_____

_____

I always find it interesting that David never had a problem asking God to "get" his enemies. Whether he was being attacked personally, physically, emotionally, or spiritually, he would implore God to contend with those who were out to get him. Psalm 35 is David in full-out tattletale mode on his enemies and crying out for justice. As evidenced in other Psalms, when God answered David's prayers, he was quick to give God thanks and praise (e.g., Psalm 21). David knew he had a fiercely protective Daddy.

Maybe it was the way I was raised—probably it was the way I was raised—but when facing "enemies," my default cry to God is: "What's wrong with me? Show me where I'm causing this situation to go wrong. Show me where I need to expand so this situation may be resolved." On the one hand, that outlook leads to growth. However, I've discovered that if I don't ask God to contend with those who hold something against me, I rob myself from the joy of having my Daddy take care of me. God is creative, and I've seen Him work resolutions where neither side loses, but the wrong isn't allowed to go unattended. To experience the joy of having God's protective arms wrapped around us during conflict is to experience the joy of His powerful love.

Is it easy or difficult for you to ask God to "get" those who hold something against you? How does thinking about God's protective nature connect you to the joy of being protected?

_____

_____

_____

_____

_____

_____

_____

_____

Tweet

To experience the joy of God's protective arms wrapped around us during conflict is to experience joy in His powerful love. #joy218ways

—— Hope in Previous Joy ——

_____

_____

_____

_____

_____

_____

Are you familiar with the Beatles' song, "Yesterday"? It's a lament of longing for the easier days of the past in the face of the troubles of today. Nearly 3,000 years before the Beatles, Psalm 42 finds the psalmist singing his blues and longing for the days he could worship at the temple in Jerusalem. Due to life's circumstances, he is downcast and is recalling a time when he was in the spiritual zone. He feels lonely and separated but even in his pain, he still calls to God. The reality that sustains him is his remembrance of previous joy.

We'll definitely have times when we don't feel close to God. Due to life's circumstances, we won't feel spiritually strong and will long for a return to easier days. In those seasons, we can stay connected to joy by looking over our spiritual shoulder and remembering when God came through in the past. Psalm 77 presents a powerful word picture to recall "the years when the Most High stretched out His right hand. I will remember the deeds of the Lord; yes, I will remember Your miracles of long ago. I will consider all Your works and meditate on all Your mighty deeds. Your ways, God, are holy. What god is as great as our God?" (Psalm 77:10–13). When life feels flat and we're disconnected from joy, recalling previous seasons of joy helps us stay connected to the hope that new joy is on the way.

Looking back, what are your spiritual "high" moments? When you go through dry seasons in your walk with God, how can recalling those times bring joy as you remember God's faithfulness?

_____

_____

_____

_____

_____

_____

When life feels flat and we're disconnected from joy, recalling past moments of joy helps us wait in the hope of new joy. #joy218ways

Clinging to Joy

Psalm 43:4

It's been days, weeks, and months; there is no end in sight. A man sits far removed from the land he loves and he's consumed with thoughts of the hardships he's faced. People are out to get him, he feels like God's been angry with him, he's depressed and longing for home. What is his response to all this pain? He refuses to accept that this is how life is going to be. He stubbornly clings to the joy he has in knowing God and believing that, even though he can't see it presently, God will somehow rescue him.

It strikes me that joy sometimes feels like a song that's stuck in our head but, for some reason, we can't remember all the words. We drive ourselves a bit crazy trying to recall the lyrics. We'll ask around if anyone knows the words and search the web to find them because we can't let it go. We know the words exist even if we don't have them in mind at the moment. And when we connect to those words after searching, we get the feeling we can move on because we are back in possession of what was eluding us. Sometimes, we need to pursue our joy in this way. God is the source of joy, so the gift of joy can be found as we pursue Him. Like the psalmist, when we don't feel joy, stubbornly clinging to God will reconnect us to Him. He is the inspiration of our exceeding joy and delight.

How strong is the "song" of joy in your life at the moment? Can you easily call up joy's sound or are you in a season of needing to search and reconnect to it?

When we don't feel joy, stubbornly clinging to God will reconnect us to Him as the inspiration of our exceeding joy. #joy218ways

—— Joy of the Church ——

_____

_____

_____

_____

At first read, this psalm may seem like a piece that would've been shared at a royal wedding in the times before Christ. However, many scholars take the position that this is a Messianic Psalm—a psalm that points to the attributes and work of the Messiah who would come. Looking at it through this filter, we see Jesus as the embodiment of the anointed king—the royal bridegroom. His bride, as we see often in the New Testament, is the church. Psalm 45 is a celebration of God's "Plan A" for reaching the world: Jesus and His church.

The description of the bride/church shows us that: She is set apart and seen as beautiful (v. 9), she is to turn away from all she's known before meeting her groom/Jesus and be devoted to Him (vv. 10–11), she is respected by the people of the world (v. 12), and she is glorious when she comes in a pure state into the presence of the king/Jesus (vv. 13–15). God gave us the gift of belonging to His church in which we can grow and find community. He did this so that we can invite others to the joy we've found (Matthew 28:19–20, Acts 2:42–47). Sometimes organized religion gets in the way of God's pure design for His bride, but we can't let human failings limit our pursuit of the joy that exists when we're a vital part of God's "Plan A."

If you are a churchgoer, how much joy does being a part of God's "Plan A" bring you? If you are not a vital part of God's "Plan A"—His church—when was the last time you explored talking to God about this?

_____

_____

_____

_____

_____

_____

_____

_____

Organized religion can mar God's pure design for His church, but we can't let human failings limit our joy at being in church. #joy218ways

Joy of Having
- a Right Heart for Worship -

_____

_____

The wedding march begins and the bridesmaids float down the aisle. They are beautiful in their gowns. Much thought and preparation has gone into how they will appear before the king. Anticipation builds as the assembly crane their necks to glimpse the bride. It is this scene that captures the essence of Psalm 45:13–15. The "virgin companions" along with the bride (daughter) represent God's church. Their virginity is highlighted as a display of the purity of their hearts as they prepare to come into the king's palace and presence.

It's remarkably easy for those who attend church to approach it so casually that the majesty of coming into God's "palace" is not even considered on a Sunday morning. Church can become something we "do" … a place we "go." If we don't spend time _before_ we arrive to church preparing our hearts for the joy of coming into God's presence, it's like being bridesmaids who stroll down the aisle in sweats and flip flops. At least we showed up, but we missed out on the special feeling that a wedding atmosphere provides. Wedding days are set apart (definition of holy) from regular days. This has nothing to do with what we wear to church; it's completely about us readying the condition of our hearts before we go to church so that we are in a holy (set apart) state of mind. It's special to come into God's house, so let's not miss out on the joy of coming in prepared!

If you are a churchgoer, what do you do before coming to church to prepare your heart for the joy of being in the presence of God? If you're not a churchgoer, would you consider praying about giving church another try?

_____

_____

_____

_____

_____

_____

_____

Before going to church, if we don't prepare our hearts to be in God's presence, we may miss out on some holy (set apart) joy. #joy218ways

Joy of Approval

Psalm 47:1

_____

_____

_____

Psalm 47 may have been written with the back-story of 2 Chronicles 20:1–30 in view. There, King Jehoshaphat was ready to lead troops to battle, but they faced an army they couldn't defeat in the natural. The king called out to God, and the Lord answered through Jahaziel. He prophesied and assured the king that, "The battle is not yours, but God's." The next day, the Lord literally inhabited the praise of the people and wiped out all their enemies. In Psalm 47, the people are called upon to clap their hands in approval of who God is and to acknowledge their incredible God. People: Give that God a standing ovation!

We all crave approval. Even if we say we don't care, that might be a real reaction to not receiving approval during our formative years. As we read Psalm 47, the thing to note is how the people are approving of God for who He is, not what He has done. Approval is a flighty accolade if we tie it to our performance. If, instead, we pursue God's approval for who we are—our character, our desire to live according to His ways—we'll have the joy of basking in approval that lasts. From the overflow of God's holy thumbs-up, what we do will be a byproduct of who we are. When God's commendation is more important to us than any affirmations from people, we walk in the joy of knowing our Father puts His holy seal of approval on our lives.

If asked, would you say that God approves of you? Perfection is not required; it's about the desire of your heart seeking the joy of God's approval.

_____

_____

_____

_____

_____

_____

_____

_____

_____

_____

Tweet

When God's holy seal of approval is more important to us than any affirmations from people, we truly have the joy of approval. #joy218ways

51

Joy of Knowing
—— Where Jesus Is ——

Psalm 47:5

In this rally psalm of praise written around 701 BC, an interesting theological truth about Jesus pops out in verse 5. As the people shout for joy at the victory God provided, He ascends back to heaven. This is a poetical way of demonstrating that, from heaven, God hears the needs of His people and He comes to advocate and fight on their behalf. This Old Testament passage points to the New Testament. In 1 Peter 3:21–22, we see the same ascending characteristic of God spoken about in relation to Jesus. "Jesus Christ, who has gone into heaven and is at God's right hand—with angels, authorities, and powers in submission to Him." The Jesus who descended to live His earthly ministry is now ascended into heaven. From there, He hears us and, seated at the right hand of God, intercedes for us.

The idea of heaven with all its mysteries can be a fascinating journey into speculation about what it's like. While we don't have a perfect physical description, we do know that heaven is where Jesus is. How can we be certain? By faith, Christians know Jesus is in heaven because of our belief that God's Word is true. Our personal view of God's Word as truth guides everything we do. As believers, we achieve a foundational joy when we settle the question for ourselves of whether we believe the Bible is the inspired Word of God.

Do you have the foundational joy of knowing that God's Word is true? If so, celebrate the joy of knowing that your Jesus is in heaven advocating for you. If not, who do you know that could talk through your questions with you?

Tweet

We achieve a foundational joy when we settle this question for ourselves:
Do we believe the Bible is the inspired Word of God? #joy218ways

——Joy in Where You Live——

_____

_____

_____

This psalm reads like a "What I love about where I live" essay. The beauty, grace, strength, and power of God are mirrored in the walls and boundaries of Jerusalem/ Mt. Zion. God's holy city elicits admiration and fear from foreign kings (vv. 4–8). Her people are invited to walk around the city and marvel at the wonders she contains (vv. 9–13). The sense of the psalmist's civic joy and pride is tangible.

We should pause to take stock of our own feelings about where we live. Would we extol the virtues of our town? More importantly, do we actively seek to see God in our hometown? If our answer is "Yes," we should offer prayers of thanksgiving for the daily blessing we receive of living there. If the answer is "No," our joy is tied to a decision tree. Will we: (a) Move. Where we live deserves honor because God created it. If we can't connect to a good feeling about our current location, then we should move. "But," we say, "We can't move." Then, (b) Pray for the wisdom, guidance, people, and opportunities that will connect us to joy where we are in the midst of not having what we want. Or, (c) Hush. If we aren't going to (a) Move or (b) Pray, then we need to avoid choosing the anti-joy of complaining about where we live. It's not God-honoring to live a life of blame and discontent. Choose a path that allows you to honor where you live with joy.

Do you like where you live? If so, share your joy with the Lord in thanksgiving. If not, are you going to (a), (b), or (c) your way to joy?

_____

_____

_____

_____

_____

_____

_____

_____

_____

_____

It's not God-honoring to live a life of blame and discontent. Choose joy. #joy218ways

The Sound of
——— Corrected Joy ———

_____

_____

Psalm 51 is one of my favorites. It's full of mercy. If it were a song, it would open with a slow, halting melody as though it's not confident that anyone would want to listen (vv. 1–2). As it continued, the tempo would quicken to a driving staccato beat of self-recrimination (vv. 3–6). With an almost startling transition, we'd hear the sweetest refrain of hope emerge in the next stanzas (vv. 10–12). It would close with a lilting upbeat sound of joy as the refrain of restoration rang from a heart that has experienced the discord of messing up followed by the sweet harmony of forgiveness.

The sound of mercy and forgiveness … when we first hear it, it usually seems too good to be true. Our tendency is to hide our sin. Sometimes, if we won't repent, God in His mercy may "crush our bones" to get our attention. It's a joy to know He cares enough to squash that sin by exposing it rather than ignoring it until we dance into a pit of self-destruction. When we've committed a major wrong and we find the courage to turn away and be open with God about it, we connect to deep joy. Barriers between us and the One who loves us beyond reason fall away, and the "sound" of that restored communication is our song of joy-filled relief.

What are you currently struggling to hide? Does confessing it to God sound like the theme song of a scary movie or an anthem of freedom? You may need to pray for a mature, loving, non-judgmental Christian to come near to help you learn to embrace the joy of God's discipline.

_____

_____

_____

_____

_____

_____

_____

When we've committed a major wrong, there is deep joy in finding the courage to turn away and be open about it with God. #joy218ways

—— Joy of Stopping Sin ——

_____

_____

David is busted. After committing adultery with Bathsheba, getting her pregnant, and arranging for the murder of her husband to cover it up, David ran from owning his sin (2 Samuel 11). It took the prophet Nathan, coming with a clever truckload of truth, for David to wake up and repent (2 Samuel 12). Psalm 51 is David's confession to the Lord about his sin. His heartfelt desire is for the separation he's caused between himself and God to heal and for their relationship to be restored.

When we're involved in a sinful choice that separates us from God, it can be difficult to let it go. We enjoy the pleasure the sin gives. At the same time, we're grieved in our souls because we know we're creating a gap between God and us. We're blocking His blessings and we know there will be consequences. How can we begin to turn when we don't even want to? The most humanly brilliant move we can make is to involve God at this stage by praying, "God: Please help me 'to want to want to' stop. Help me to want to return to the pure joy of living Your way." While God gives us free will to make our choices, He will begin to send people, events, ideas, and resources. He'll grant a "willing spirit" in that prayer space. We'll never regret the steps we take to draw closer to God, but we'll always have some type of regret when we harbor sin in our lives.

What sin in your life has been the most difficult to turn from? Did you experience the joy of feeling restored in your relationship with God when you put it behind you?

_____

_____

_____

_____

_____

_____

_____

_____

_____

_____

_____

While God gives us free will to make our choices, it's His joy to send what we need to strengthen us when we turn from sin. #joy218ways

Joy of Missions

_____

_____

_____

_____

God is so good. That's the theme running through Psalm 65. The goodness of God's moral character shines in verses 1–5. Verse 8 is interesting because God's ability to reach all the people of the Earth is lifted high. "Where morning dawns and evening fades" refers to God's reach from the east to the west. God is good, His creation is overwhelming, and His all-inviting love extends to people in every corner of the world.

As Jesus prepared to return to heaven after His resurrection, He stood with His disciples one last time. In Acts 1:8, He told them that when they received power from the Holy Spirit, they would be His "witnesses in Jerusalem, and in all Judea and Samaria, and to the ends of the earth." They would start in Jerusalem—their own zip code—and share the story of God's amazing invitation. From there, He called them to branch out in ever-widening circles until the whole world heard the message. It's over 2,000 years later, and there are still people who don't know about Jesus, starting with people in our own zip code. When we have the opportunity to share the story of God and His love, we touch the joy of Jesus' missional heart. Let's always be on the lookout for where we can share the gospel, and let's be supportive of those who do God's mission work at home and around the globe.

When was the last time you had the joy of sharing the story of God's love? How often do you pray for opportunities to invite not-yet believers to take their next step toward God?

_____

_____

_____

_____

_____

_____

_____

_____

_____

When we get to share the story of God's love with others,
we get to experience a natural joy-high! #joy218ways

Joy of Being
— a Good Earth-Steward —

_____

_____

_____

God is an excellent steward of His creation. Verses 9–11 list the ways in which the Master Gardner tends His land, earth, crops, pastures, grasslands, hills, meadows, and valleys. This reminds me of Romans 1:20: "For since the creation of the world God's invisible qualities—His eternal power and divine nature—have been clearly seen, being understood from what has been made, so that people are without excuse." If God didn't take care of His creation, we couldn't enjoy all the plants and trees— there's no way we could water all of them! God demonstrates His power in the way He nurtures nature. God's creations respond with a sound—a song—to their maker, and their praise is one way that God draws people to Himself.

As a reflection of God's stewardship of His creation, we are called to attend to the areas that He entrusts to us. In big ways or small, everything we do to care for our environment helps maintain the planet God gifted to us. We can't take the rustle of crop leaves, the sighing of tree limbs, and the myriad voices of animals for granted. We are here to partner with God in preserving this beauty. As we listen to nature's joy-filled shouts and singing, our joy comes in knowing that we are part of caring for this symphony.

What intentional steps do you take to be a good steward of God's creation? Are there any ways you could expand your joy in being a good Earth-steward?

_____

_____

_____

_____

_____

_____

_____

As we care for nature and listen to its sounds and song, our joy comes
in knowing that we are part of the symphony. #joy218ways

—— Joy of Discipline ——

_____

_____

At a moment in history, a group of God's people needed correction. Rather than complain or question why it happened, the psalmist recognized that God was disciplining the nation for their corporate good (vv. 8–12). As a member of that nation, the writer owned that he was going to make good on all the prayer-promises he gave God when they were in the thick of the trial (vv. 13–15). The theme of people going their own way, God intervening with discipline and eventually working it for their good rises from Psalm 66. That the psalmist trusted God is evidenced by how he opened the psalm. He wanted God's goodness shouted with joy so all the earth could witness His glory.

As we reflect on the theme of Psalm 66, we may be able to relate to times when God refined or tried us. Whatever direction we were headed, God—the perfect parent—knew there were life lessons we needed to learn. Rather than let us become an ugly version of ourselves, He provided redirects that caused us to move toward a positive path. None of us like to be busted or for God to spoil our "fun" but all of us want to live our best life. Learning to find joy when (not after) God disciplines us is a mark of maturity. That kind of a trusting relationship with God will be a "shout of joy" to everyone we encounter.

What is your reaction when you receive discipline? Does it help you embrace the joy of God's discipline to know it's because He loves you too much to leave you in something that will hurt you?

_____

_____

_____

_____

_____

_____

_____

_____

_____

_____

Learning to find joy when (not after) God disciplines us is a mark of maturity. #joy218ways

Joy in Leadership Salvation

National pride is a beautiful sentiment. Seeing my flag, hearing my anthem, and taking part in the things that are good in my country stir areas of my joy that nothing else can touch. Nations have kingdom value. The prayer in Psalm 67 asks that God's favor would shine through His people so that His gift of salvation and praise would fill the earth (vv. 1–5). We read the simple and clean acknowledgment that God rules and guides the nations (v. 4). Being recognized as the One in control, His response is to bless the people (vv. 6–7). God designed the nations to be a platform through which His kingdom work can shine.

In our culture, it seems many leading intellectuals and powerful people make the truths of God appear, at minimum, difficult, and at most, non-existent. They rely on themselves and aren't willing to humbly acknowledge God or trust Him. From their positions of influence, they persuade or force nations to follow their non-biblical ideology. What hope do we have? Fortunately, our hope is in Jesus, not in leaders. Think of the impact a God-honoring leader would make on the political landscape. Are we praying for the salvation of those in power? I think we've gotten so beaten down by culture that we're almost surprised to (a) find a Christian in national leadership and (b) think a not-yet believing leader would stop rejecting Jesus' offer of love and forgiveness. Let's Christian up and rekindle our joy by praying for our leaders' salvation!

During difficult times, is simply knowing that you are saved enough to maintain your joy? Do you trust that God's salvation is what would turn off-track leaders into national heroes?

When not much in the world makes sense, sometimes the joy of our salvation is all that keeps us afloat. #joy218ways

–Joy of Not Happy-Hoping –

...it's as though we're listening in on a prayer offered up by a gray-haired man in a rocking chair. At first glance, he looks like a gentle grampa. However, as we listen in on Psalm 71, we find that he evidently still has enough spit and vinegar in him that he's got some enemies (vv. 9–13). His declaration in verse 23 is the joy of a man who has the confidence of knowing that, based on his long relationship with God, the Lord will answer his cry for help. He looks forward to being on the other side of this problem as God walks him through it.

How do we pray when big situations press in on us? One option is to pray in a sort of wishy-washy-hoping mindset. It sounds something like, "God. I know You're there. Please help." In the background of our mind, however, is the niggling fear that God might not be able to handle this. We know it's better to pray than not to, so we cover our bases and wallow in our wondering. The flip side is to attack our problem with the weapon God provides—a prayer full of belief that our God will move on our behalf. We have to let God be God and trust that He will answer in the way that is for our best. We release joy that's being held prisoner behind our wall of fear when we pray with confidence that God is on the move.

When hard situations hit, do you pray with wishy-washy-hope or confident expectancy? If confidence that God is moving on your behalf is not your default, up your joy by inviting the Holy Spirit to strengthen your confidence in Him.

We release joy being held prisoner behind our wall of fear when we pray confidently knowing God is on the move. #joy218ways

Joy of Legacy

Legacy: Something transmitted by or received from an ancestor or predecessor or from the past.

In Psalm 81, Asaph says, "Sing for joy to the God who has led our people for centuries!" He reminds the Israelites of the mighty way their God rescued them in the past (vv. 3–7). With the wisdom of one who has a solid history of walking with God, Asaph closes by giving them a taste of how the Lord stands ready to bless them if they turn from their ways and follow Him (v. 16).

Those who have journeyed long with God through hard times have a legacy of wisdom to pass to the generations that come behind. Their wisdom illuminates an efficient pathway to our best life if we heed it. Perhaps we didn't grow up in a Christian home where this kind of wisdom was shared. Our call, then, is to birth a legacy that will change the course of the next generations. If we were blessed to have Christian parents/grandparents/guardians who shared their faith and wisdom, our call is to build on the legacy they passed down to us. The only course that we must avoid at all costs is to break a legacy of faith our elders gave us. That is the definition of a fool. Joy is found in birthing and building legacies while lovingly praying for those who have broken with theirs.

Which connects with you the most: birthing, building, or breaking a legacy of faith? If you are birthing, pray for the joy of seeing it multiply. If you are building, thank those who gave you this joy. If you have broken with a legacy of faith, what would have to happen for you to take a step toward embracing it again?

Joy is found in birthing and building legacies of faith while lovingly praying for those who have broken with theirs. #joy218ways

Recharge Your Joy-O-Meter

_____

_____

"You're asking for it." When that phrase flies through the air, usually people are about to get more trouble than they bargained for. Psalm 86, however, puts a different spin on this. In the face of a troubled time (vv. 7, 14), David lays a series of requests in front of the Lord that is supported by the reasons he feels confident to ask for them. He asks God to hear him for he is poor and needy (v. 1). He asks God to guard (preserve) his life and have mercy (be gracious) for God is the One whom David calls on and trusts in. I especially love verse 4, "God, bring joy (gladden) me for my soul worships you." David is saying, "God, I'm sitting on empty. I need a spiritual fill up, and I'm asking for it."

When our joy-o-meter is on "low," we need a way to recharge it. One option is to choose activities that distract us from whatever drained our joy. That actually does work—at least for a time. However, it's not sustainable; when it fades, we hit empty. David models an uncomplicated solution for renewing a depleted tank. If we feel low on joy, we simply need to go to God and ask Him to fill us up. This may sound too easy but if we haven't tried it much, we can't really say it won't work. Ask Him; we might just get more joy than we bargained for!

How full is your joy-o-meter at the moment? Do you think getting a recharge of your joy is as simple as asking God to bring it to you?

_____

_____

_____

_____

_____

_____

_____

_____

_____

_____

_____

_____

If our joy-o-meter is on "low," we simply need to ask God to fill us up. Sound too easy? Try it. You might like it. #joy218ways

"But Life" Joy

_____

_____

Christians have a saying: All God's promises are true. It's rooted in scriptures like Deuteronomy 7:9, "Know therefore that the Lord your God is God; He is the faithful God, keeping His covenant of love to a thousand generations of those who love Him and keep His commandments." Psalm 89 finds Ethan the Ezrahite praising God's creation. He's amazed that even Mt. Tabor on the west of the Jordan to Mt. Hermon in the east sing for joy. As the psalm develops, he seems to be reminding God of the covenant He made with David and his descendants. In verses 38–51, however, some major life event has occurred, and it appears that God is withholding His favor. Ethan knows God's promises are true, but life has caused a delay of game. He wonders how long it will take for these promises to become a reality.

God's promises are true, but life has a way of squelching joy when pressures mount. Sometimes joy is found by staying in touch with what we know to be real even when we can't see or feel it. In Matthew 22:37, Jesus said we are to "Love the Lord our God with all our heart and with all our soul and with all our mind." In seasons where our heart hurts and it isn't well with our soul, we can maintain a quiet joy by loving God with our mind as we reflect on His promises. We may not connect to _feeling_ joy, but as we use our minds to remember God's faithfulness, we connect to the assuring joy that God is a promise keeper.

How does the idea of loving God with your mind by recalling His promises help connect you to joy?

_____

_____

_____

_____

_____

_____

_____

_____

_____

When our heart hurts and it isn't well with our soul, quiet joy is found in loving God with our mind. Recall His faithfulness. #joy218ways

— Unfailing Love Gives Joy —

_____

_____

_____

_____

God is awesome. By His word, the earth came *ex nihlo*—"out of nothing" (vv. 1–2). He holds the days of our lives in His hands (vv. 3–6). He is outside of time, as we understand it (v. 4). He is holy and is the standard by which good is measured (vv. 7–12). He is loving and patient (vv. 13–17). While the psalmist weaves these good attributes of God throughout Psalm 90, his words also demonstrate his understanding of the power of a holy God who does not bend to accommodate human sin. The posture of the psalmist is one of worship as he acknowledges God's awesome presence. In the midst of all his reverence he makes a request on behalf of the people: God, let the thought of Your unfailing love satisfy us in the morning and be our joy (v. 14).

Is the thought of God's unfailing love enough to fill us with joy when we open our eyes in the morning? The right answer is, "Of course." Being honest, however, we often either (a) don't entertain that as our first thought or (b) think we need His unfailing love *plus* a lot of issues handled before we'll be satisfied enough to sing for joy. None of us would look God in the eye and say, "Sorry, Your love isn't enough. Give me more if you want to hear me sing." If we wouldn't say it, then we'd better not live like it. God has unfailing love for us. That is enough to give us a reason for joy today.

What was your first thought this morning? Give God a prayer of thanksgiving and joy that His love for you is unfailing!

_____

_____

_____

_____

_____

_____

_____

_____

_____

God has unfailing love for us. That, by itself, is reason
enough to sing for joy today. #joy218ways

——— Joy in the Sabbath ———

Psalm 92:4

_____

_____

_____

_____

As the title says, this is a psalm for the Sabbath—the day of the week set aside for rest and worship (Exodus 20:8–11). As the people declared the words of this song, they were reminded to praise God for His love and faithfulness, His righteous judgment on the wicked, His provision, and His defense of His people. Members of the assembly cried out together, "I sing for joy at what Your hands have done. You, O Lord, are exalted forever" (vv. 4, 8). What a rush of joy to focus on God and set aside all the cares of the world for a moment. It's always good to give God praise for the work of His hands, but it's especially important to do on the Sabbath as He intended.

In our modern culture, people observe the Sabbath in varying ways and degrees. On one end of the continuum, denominations have formed around their interpretation of the correct way to observe the Sabbath. Solid guidelines and rules regarding how to keep the Sabbath on a certain day govern the people who follow that religion. Conversely, many others have no regard for the holiness of the Sabbath thinking it belongs to a forgotten era. For them, the day is like all the others of the week. We live in a busy, hurried, connected world. God's command to keep the Sabbath holy is an invitational gift rather than an oppressive mandate. Having the margin to pause and focus on the work of God's hands—whether in nature, in rest, or in relationships— activates a joy that gets buried under the burden of a busy week.

How do you observe the Sabbath? What are some ways you could activate more joy on the Sabbath?

_____

_____

_____

_____

_____

_____

_____

_____

Tweet

Pausing on the Sabbath to focus on the work of God's hands activates
a joy that is hidden throughout a busy week. #joy218ways

—— Joy during Anxiety ——

_____

_____

Even the strongest believers feel attacked and anxious at times. In Psalm 94, we get a "behind the scenes" look at a scary time in the life of one such person. How do we know this psalmist is a strong believer? He is close enough to God that the Holy Spirit chose him as the author of a chapter in the Bible—that's a pretty decent credential. The psalmist notes how the leaders within his nation are oppressing the people (vv. 1–8, 20–21). He cries out against them but we get the sense that he is powerless to stop them. He knows and declares that only God can do it (vv. 9–17, 22–23). At his lowest point, the psalmist feels unsettled and anxious but he discovers a fresh joy when he feels God draw near (vv. 18–19).

Even if we don't order attacks and anxiety off Life's menu, some still gets put on our plates. Thank God He is there to help us navigate them. Check out verses 9–11 in Psalm 94. When attacks are coming from people, do they really think God won't hear, see, and know all they're up to and punish them? I see God sort of shaking His head. Notice, in verse 19, where the joy for those moments comes from. God doesn't necessarily grant us joy by changing our circumstances; joy comes from the consoling sense of His abiding presence. Picture it as Life giving us an unasked for triple-decker sandwich of anxiety. God won't eat it for us but His presence will be the special sauce that helps us digest it bite by bite.

Is anxiety a stronghold in your life? How can knowing God is with you and understands your situation help you connect to His consoling joy?

_____

_____

_____

_____

_____

_____

_____

_____

When life gives an unasked for triple-decker anxiety sandwich, God's presence is the special sauce that helps us digest it. #joy218ways

—— Joy of a Huge God ——

Psalm 95:1

At 36,070 feet below sea level, the Challenger Deep in the Mariana Trench is the deepest known point in the Earth's oceans. To put this in perspective: Mount Everest is the highest mountain on Earth and would be covered by a mile of water if it were placed in this trench.[1] In light of this fact, consider the words of Psalm 95:4–5, "In His hand are the depths of the earth, and the mountain peaks belong to Him. The sea is His, for He made it, and His hands formed the dry land." Can you even begin to wrap your head around the incredible power of a God who holds mountains and oceans in His hand, and still pays attention to the salvation status of each one of us?

"He's got the whole world in His hands." A mind-blowing joy awaits us when we focus on who God is. To enjoy this holy time-out, we have to intentionally say "Please hold" to the issues in our lives. We choose, instead, to go into His throne room with praise music and prayer. We allow no head space for our problems when we immerse ourselves in intense worship of Him. God is more immense than we can fathom. To consider the works and nature of God requires that we concentrate on Him to the point that we blot all else from our minds. Moving into focused worship of the Creator of the world shines perspective on the problems in our worlds. God is hugely good. Every once in a while, it's good to enjoy the joy of worshiping this huge God.

When was the last time you immersed yourself in the joy of intensely worshiping your hugely good God?

_____

_____

_____

_____

_____

_____

_____

_____

_____

_____

Tweet

A mind-blowing joy awaits us when we focus on how
hugely good our God is. #joy218ways

[1] "Deepest Part of the Ocean." Geology.com. Accessed September 15, 2017. http://geology.com/records/deepest-part-of-the-ocean.shtml.

-Joy of Future Redemption-

_____

_____

_____

_____

No sports team or dance troupe will ever be as tightly in sync as an acre of crops moving by the wind of God's breath. His glory is evident when a person's eyes are attuned to witnessing the "fields be jubilant." Even the trees, which have no human voice, sing and broadcast the joy of knowing one day all the earth will be restored and redeemed (Romans 8:19–22). Psalm 96 shouts praise to the Creator God who is in all things and reigns over all things. It puts into words how worthy and deserving God is of our worship. It also expresses a longing for the day the Lord will come to rule—the day He will restore and redeem all that is broken.

As I sit outside on a gorgeous late summer day, I'm basking in the blues, greens, and golds of God's earth. It's as though He has His arm around me directing my gaze and saying, "See? I made this … and this … and this…" How can He be denied? And, as real as the natural elements are that fill my vision, God's returning to judge the earth is also a powerful coming reality. That thought could elicit fear in those who are not connected to a relationship with Him. However, for believers, the thought of the Lord coming to destroy all that is evil by establishing His right ways on earth should stir the joy of anticipating His restoration and redemption!

What emotions stir in you when you think about God judging the earth? Like the trees in Psalm 96, do you sing for joy? If the thought stirs any fear, spend time talking to God about that.

_____

_____

_____

_____

_____

_____

_____

_____

_____

The thought of the Lord returning to destroy all that is evil stirs the joy of anticipating His restoration and redemption! #joy218ways

Joy of Alignment

Have you ever driven a vehicle that is out of alignment? Perhaps it's out of whack from a nasty encounter with a curb or it may be worn down from lack of maintenance. Either way, you find yourself having to constantly pull the steering wheel to the left or right to compensate for the problem. With wisdom and experience, you know if you let the car go its own way, you'll be off-roading in no time. Psalm 97 is about the power of God and about being in alignment with His will and His ways. I kid around sometimes and say that if we don't do things God's way, we're in for a "lightning spanking." But, reading verses 3–4, maybe we'd better watch our backsides!

Often, we're quicker to take an actual out-of-alignment vehicle in to the repair shop than we are to realign our off-track lives to God's ways. We know that a car in need of adjustment is deadly if it's allowed to go its own way. But, if we're off course, it's not as critical, right? Psalm 97 shows the danger in that wrong thinking. One of the blessings for obedience to God's ways is the joy of being "upright in heart." When we know with certainty that something we chose was in alignment with God's will and we act on it, we experience the joy of being in alignment with our God.

How is your alignment with God and His ways? Are there areas in which the Holy Spirit is trying to correct your course? Can you think back to times you aligned to God's ways and felt the joy of being "upright in heart"?

Joy of alignment: Knowing something is in alignment with God's will and acting on it—even when it's hard to do! #joy218ways

Joy to the World; God of Our Past

In 1719, Isaac Watts published a book called *The Psalms of David Imitated in the Language of the New Testament*. Included in it was "Joy to the World"—the popular hymn we sing at Christmas. While Watts intended the song to be about the second coming of the Lord, the words fit equally well as a song of joy about Jesus' initial advent. Isaac Watts was inspired to write the words based on Psalm 98. In it, we see three interactive time spans between God and His people: God is praised for saving Israel in the past (vv. 1–3), He is praised for being the King of the present (vv. 4–6), and all the earth looks forward to praising God when He comes to judge in the future (vv. 7–9).

As we reflect on these movements of God, there is a deep joy in recalling the "marvelous things" He has done in our past (v. 1). First and foremost, He granted us salvation when we could do nothing to deserve it (v. 2). As if that wasn't enough, even when we fail Him, He continues to love us and is faithful to rescue us (v. 3). It's good to remember the times when God has brought us through sticky situations in our past. Keeping all He has done in mind, we, like the psalmist and Isaac Watts, will sing praise and "repeat the sounding joy."

What "marvelous" things has God done in your past? Do you remember the day you made the decision to believe in Jesus? Praise God for the joy of Him being a part of your past.

God of our past: There is a deep joy in recalling the marvelous things God has done in our lives to rescue and redeem us. #joy218ways

— Joy of What's Possible —

_____

_____

_____

I wonder what it would sound like if every person on the planet burst into song at the exact same moment. We'd have to set it up so that all automated machines were silenced and all transportation came to a standstill. With timing coordinated around the globe, the "jubilant song" would begin. Some would sing in the bright light of day while others would lift their voices through the covering of night. Not only would we hear the hum of humanity, we'd also have string and brass instruments merge with our vocals to create an unforgettable moment. The power of this song would drown out every sorrow.

It would be easy to cruise by the words of Psalm 98:4–6 without considering how they apply to our present lives. The idea of a mass moment in which the whole earth focused on God is, to us, impossible. Yet, the more we wear the Cloak of Impossibility, the less we wear our Cape of Dreams. Impossible leads us toward saying, "What's the point? We'll never see a time when everyone believes in Jesus." Yet, Psalm 98 presents a different reality forecast. It's God's desire that all would be in a relationship with Him (2 Peter 3:9); it's that truth that makes the idea of an all-earth worship set a possibility. In our day-to-day world, let's be reminded of what's possible and not miss opportunities for our lives to shout about the joy we've found in Christ.

Who, around you, needs to see your life shout with the joy you have in your relationship with Jesus? Now is a great time to pray for him/her/them and to commit to letting your joy point them to Jesus.

_____

_____

_____

_____

_____

_____

_____

_____

As we live in our day-to-day world, let's not miss opportunities for
our lives to shout the joy we've found in Christ. #joy218ways

—— Joy of Being Unique ——

_____

_____

As I studied Psalm 98, I came across an interesting note: The metaphor of the rivers clapping their hands occurs only in this verse. In Isaiah 55:12, the trees are asked to "clap their hands," but only here in the entire Bible is the idea of clapping rivers written in. The next time you stand by any body of churning water, listen to the joyful sound of aquatic applause as its waves break into each other. You'll be sharing in one of God's unique joys.

All of us are uniquely made. Some of us are more in touch with this truth than others. Among us, some actually believe this might be true about other people, but it isn't true about us. It may be that we had negative people in our lives who were too lazy and self-centered to encourage us to discover our giftedness. We may have found safety in conformity. Yet, we always look to God's word for truth. Psalm 139:14 says, "I praise you because I am fearfully and wonderfully made; your works are wonderful, I know that full well." And Psalm 111:2 says, "Great are the works of the Lord; they are pondered by all who delight in them." With joy, we need to embrace the fact that we are a "work" of the Lord. Our God creates delightfully unique works, and each one of us is one of them.

What is unique about you? Do you take joy in celebrating the great and unique way God made you? If it's difficult to get in touch with that joy, ask the Lord to show you what is blocking this joy.

_____

_____

_____

_____

_____

_____

_____

_____

_____

Tweet

With joy, we need to embrace the fact that we are a work of the Lord, and our God creates delightfully unique works. #joy218ways

Joy in the Goodness of God

Psalm 100:1

_____

_____

The psalmist begins with a shout of praise pointing to God's goodness (v. 5). Yet, sometimes, His goodness doesn't fit our definition of what's good. Another psalm provides a window into the tension of accepting God's ways. Psalm 73 is an intimate look at a person struggling to understand the goodness of God. The first half is full of complaints about life not being fair. It turns in verse 21 with the confession that complaining did no good. The end of Psalm 73 gets to the core of God's goodness: It's about being so near to Him that we are connected to good regardless of what life does to us.

The goodness of God is sometimes understood with our heart, sometimes with our soul, and often with our mind (Matthew 22:37). When we have all we need and our relationships are flourishing, we feel the goodness of God in our hearts. We know His goodness in our souls when we sense our relationship with Him is thriving. However, if we think the goodness of God should mean the absence of pain, difficulty, trouble, sorrow, ill health, or poverty, we'll question His goodness when those challenges hit. In those times, we need to tap into the joy of knowing God's goodness through trusting what He's told us about Himself. In Romans 8:28, God tells us that He works "all things for the good of those who love Him, who have been called according to His purpose." We may not know _how_ He will bring good, but we walk in joy when we trust _that_ He will.

How do you define God's goodness? When life is hard, is it easy or difficult for you to connect to the joy of trusting that God will work to bring good from the pain?

_____

_____

_____

_____

_____

_____

_____

_____

_____

Tweet

When life is hard, we may not know HOW God will bring about good. We walk in joy by trusting THAT He will. #joy218ways

Joy of Historical
——— Faithfulness ———

_____

_____

Psalm 105 is a historical remembrance of God's faithfulness to the people of Israel. In verse 43, the "shouts of joy" came as Israel exited Egypt following hundreds of years in slavery. God's people left their bondage behind with joy-filled clamor because they were free and they knew it was because God made it happen. Pharaoh eventually was the one who released the Israelites but only after God brought so much pressure he had no choice. God may work through people to accomplish His will. He orchestrates their works and those works are for the benefit of His kingdom.

God is faithful; we need that reminder when we face fresh difficulties. If we stop and consider everything He's done in our lives, it will stoke a new enthusiasm to look forward to what He's going to do. Unleashing the joy of recalling God's faithfulness is a practical application of joy. Often, the situations in our lives look bleak. We don't see a way out and hopelessness sets in. In Psalm 105, we read how God moved on behalf of His people over and over, but I bet they felt overwhelmed while they waited. As God's chosen people (1 Peter 2:9), we are heirs to His faithfulness. When we've waited a long time for our prayers to be answered, our joy is rekindled when we remember God's past faithfulness—not only in our past but in the past of those who went before us. When life is hard, get historical, not hysterical!

In your past, when did God show up and move on your behalf? How does remembering that historical faithfulness help rekindle your joy as you wait for Him to move in any current situations?

_____

_____

_____

_____

_____

_____

_____

When we've waited a long time for our prayers to be answered, our joy
is rekindled when we remember God's faithfulness. #joy218ways

–Joy of Not Acting Spoiled –

_____
_____
_____
_____

Have you ever seen a child pitching a fit because his parent will not give him the candy or toy he wants? Do you sympathize with the parent or the child? I am always Team Parent! It's my default belief that there is a reason the parent said, "No." In Psalm 106, the psalmist begins with praise to the Lord—the perfect parent. He wants to share in the joy of being God's chosen. Yet, as the psalm reveals, God's people can pitch a fit when things don't go their way. Verses 13–39 reveal details of Israel's ingratitude and faithlessness in response to the times God came to their aid.

What about us? Do we pitch a fit when God doesn't answer our prayers the way we've requested? We want to share in the joy of being His chosen kids, but we don't always want to trust that no matter how He answers, it's for our good. Psalm 106:13 says, "But they soon forgot what He had done and did not wait for His plan to unfold." We can be like the Israelites. We want God to give us what we asked for and we want it now. When we choose trust over pouting, we tap into the joy of not acting spoiled and of waiting in peace. Because we watch with patient eyes, we don't miss the way God answers—even if He does it differently than we asked.

Do you have a patient approach or a pouting attitude as you wait for God to answer your prayers? Does it hit close to home that you may be trading your joy due to forgetting all God has done and not waiting for His plan to unfold?

_____
_____
_____
_____
_____
_____
_____
_____
_____

When we choose trusting God over pouting that He hasn't answered, we tap into the joy of waiting in peace. #joy218ways

Joy of Unending
——— Rescue-Relief ———

This verse nestles in a four-part song of deliverance found in Psalm 107:4–32. God's people rebelled then called out for help. From direction out of the desert (vv. 4–9), to freedom from prison (vv. 10–16), to healing from illness (vv. 17–22), to guidance out of troubled waters (vv. 22–32), God rescued His people. They cried out; He answered. It's a good thing His well of mercy and redemption never ran dry.

It seems clear that the consequences that came the Israelites' way were a result of them not doing things God's way. It's like a face-palm to the forehead to see how shortsighted they were. Who really thinks they can prosper if they go against the God who knows all and sees all? Oh, wait a minute. We do that, too. Reading a scripture like Psalm 107 renews and reminds us that God delivers His people time and time again. He did it for them back then and He'll do it for us as well. When we're tempted to think we've messed up too many times for God to want to hear from us again, we need to remember the joy of knowing He never runs out of rescue-relief. He is simply waiting to hear us acknowledge that we need Him … again.

How many times has God come to your rescue? Do you ever feel you may have messed up so many times that God will not help you again? How does understanding God's unending well of rescue-relief point you to joy?

We can think we've messed up too many times for God to help us again. Joy comes in knowing He never runs out of rescue-relief. #joy218ways

Joy in Being Under —— Righteousness ——

_____

_____

_____

The word righteous in this verse comes from the Hebrew word _tsaddiq_ (tsad-deek'). In this context, it specifically means "righteous, as justified or vindicated by God." Psalm 118 was originally a victorious processional celebrating God's consistent triumph over Israel's enemies. Like the Israelites, we also have battles in our lives. When we are still in the thick of them, we need to recall verses 5–14 and say, "The Lord is with me; I will not be afraid. What can man do to me?"

Rather than fighting back against unfair attacks, our next level of power comes from understanding what it means to be "in the tent of the righteous." It's not about us being right; it's about us being right with God. The lure to match ugly word for ugly word will drag us out from under that tent and we remove ourselves from God's covering. At that point we're on our own, and that rarely turns out well. We may think we have victory after letting loose on our opponents, but the charred relationships we leave behind smell of loss. Our best shot at true victory is to stay inside the tent of God's righteous covering. Practically, this means that in conflict, we don't say a word unless we know the Lord would be pleased. Under God's righteous covering, we'll experience the joy of learning how conflict leads to deeper relationships rather than destroyed ones.

How easy is it for you to seek God's help before entering/continuing an argument? Is it more important to be right or to be righteous? If you desire more of the joy of seeing how conflict can lead to deeper relationships instead of destroyed ones, ask the Holy Spirit to help you pause and pray when attacks occur.

_____

_____

_____

_____

_____

Under God's righteous covering, joy comes in learning how conflict can lead to deeper relationships rather than destroyed ones. #joy218ways

——— Joy of God's Word ———

Psalm 119 is the longest psalm and the longest chapter in the Bible. This extended hymn is written in stanzas of eight verses. The stanzas take us artfully and alphabetically through the Hebrew-language characters as each section begins with one of its twenty-two letters. Psalm 119 celebrates the power and life-giving beauty of God's Word. Within it we find ten synonyms that reference God's blueprint for how He instructs His people to live. Through them, the Lord lovingly invites His people to freedom from bondage to sin. The ten words to watch for in Psalm 119 are law, command, decree, judgment, precept, statute, word, saying, way, and path.

Many Christians say, "I really need to read my Bible more." Others say, when needing or giving guidance, "Well, I know it's in the Bible somewhere..." In order to organically operate in the power of God's ways, we need to know God's Word. If we approach spending time in the Word as a "to do," we are not approaching it prayerfully. God's Word is not a burden for believers who want to know God and His ways; it is food for our soul. Billy Graham said, "The Bible teaches that there will be a famine of the Word of God in the last days ... spiritual starvation leads to spiritual death." Let's not be spiritually skinny people. May the gift of God's word be the joy of our hearts.

How dynamic is your approach to God's Word? Do you feel spiritually starved or are you on a steady diet of good "food"? If spending time in the Word seems like a chore, fight against the spirit that is distracting you by praying right now for the Holy Spirit to help you "Taste and see that the Lord is good"! (Psalm 34:8)

_____

_____

_____

_____

_____

_____

_____

_____

_____

God's Word is our spiritual food. Let's not be spiritually starving people.
May the gift of God's word be the joy of our hearts. #joy218ways

——— Joy of Restoration ———

_____

_____

_____

_____

God's restoration is something to celebrate! The opening verse of Psalm 126 sets the tone for this psalm of joy. God had brought back/restored His people to their land. He regarded them as His fortune, and it caused all those who recalled that powerful time to laugh and sing songs of joy. Not only were the people restored, but God also redeemed their shame from all the years lost to bondage. Others from lands outside Israel looked at the former captives and said, "The Lord has done great things for them." The story of God's redemption in our lives is our testimony to the world.

We all go through rough times. Sometimes it's of our own making due to choices we've made. We put ourselves in bondage to a variety of things: drugs, alcohol, co-dependency, sexual sin, working too much, believing lies about ourselves, broken relationships, and so on. It can seem like God isn't working with us or for us. Yet, as we continue to pray—whether powerfully or simply—we show God we trust Him. When He delivers, it's often in ways we never could dream. We wouldn't creatively bless ourselves like God can … to the point "our mouths are filled with laughter, our tongues with songs of joy." God stands ready to restore us and to redeem any time we've lost due to unholy distractions (Joel 2:25). His restoration is our joy!

Do you currently have anything that you need God to restore? Spend time opening your heart to the truth that God is able to do more than you could ask Him for or imagine (Ephesians 3:20). If you do not have a current struggle, praise God for how He has restored you in the past.

_____

_____

_____

_____

_____

_____

_____

_____

We'll never be able to creatively bless ourselves like God can. His restoration is our joy! #joy218ways

—— Joy of Right Focus ——

Psalm 126:3

_____

_____

How can the psalmist say, "The Lord has done great things for us"? The only way he can do it is if he focuses his mind on the powerful ways he's seen God move. Reading through the rest of Psalm 126, we see the psalmist is still waiting for God to do some things such as "Restore our fortunes" (v. 4). However, he continues to flex the power of right-thinking by focusing on what God has done as he waits. He also practices the power of visualizing a brighter future (vv. 5–6). God has what they need; they need to come and get it.

I always say that God is a gentleman. He will not make us love Him, and He will not make us have joy. Experiencing His joy is a partnership, and our responsibility in that partnership is to decide what gets our focus. If we concentrate on the ways we are seeing God at work, our spirits are open for fresh deposits of His joy. If, instead, we choose to focus on those things that are not going our way, we become so hard and closed that joy can't take root. Rather than asking God to change everything around us so we can have joy, we travel a more joy-acquiring route if we pray for strength to focus on right-thinking.

Do you struggle to be open to fresh deposits of God's joy due to focusing on what's not right? If you took a solid ten minutes and did nothing but focus on everything that is not going your way, would you experience more joy? Every minute that we give to wrong focus is a minute we separate ourselves from God's joy. Ask the Holy Spirit to tap you on the shoulder when you start drifting into wrong focus.

_____

_____

_____

_____

_____

_____

_____

_____

Tweet

We travel a more joy-acquiring route if we pray to focus on right-thinking instead of asking God to change everyone else. #joy218ways

Joy of Praying
— Outside Our Sandbox —

Psalm 126:5

_____

_____

"We only die once, so it might as well be for Jesus."
—Werner Groenewald

South African pastor Groenewald spoke those words to an international group of co-workers in 2014. One month later, the Taliban killed him and his children in Afghanistan, where he had served as an aid worker for over a decade. In some translations of Psalm 126, verse 1 talks about God bringing back those who have been in bondage. It made me think of the persecuted church around the world. We can be certain there are tears sown into the fabric of the kingdom over the injustice of their suffering.

How often do we pray outside our own zip code? How often do we pray for those in chains of all sorts? I think this is an interesting look at joy. When we intentionally pray for those we may never meet, we experience the joy of praying outside our sandbox. It begins with an honest assessment of whether we believe prayer is effective. If we do, then the idea of praying for a brother or sister being attacked for his/her faith will bring us a somber joy. It's the joy of knowing that while we are helpless to alleviate their suffering, we know we can help by lifting their situation before the Lord. We never know how God will move, but we'll certainly never know if we don't ask.

Has God connected your heart with an area of the world where Christians are being persecuted? If so, lift them in prayer now and breathe in the joy of knowing you are helping them. If not, would you open your heart to asking the Lord for where and how to pray?

_____

_____

_____

_____

_____

_____

Tweet

If we feel helpless to alleviate someone's suffering, there's joy in knowing we help by lifting their situation to the Lord. #joy218ways

Joy of Planting
——— Seeds of Sorrow ———

_____
_____
_____
_____

I grew up in a small farming community in Illinois. I was a "townie," but as many of the families in my church were farmers, everything revolved around the seasons. When it was planting time, church meetings and practices shifted to accommodate the seed-sowing schedule. In the same way, during fall harvest, combines and tractors had the right of way on the roads and community life was on farmer-time. The faith of the farmers was something to behold. They knew their livelihood was partially about their hard work, but primarily about God's weather patterns. Once they sowed, there wasn't much they could do except pray. Most years after the right amount of time had passed, they saw their prayers answered. Other years, they experienced setbacks, but their faith never wavered.

Many of us are afraid to depend too much on God. We want to have control. The amusing reality is that even if we think we've got everything in hand, it only takes a hiccup in the universe for things to spiral out of control. When these types of situations hit, weeping is but one of the heavy ways we let our emotions spill out. How did this happen? Is this really our life? Psalm 126:6 offers hope. Go ahead, cry and ask questions. Ultimately, though, take those seeds of fear and doubt and sow them into the soil of trust with prayer. God's promise is that He will transform those seeds of sorrow into a harvest of joy.

What/who is weighing on your heart? Take this Godpportunity to prayerfully sow your fears, concerns and doubt into the soil of trust. Believe that you will see a harvest of joy in God's perfect timing.

_____
_____
_____
_____
_____
_____

When we plant seeds of sorrow and fear into the soil of trust in God, He will give us a harvest of joy in His perfect timing. #joy218ways

— Joy of Worship in Church —

Psalm 132:9

_____

_____

_____

_____

Psalm 132 talks about the resting place for the Ark of the Covenant. David and the people he led had a passion for creating a sacred space that would house the ark and be a house of worship. They navigated the fine line between honoring God's treasure and not allowing the ark to become an idol they worshiped. We see this in how they ascribed the focus of their worship as longing to go into "His" dwelling place and wanting to be at "His" footstool. Out of their love for God, they desired to gather as a community in His house united for a common purpose.

Walking into a church filled with lovely artifacts is a comfort to many Christians. It allows us to feel we've walked into a sacred place, and it helps us get into a worshipful state. For others, the absence of those types of artifacts in our houses of worship is equally important. We feel the artifacts are a barrier or a distraction to coming before the Lord. Ultimately, the style of our church is never as important as the One we worship. God wants us to gather and be united for the common purpose of growing and reaching people with His truth and love. This weekend, let's pray for our church leaders to be clothed in God's righteousness as they lead us in putting the gospel into action. Focusing our worship on God, let's set aside all the concerns of the world and sing for joy in His church.

Do churches filled with artifacts bring you joy or are they a distraction/ intimidation to your joy? How does the reminder that worship is about God and not the surroundings affect the way you worship?

_____

_____

_____

_____

_____

_____

_____

_____

Tweet

As we focus our worship on God, we can set aside all the concerns of the world and simply sing for joy in His church. #joy218ways

Joy of Salvation

Psalm 132:16

God chose Zion as His "resting place." In a literal sense, Zion/Jerusalem is the actual city in Israel that is steeped in historical importance. However, through study of related scriptures, we see that Zion is also symbolic of God's church.[1] In looking at Psalm 132 through this filter, we can understand that God's chosen resting place is in the people of His church. It is His plan for the message of salvation to flow through His church leaders and for the song of salvation to spill out from those who believe.

Some songs are instantly recognizable within the first notes. Think of "Celebration," "Eye of the Tiger," or "Bohemian Rhapsody." People at a wedding reception, for instance, are immediately attracted to the song and throw their heads back to join in singing. What a picture of how our salvation song should sound! As God's chosen people, we are His bride.[2] We have the joy of inviting people to our never-ending wedding reception. As people come, they find their feet tapping along to the rhythm they hear in the lives of those who invited them. When, in a life-changing moment they choose to begin singing along, the angels rejoice (Luke 15:10)! There is nothing like the feeling of hearing people begin singing their salvation song for the first time because your joy pointed them to Jesus.

When not-yet believers observe your life, is the joy of your salvation apparent in the way you live? If so, for which not-yet believers are you praying? If not, ask the Holy Spirit to help your joy be evident in your life-song.

_____

_____

_____

_____

_____

_____

_____

_____

Tweet

When someone begins singing their salvation song for the first time
because your joy pointed them to Jesus, that is pure joy! #joy218ways

[1]   Hebrews 12:22, John 12:15, 1 Peter 2:6
[2]   2 Corinthians 11:2–3, Ephesians 5:22–27, Revelation 19: 7–8

The Pain of
—— Remembered Joy ——

_____

_____

_____

Psalm 137 isn't a psalm of joy, it's a very human cry about remembered joy that has been taken away. The psalmist is crying out to God from his place of captivity. He has been enslaved, taken from his land and forced to work for his captors. He longs to be restored to Jerusalem and he passionately tells God how he'd like Him to repay those who stole his joy.

Many of us can relate to times in which we had joy, and then something cruel came into our lives and took it away. Death, divorce, job loss, accident, illness, natural disaster, broken dreams—all these and more can leave us feeling robbed of our joy. In times of intense loss, our only defense is God. We come to a point of saying, "I've lost everything that matters; all I have left is God." We get in touch with understanding that our situation isn't going to change, but our ability to have joy is 100 percent within God's power to sustain and restore to abundance. In the same way life took our joy captive, we need to take captive every thought that keeps us distanced from the One who can help us rebuild (2 Corinthians 10:5). May we lean in to God's ability to create new mosaics of joy from the shattered pieces of our brokenness.

As you read this, what loss comes to mind as the most painful in your life? If you have seen God work a new mosaic from that broken time, spend time thanking Him for creating new joy. If you are still reeling from the loss, cry out and ask the Lord to restore, redeem, and rebuild a deeper joy in you as a result of this pain.

_____

_____

_____

_____

_____

God has the ability to create new mosaics of joy from the
shattered pieces of our brokenness. #joy218ways

— Joy of Spiritual Oxygen —

Psalm 137:6

This man is homesick. Being held in Babylon by his captors, he longs for his land and his former way of life. Perhaps we can relate because of a move in which we left friends and family behind. Maybe it happened when we started college, changed churches or small groups. We look back to the times of joy, and the pain of separation is a stark contrast. The psalmist clings to joy by laying out his pain to God in a raw, harsh way (see verse 9). It's not pretty, but he knows God is the one who can handle his pain.

It's interesting how abruptly this psalm ends. I don't see a big, booming reply coming back from God, and I can relate to that. I've had sessions in which I cried so hard I couldn't breathe through all the snot and tears. After being raw with God, I didn't get anything back from Him. I didn't get a word, an impression, a voice, and certainly no burning bush. But—and this is more important—neither did I get the feeling of being condemned. God was there and listening. I may have felt depleted at the end of those outpourings but I needed to empty out the ugliness to make space for God to fill me with something better. Joy isn't only found in the high, happy places of life. Sometimes, joy is the almost silent heartbeat of "I'm here" from God. It's the spiritual oxygen we need until we can breathe on our own again.

Can you relate to a time when you felt God helping you through a difficult time of pain? Did you recognize the joy of Him being there to simply listen? Do you feel any emotion is off limits to share with God?

Tweet

Joy isn't only found in the high, happy places of life. Sometimes, it's spiritual oxygen until we can breathe on our own again. #joy218ways

— Break-in-the-Action Joy —

_____

_____

A day in the life: Wake up, coffee, get the morning going, be productive at work, at school, or at home, spend time at family/friend activities, handle details of life, sleep, repeat … it's easy for routine to become life. Psalm 149 is refreshing with its "I'm loving on you" flow from God to His people and theirs to Him. It reads like a beautiful break-in-the-action-from-life psalm. This scriptural moment is deep, celebratory, and powerfully relational. As the psalm closes, the depth of the people's love finds expression in their fierce desire to protect the name of the One they adore (vv. 6–9).

Even in the best of relationships, day-to-day rhythms of life can bog us down. Communication becomes dull, mundane, and primarily functional. We get to the point we don't feel we have anything new to say. Rather than seek ways to jumpstart the drained battery of our relationship, we sit beside each other in the front seat of our dead car on our phones. Break-in-the-action moments rekindle our joy and remind us why we are important to each other. I have a few people in my life who, periodically, send a quick word to interrupt the humdrum pattern of my day. Sometimes it is a loving message, other times it makes me laugh. Either way, hearing from them resets our relationship clock and affirms why we do life together. Taking our cue from the God who delights in us (v. 4), let's share break-in-the-action joy with those we love.

In your circle of family and friends, whom could you share a break-in-the-action joy moment with today?

_____

_____

_____

_____

_____

_____

_____

_____

_____

In relationships, break-in-the-action moments rekindle our joy and remind us why we're important to each other. Be the surprise. #joy218ways

Joy of a Wise Kid

Proverbs 10:1

_____

_____

Two trains of thought come to mind as I study this verse. First: Fathers and mothers equally share in the joy a wise child brings, and they grieve equally when a child's foolishness disrupts the family. In proverbial literature, the word "but" is a connector, not a divider. The parents' shared joy/grief is, however, assuming they are a God-honoring team that teaches their children to live God's way. That understanding led me to the second track. I've known many people who were not raised in a Christian environment. As adults, they decided to follow Jesus. Often—even though they now live wisely from a Christian perspective—their non-believing parents consider them to be foolish.

I had the great fortune to be raised by a Christian mom, and it was my joy to live according to her teaching. I poured that same instruction with even more intentionality into my kids as I raised them. My oldest, however, took a turn off the path for about four years in his teens. While he's on a good path now, that dark period became so difficult I couldn't read the book of Proverbs because I'd get smacked in the face with verses like this. I know the pain of having a child reject your beliefs. If you're in a similar struggle, keep praying. Stay connected to the joy of knowing that praying is taking action on his/her behalf. Similarly, if you have parents who reject your Christian beliefs, keep praying. Don't fight _with_ them to get them to accept the truth you've found; in prayer, fight _for_ them.

How were you raised? Do you now make choices that are wiser or more foolish? Does that bring joy or grief to the parents/grandparents/mentors in your life?

_____

_____

_____

_____

_____

_____

_____

_____

_____

_____

Tweet

If those you love reject your Christian beliefs, don't fight with them.
Stay connected to joy by praying for them. Enjoy them. #joy218ways

– Joy of Killing Wickedness –

_____

_____

"I'll get you my pretty!" Green, ugly and full of warts, the Wicked Witch of the West screamed this iconic threat at Dorothy in _The Wizard of Oz_. The witch expected her power to bring her wicked desires to reality. However, with a simple pail of water from good, little Dorothy, her life perished in a green cloud of nothingness. When we have desires, do we trust in our power or God's? If any of us—whether righteous or wicked—try to go against Him, ultimately, God's ordained ways win out. People may "hope" to get away with wicked deeds, but unrighteousness is always exposed and, whether in this life or the next, consequences follow.

Even committed Christians sometimes act wickedly, so this verse isn't exclusively for nonbelievers. Christians should be more aware of the "nothing" factor because wicked actions will not bear fruit (Galatians 5:22–23). When we make mistakes, we need to repent and ask the Holy Spirit to fill that sin spot with His power and strength. God, then, gets the glory because, as we turn from that bondage, it is His work in us that empowers us to live righteously instead of wickedly in that area. Another way to render Proverbs 10:28 is, "The hope of good people is their joy." When we're presented with the opportunity to do something wicked, may the joy of our hope in Christ be the pail of water we reach for to kill off wicked temptation.

What areas in your life most tempt you toward wicked behaviors? Just as the pail of water was a practical thing to destroy wickedness for Dorothy, what practical steps can you take to keep your joy strong when temptation hits?

_____

_____

_____

_____

_____

_____

_____

_____

When we're presented with the opportunity to do something wicked, may the joy of our hope in Christ kill off the temptation. #joy218ways

Joy of Knowing God is on —————— Your Side ————

Proverbs 11:10

This immediately makes me think of war. When our country prospers in battle, we rejoice. When our enemies perish or are brought to justice, we shout for joy. However, those who oppose our nation in the conflict see it exactly the opposite. When they prosper, they rejoice; when we perish, they shout for joy. Who is right? Whose side is God on? Usually, we find both sides claiming God is on theirs.

The above calls to mind a biblical example of a time when people needed to see if God was on their side. Abram and Sarai were waiting for God to deliver their promised child (Genesis 12:7, 13:16, 15:4). After giving God ten years to carry through, seventy-five-year-old Sarai came up with a way to get God's promise. Following the custom of the day, she gave her maidservant, Hagar, to Abram so Hagar could give them a child. They believed God would create a son from eighty-five-year-old Abram, so their faith was in the right place, but it was in the wrong plan. They got what they wanted, but due to not asking God if it was the way *He* wanted to provide the answer, their scheme failed miserably (Genesis 16). This lack of trust has ushered in generations of fallout. We access our joy more efficiently when we ask God what is right in order to know if our choices are righteous or wicked.

Have you ever tried to "help" God by creating your own plan to get what you wanted instead of trusting His timing? If so, what lesson did you learn? If you haven't had this kind of experience, where do you get your strength to trust His timing?

_____

_____

_____

_____

_____

_____

Tweet

We access our joy more efficiently if we ask God who/what is right so we may know if we are acting righteously or wickedly! #joy218ways

—— Joy of Battling Evil ——

_____

_____

_____

_____

Originally written in Hebrew, the word in Proverbs 12:20 translated as "plot/devise" is *charash*. Its root means "to scratch or plow." When a person plots evil, he plants seeds of discord, selfishness, and immorality through his words and actions. A person's true character cannot be hidden. As Jesus said, "The mouth speaks what the heart is full of. A good man brings good things out of the good stored up in him, and an evil man brings evil things out of the evil stored up in him" (Matthew 12:34–35). When peace is the pursuit of a heart, God rewards that heart with joy.

When I look at this proverb, I don't see it as instruction or correction, but simply a statement of fact. It's sad because people with evil in their hearts don't desire God's joy so they're not motivated to live differently in order to obtain it. If they're not self-motivated, what will change them? Pessimistically, nothing will. Spiritually speaking, God. God graciously gives all humans free will to reject His offer of love and forgiveness, but He also pursues us. God can do anything, and we must remain faithful. We gain a new understanding of joy when our response to evil people is to pray for them. Pray for the evil in them to lose out. Pray they accept Jesus as Savior and Lord. Pray that their battle becomes against their old ways and not against the God who loves them. In the presence of evil, our joy is untouchable when we passionately stay connected to God in prayer.

Do you know anyone who—from what you can see—is sowing evil into the world? Would you pray for him/her? If you don't know anyone personally, pray for the evil that attacks your community.

_____

_____

_____

_____

_____

_____

_____

In the presence of evil, our joy is untouchable when we passionately stay connected to God in prayer. #joy218ways

—Joy during Loneliness—

Proverbs 14:10

_____

_____

Loneliness is like being on a minuscule island in the center of a black sea that won't even ripple a reply when we touch it. The darkness robs all the color from our world. Escaping the island or finding a way to get people to visit becomes all-consuming as we go about our ordinary lives. Who sees us? When we have wonderful things to share, whom can we tell? "It would be too easy to say that I feel invisible. Instead, I feel painfully visible, and entirely ignored," wrote David Levithan.[1] Who understands? We long to be known yet we're afraid to trust.

Loneliness is overwhelming, so our prayers for relief need to be simple. It's about asking the Lord to send those who will listen and allow us to "be" without requiring us to "be ok." C. S. Lewis said, "God whispers to us in our pleasures, speaks in our conscience, but shouts in our pains: it is His megaphone to rouse a deaf world."[2] Sometimes, the Lord provides a person to be our island-mate. Other times, He is the one who comes. His presence becomes more evident in the absence of human noise. Ultimately, only God can know and relate perfectly to the depths of our bitterness and to the heights of our joy. Whether through a person or His presence, we experience joy in the midst of loneliness by keeping our eyes open for how God responds to our prayer. When two inhabit the Isle of Loneliness instead of one, everything changes.

When have you felt lonely in your life? Are you currently inhabiting this island? Pray now and ask the Lord to send His relief. Prayerfully keep your eyes open for the joy of how He responds.

_____

_____

_____

_____

_____

_____

_____

_____

Tweet

Whether through a person or the joy of God's presence, when the Isle of Loneliness becomes inhabited by two, everything changes. #joy218ways

---

1   Levithan, David. _Every Day_. New York, Alfred A. Knopf, 2012.
2   Lewis, C. S. _The Problem of Pain_. New York, NY, HarperCollins, 2014.

Joy in Grief

Proverbs 14:13

Loving deeply. When our soul connects to another's, we experience joy in ways we can't attain on our own. At the point, through death, divorce or distance, a relationship ends in loss, our joy crashes headlong with grief. Following the death of his wife, C. S. Lewis wrote: "No one ever told me that grief felt so like fear. I am not afraid, but the sensation is like being afraid. The same fluttering in the stomach, the same restlessness, the yawning. I keep on swallowing. At other times it feels like being mildly drunk, or concussed. There is a sort of invisible blanket between the world and me. I find it hard to take in what anyone says. Or perhaps, hard to want to take it in. It is so uninteresting. Yet I want the others to be about me. I dread the moments when the house is empty. If only they would talk to one another and not to me."[1]

How many times have we pasted a smile on our face to mask the pain of our loss? It seems people around us need us to be okay before we have the ability to be so. While none of us want to stay enveloped in the "invisible blanket" of our grief forever, it becomes more ensnaring if we attempt to get untangled on someone else's timetable. At times, we may observe others' grief and, mistakenly, try to help them get over it. We are better instruments of joy if we simply stay near as they discover how to be comfortable outside the invisible blanket of their grief.

Have you experienced a deep loss? Did you extend yourself grace for your journey? Did you have the joy of receiving grace from others or did you learn how not to journey with a grieving person by others' poor example?

_____

_____

_____

_____

_____

_____

_____

_____

_____

Tweet

When we lose someone—whether to death, divorce or distance—our portal to quiet joy is giving ourselves grace as we grieve. #joy218ways

---

[1]   Lewis, C. S. *A Grief Observed*. London, CrossReach Publications, 2016.

— Joy in Not Being a Fool —

Proverbs 15:20

As Proverbs 10:1 is almost identical to Proverbs 15:20, see page 88 for a look at how this verse applies to family dynamics. In the book of Proverbs, a fool is defined as someone who actively hates and avoids wisdom, instruction, and discipline.[1] As much as it grieves parents' hearts when their children act foolishly, how much more anguish must God feel when we, His children, actively avoid His wisdom and instruction?

It's funny, but when a pastor's sermon speaks about negative character traits, we often think about people we know who fit that description. If the topic is lying, we think about the people who have lied to us, but not so much about the lies we've told. If the topic is anger, we get mad thinking about the people who struggle to keep their anger in check. Hopefully, we get around to seeing the log in our own eye (Matthew 7:3). God didn't give us His Word so we could beat others up with it. It's given to each of us to be a mirror. If our goal is to become more like Christ, we need to check how well our reflection matches the Word's perfection. Our petition should be, "Mirror, mirror, God's Word my guide and rule, show me any area in which I act a fool." We are God's kids and Jesus died for us. Out of love and respect, may we turn from our foolishness so we bring joy to our Father.

Knowing that God only wants what is best for you, are you willing to pray in the mirror of God's Word and ask the Holy Spirit to reveal any areas of foolishness in you?

_____

_____

_____

_____

_____

_____

_____

_____

_____

_____

Tweet

We are God's kids and Jesus died for us. Out of love and respect, let's turn from foolishness so our lives bring joy to our Father. #joy218ways

[1] Proverbs 1:7, 1:22, 12:1, 12:15

Joy of Wisdom

Proverbs 15:23

When someone solicits our advice, it's a sign of their trust and respect. It's a joy to share wise words that point someone to greater peace, power, and purpose. As in all things, we need to stay humble when we're given the privilege of sharing a timely word; the only insight we have is from the wisdom God imparts. As a good steward of that wisdom, we need to prayerfully consider how we handle it. Fulton J. Sheen said, "Counsel involving right and wrong should never be sought from a man who does not say his prayers."

The timing piece is critical. When I was younger, if a person asked my advice and the pathway forward was evident to me, I'd share what I was seeing. On a few occasions, the wisdom was too meaty and hard to digest for the one asking. As a result, he/she distanced from me and I was left wondering what happened. God opened my eyes to the importance of timing. Now, when the question, "Lisa, what do you think?" pops up, with wisdom I say, "I do see some things, but I think they might be hard to hear. Do you want me to share them or hold off for now?" This lets the one asking to be in control. Most of the time, they want to know, but since I've respected their emotional state in advance, our relationship weathers the wisdom. Occasionally, people say, "I can't take anything more right now." I lovingly respect that. They know I'm here when/if they are ready. Wisdom is a precious gift that we have the joy of handling with prayer.

When you are asked for advice, do you pause and pray before sharing? Do you consider yourself to be a wise person? If not, how do the words of James 1:5–8 point you to acquiring wisdom?

Wisdom is a precious gift that we have the joy of
handling with prayer. #joy218ways

–Joy-Filled or Joy-Sucking–

Proverbs 15:30

_____

_____

_____

_____

Mornings are not my jam. I prefer to stay up late and would love to sleep until I'm Ready o'clock. However, children and the entire package that accompanies their arrival conspire against we night owls. And then there's that work thing ... apparently the world doesn't work on LMR time. What does this have to do with a "cheerful look/ light in a messenger's eyes" you ask? I look at this verse through the filter of giving a cheerful look as opposed to receiving it. In the mornings, my default look is Grumpy the Dwarf as opposed to Happy the Pastor. I think my eyes communicate my earnest longing to be horizontally in my bed, and my look often robs my family of some joy instead of bringing it to them.

To all you morning people out there reading this and thinking to yourselves, "I'm glad I'm not like her" ... Oh yeah? Have you seen yourselves when you're kept up past your early bird bedtime? Some of us are lovin' life at midnight while others would take a life if forced to stay awake. Either way, at some point in the day, most of us hit a wall and have a choice to make. If we focus on ourselves, our tiredness, and our absolute lack of desire to be in the moment, we turn into the dreaded Joy-Sucker. Our facial expressions are our responsibility and they set a tone. Will we be a joy-filled light or a joy-sucking ogre to those around us?

How aware are you of what your face communicates? Is this an area in which you can grow in sharing your joy in the Lord?

_____

_____

_____

_____

_____

_____

_____

_____

_____

Tweet

Our facial expressions are our responsibility. Will we be a joy-filled
light or a joy-sucking ogre to those around us? #joy218ways

— Show Joy Not Judgment —

Proverbs 17:21

Are you familiar with what I call the Christian Parenting Formula (CPF)? It goes something like this: To raise kids who turn out well, you need to have your kids dedicated or baptized, raise them in church, read Bible stories together, help them memorize scriptures, pray together, put them in sports (ideally Christian run), send them to Christian camp, encourage them to be Christian leaders, only play Christian music, serve together, and model your love for the Lord. The CPF has to work, right? But, here's a question: What about families who authentically apply the CPF and the result is a child who is a fool?

I've seen families exhaust themselves trying to cover all these bases. (Color me a little guilty...) The problem becomes when we trust the CPF more then we trust God. Even when we apply the CPF with sincere hearts and true joy, only our kids can choose whether they will follow Christ at the end of the day. We may invite our kids to the joy of salvation, but we can't make the choice for them. If you are aware of a family struggling with a child, rather than deciding they must not have applied the CPF correctly, have compassion for their journey. Joy is a scarce commodity in a home when a child is living the life of a fool. Christians should pray a blanket of soothing joy around the hurting hearts of these families. We truly never know if we may need that encouraging joy ourselves one day.

Before enrolling or directing your children to engage in a program, do you ask God if that's what He wants for them? Have you ever judged a family that is struggling with their child? How can you show encouraging joy to a hurting family?

Tweet

Joy is a scarce commodity when a child is making bad choices. Pray a blanket of soothing joy over the parents' hurting hearts. #joy218ways

——Joy of the Righteous——

"Right is right, even if everyone is against it, and wrong is wrong, even if everyone is for it," said Pennsylvania founder William Penn (1644–1718).[1] Most of mankind shares an overarching sense of what's right and what's wrong. Even for those who are not Christians, there is a common understanding that murder, for example, is wrong. On the whole, people understand that right-standing people have no reason to fear justice but evil people do. It's here—in God's Word—that we see the root of "why" we all know this to be true. It's a God-thing; it's His principle.

I believe verses like this make the case for God's existence. He created us to innately understand that righteous people celebrate justice while those who intend harm quake when justice interrupts their plans. Romans 1:18–20 is another scriptural screen shot of this truth: "The wrath of God is being revealed from heaven against all the godlessness and wickedness of people, who suppress the truth by their wickedness, since what may be known about God is plain to them … For since the creation of the world God's invisible qualities—His eternal power and divine nature—have been clearly seen, being understood from what has been made, so that people are without excuse." At times, the righteous will have to wait for justice to come, and the waiting is hard. During times of praying for a wrong to be made right, our joy comes in knowing we are waiting on a God who loves justice.

If you've ever had to wait for God to work justice for you, were you able to stay connected to the joy of knowing that the God of Justice was moving on your behalf? Is that a comforting or frustrating thought?

_____

_____

_____

_____

_____

_____

_____

During times of waiting for a wrong to be made right, our joy comes
in knowing we are loved by a God who loves justice. #joy218ways

---

[1] "Quotations from William Penn." Ushistory.org. Accessed October 9, 2017. http://www. ushistory.org/penn/quotes.htm.

——Joy of a Joy Account——

The book of Proverbs is not short on blunt instruction for fathers, mothers, and kids. This verse is part of the Thirty Sayings of the Wise found in Proverbs 22:17–24:34. In Proverbs 23:22–25, the child is directed to honor his mother and father and to seek truth, wisdom, discipline, and understanding. The parents have a passive role, yet we can only assume they have sown a legacy of right-thinking into their son. In order for them to recognize righteous character traits in him, they themselves would need to possess them.

There are no shortcuts to parenting. Even if you don't have kids of your own, it's likely you have influence on younger people around you. Every day, we have hundreds of opportunities to show righteousness and wisdom to our kids. When we choose to do right, we make deposits into their character banks on which they can draw when making their choices. However, when we choose to handle a situation poorly, we potentially cause a withdrawal … a withdrawal from their sense of personal worth and a withdrawal from us. While we'll never be deposit-only parents/adults who handle every situation correctly, our best shot at becoming better is to allow the Holy Spirit to invade our lives. If our account is empty, how can we make deposits into the kids'? We'll still have withdrawals—we're human. But when God is involved, He'll be that action-halting-pop-up screen that says, "Are you sure you want to make this withdrawal?" It's good to have God as our joy-banker.

How is your joy account? Are you enjoying a healthy balance or is it running low? Ask the Lord for new deposits so that you can pour into those around you.

The closer we are to God, the fuller our joy account will be. We'll still have withdrawals, but He refills on request! #joy218ways

—Joy of Stinking Nicely—

_____
_____
_____
_____

I love to bake. I'd do it if only for the joy of trading pure oxygen for the smell of heated sugar. On cookie days, every room wraps you in a hug and lures you toward the kitchen to sample that sugar-momma-carb-kiss sitting on the counter. The way something smells communicates beyond words. Paul understood the power of scent: "But thanks be to God, who always leads us in triumph in Christ, and manifests through us the sweet aroma of the knowledge of Him in every place. For we are a fragrance of Christ to God among those who are being saved and among those who are perishing; to the one an aroma from death to death, to the other an aroma from life to life" (2 Corinthians 2:14–16). Without a word, the way we smell communicates what we're about.

Think of walking by a person wearing his/her favorite perfume or cologne. Sometimes that's an enjoyable walk by; other times their cloud leaves us gasping for air. While not available in a bottled form, our attitude communicates our aroma. If we layer Proverbs 27:9 and 2 Corinthians 2:14–16 together, we're challenged to live in such a way that our "perfume/fragrance" brings joy to the hearts of those near enough to smell us. The inescapable truth is that we emit an aroma at all times. Will our fragrance smell like the joy of a person connected to an amazing God or will we stink like one who forgot to shower in that joy today?

As a member of Christ's body, check your body odor. Are you attracting or repelling people with your attitude-aroma?

_____
_____
_____
_____
_____
_____
_____

We either smell like the joy of a person connected to an amazing God or stink like one who forgot to shower in that joy. #joy218ways

—— Joy of Special Needs ——

_____

_____

_____

This one hits close to home. When my little guy was growing up, he bounced. The idea of walking a straight line did not compute. He sort of rendered his kindergarten teacher a quivering mess by the end of the school year. My remedy was to discipline him to the kabillionth power, but he still bounced. Fortunately, his first-grade teacher gently led me to see that my sweet boy had ADHD, and the difficult trajectory of his school years ensued. Those who judged him on his behaviors often treated me with contempt: "If you would discipline him more..." My exhausted heart had no reply. They had no idea how structured and diligent we were in raising him. They weren't there at night to hear him pray, "God, please help me not get any checks tomorrow."

Kids with special needs are often misunderstood. The effort it takes for them to live in "normal" society is a tremendous strain. Even though I firmly believe they are "fearfully and wonderfully made" (Psalm 139:14), some make them feel "freakishly and wackily made." Over the years, my son has brought me incredible joy _because_ of the way God made him. I've observed other families of kids with special needs stubbornly find joy in the gift of their children even when they're on the receiving end of contemptuous glares from "norms." When children stretch the boundaries of normalcy—whether physically, socially, emotionally or mentally—we collectively increase our joy by withholding contempt. Instead, we release new understandings of joy as we celebrate their unique contribution to our world.

Do you have loved ones with special needs? Maybe you, personally, are one such wonderfully made person! Pray for opportunities to celebrate a person with special needs and increase their joy in the way God made him/her.

_____

_____

_____

_____

_____

_____

When children stretch the idea of normalcy—physically, socially, emotionally or mentally—we release joy as we celebrate them. #joy218ways

Joy in the Wisdom-Package

Proverbs 29:3

_____

_____

_____

_____

Dear God: I think You must look down at this world sometimes and say, "Duh." Lord, we know it's obvious that "wisdom" and "prostitute" aren't congruent. How it must break Your heart to have to tell Your creation the same. How do You do it? How do You keep loving Your sons and daughters when we chase after sin that wastes what You've entrusted to us? I mean, this is only one example and You see billions of sins every day. I can't grasp how tremendous Your mercy is. It defies logic, but its brilliant beauty dazzles when I stop to consider that without it, all we take for granted would never exist. From a grateful heart, I pray for a renewed desire to love Your wisdom and to bring You joy.

Dear sons and daughters of God: When we look at ourselves in the reflection of this verse, do we bring joy to God as His children? Do we love wisdom and all that comes with the wisdom-package? Is it our joy to turn from wasting the resources of money, time, and talent on things that do not bring glory to our Father? In many ways, we can celebrate how far we've come on our journey toward bringing joy to God. And, with acknowledgment that the journey isn't over, we humbly continue to ask the Holy Spirit to help us be more like Jesus every day. We want to be sons and daughters who bring joy to our Father.

Do you love wisdom and all that comes with the wisdom-package? What areas of previous struggle do you celebrate as victories in your journey of becoming more like Christ? Is there a current issue that causes a detour to your journey?

_____

_____

_____

_____

_____

_____

_____

_____

Tweet

When we love wisdom and all that comes with the wisdom-package, it's our joy to stop wasting the resources of our time and money. #joy218ways

Joy in the Basics

_____

_____

_____

_____

_____

Confession of a responsibility-aholic: My initial reaction to this verse is, "Come on. Nothing better than to eat, drink, and be glad? What about duty, responsibility, sacrifice, doing the right thing, and working hard?" Being honest, I know my outlook is a bit heavy on the sour. Solomon's is sweeter, yet still practical. In chapter 8, he talks about the mysterious contradictions of life. The righteous don't always get rewarded but sometimes, the wicked do. How can we respond to the age-old dilemma of "Why do bad things happen to good people?" Solomon offers a palatable way to navigate this world: Since we have no control over every outcome, find joy by focusing on the gifts God provides in our day-to-day living.

Christian joy is not an escape mechanism, and it doesn't immunize us from being infected by the evil in the world. It is, however, accessible through the daily joys God provides. When our basic needs are met, we often forget to find joy in them. We might be grateful, but do we take joy in them? Going about our daily toil—work, school, volunteering, homemaking—do we find joy in the basic need of having purpose? If we set entitlement to the side, this is an easy joy to own. Enjoying the basics is much sweeter than sourly plugging through the day.

Do you do a good job of finding joy in your basic needs being met? Is your work a source of joy? If joy is lacking in either of these areas, take an honest look to see if you think you're entitled to something more.

_____

_____

_____

_____

_____

_____

Christian joy isn't an escape mechanism. It doesn't happen by burying our head in the sand and it isn't fake. It's simply real. #joy218ways

Joy of Youth

Ecclesiastes 11:9

_____
_____
_____
_____
_____

"I can't wait until…" Too many of us live in this state. Students "can't wait" for graduation. People in careers "can't wait" for promotion. Potty training parents "can't wait" for undies to replace Huggies. When life is comprised of can't waits, we trade the joy of living in the now. It's great to set goals and look forward to them, but if they consume our focus, we delay owning joy that is available today. At every opportunity, let's encourage each other—but especially young people—to soak in the joy of the present age. Once it's gone, only the memory of how we lived it remains.

The phrase "Follow the ways of your heart and whatever your eyes see" might sound like, "If it feels good, do it." However, that would be to misunderstand what is meant by heart. The Hebrew word for heart is _leb_ (labe), and it's used figuratively to convey the idea of our feelings, will, and intellect. With this in mind, the idea of verse 9 is more "Think through what you will do, then do it." If the desire of a person's heart is to honor God, then he will have God's pleasure and judgment in mind when following the ways of his heart. In our efforts to guide young people around us, let's encourage them to own today's joy by enjoying the truly good things in life.

If you are in a stage of "can't wait," how can you relax into the joy of today? Are there people younger than yourself whom you can encourage to enjoy the truly good things of life?

_____
_____
_____
_____
_____
_____

In our efforts to guide young people around us, let's encourage them to own joy by enjoying the truly good things in life. #joy218ways

——— Joy of the Light ———

Several years ago, I accompanied the Boy Scouts on a cave adventure. Using only my elbows, I drug my nearly six-foot frame through a tunnel all of thirty inches in height. As I grunted over the jagged, slime-covered floor, I found myself muttering, "I'd rather give birth," and I meant it. Forty-two thousand hours later—or so it seemed—a surprising payoff occurred. Deep in the belly of the earth, we boarded boats and set out on the underground river. A few minutes in, the captain extinguished all the lights. For the first time in my life, I experienced absolute darkness. No matter how long we sat there, our eyes never adjusted to the dark due to the complete absence of a light source. About five minutes later, one of the crew lit a single lantern and our eyes were like moths to a flame. That one light pierced the darkness.

Isaiah 9 begins with the prophecy that "the people walking in darkness [would] see a great light." In the short run, this was directed to the first of Israel's northern tribes when they experienced the Assyrian invasion (722 BC). In the bigger picture, the prophesy in Isaiah 9:1–7 speaks about the light of Jesus Christ shattering the world's sin-black darkness. When we recall our darkest sin moments, shame often lurks in the shadows. Yet, instead of focusing on the darkness, our joy comes as we turn our eyes to the light of Jesus' forgiveness. That one light pierces our darkness.

Not that it's a joy to think of this, but what has been your darkest sin moment? Which is more powerful for you at the current moment: shame for the sin or joy for the forgiveness?

_____

_____

_____

_____

_____

_____

_____

_____

When we recall our darkest sin moments, shame often lurks in the shadows. Joy comes as Jesus' forgiveness pierces the darkness. #joy218ways

Drinking Joy from the Well

_____

_____

_____

Ladies and gentlemen: Allow me to introduce you to one of my favorite verses in the Bible. If asked to name my number one pick in *218 Ways to Own Joy*, Isaiah 12:3 would be it. Paired with Isaiah 12:2, this scripture provides an unshakable foundation on which to anchor our lives. These verses sing across the centuries: Our joy is in our salvation! When life gets tough, when circumstances are hard, the more we focus on the foundational truth that Jesus saved us, our problems become what they truly are: a situation we need Jesus to help us through. We can become so impressed with our mess that we leave little room to be blessed.

When we go to the well of our salvation, we need to know we'll always have water to drink. How deep are our wells? Some draw from the Well of Condition. They believe the well provides water *so long as* they have more good deeds than bad to their credit. Others draw from the Well of Behavior. They believe the well dries up when they mess up. Neither is true. God is the one who digs the well. If it depended on us, we wouldn't have the power to break ground; we can't save ourselves. When we accept Jesus Christ as our Savior, God reveals a well of salvation that never runs dry. In seasons of spiritual and emotional drought, visualize coming to this well. Its living water is so pure it clears the mind and makes it easier to breathe again. The joy from this well is always available, and it never runs dry.

When was the last time that you felt spiritually and/or emotionally dry? When did you last visit the well of your salvation and "drink" in the pure joy-knowledge that you are saved?

_____

_____

_____

_____

_____

_____

_____

_____

When we accept Jesus Christ as our Savior, God reveals a well of salvation that never runs dry. With joy we draw from His well. #joy218ways

—— Joy in the Holy One ——

Isaiah 12:6

_____

_____

_____

This verse celebrates the One who would bring the prophecies of Isaiah 11 to life. In response to God's great works, the people of Zion are to spread the message of His great love from Israel to all the nations through their proclamations and song (12:4–6). Written more than 2,700 years ago, these words remain true for you and me because God has adopted us into His people (cf. John 1:12–13, Galatians 3:26, 29). In this verse, Zion is literally Jerusalem, but it also means God's church in a spiritual sense. Through our witness of the way He works in our lives, we—God's people—continue the spread of the Gospel.

Not only do we have a message to share, we have the incredible presence of the Holy One of Israel among us. How clearly and how powerfully do we feel this Holy One? He is always with us, hearing our words, knowing our inner thoughts and observing our choices. I wonder: If we could see Him physically in the room, would that change anything about the way we act? I heard Pastor Tony Evans say that, as a teen, when he got ready to go out with his friends, his father would say, "Remember, son, Jesus is coming along. Make Him proud." Awareness of the Holy One at our side should motivate us toward the joy of living in ways that make Him proud. He is among us, so may our lives be a joy-filled reflection of His presence!

Do you find yourself tuned in to the Holy One's presence every moment? How can an increased awareness of Him being at your side lead you to the joy of making Him proud?

_____

_____

_____

_____

_____

_____

_____

_____

Tweet

Awareness that the Holy One is right beside us should motivate us toward the joy of living in ways that make Him proud. #joy218ways

—— No Joy over a Wreck ——

Isaiah 16:9

_____

_____

_____

_____

_____

When approaching a hairpin curve on the road marked Wisdom, some folks would rather drive off a cliff to see what happens than proceed with caution. Seasoned drivers try to warn them but they prefer risking a hair-brained crash over listening to dire predictions. When the inevitable occurs, we wouldn't expect to see seasoned drivers standing over the wreck and laughing at the carnage. Instead, we'd expect to see them shaking their heads in great sadness over the waste of wisdom. This is Isaiah's tone in chapters 15–16 as he prophesies the destruction of Moab. Even though Isaiah belongs to a different nation, he finds no joy in seeing the spiritual revelation of Moab's coming disaster. God warned and invited Moab to follow Him, but the nation chose to drive off the cliff.

How many of our friends or family come to mind when we think about people who are reckless with their lives? We try to tell them that living in opposition to God will eventually lead to a wreck. In spite of our pleading, they continue to knucklehead their way through life. Like Isaiah, compassion needs to be our tone. Rather than gloat or sound holier-than-thou, our hearts should break as we view the path they're choosing. While we need to speak truth, sadness at their impending and predictable outcome should be our motivator. No one rejoices at the sight of a wreck—even if it could have been avoided.

Who needs your prayers for redirection in his/her life? If you've already been praying for this person, continue to ask the Lord for opportunities to point compassionately to His truth and to keep your heart engaged.

_____

_____

_____

_____

Tweet

Our hearts should break if someone's on a bad path. There's no joy at the sight of a wreck—even if it could have been avoided. #joy218ways

Joy of the Hedad

The nation of Moab had orchards, vineyards, and wineries. During seasons of prosperity, the hoot of the *hedad* (Hebrew word for "shouting") rang from the fields during harvest and wine making. Workers cheerfully whooped this shout of joy as they converted the abundant grapevines into wine. However, in a drastically different season, sorrow converted the *hedad* into silence. As punishment for not responding to the invitation to follow His ways, God pronounced judgment on Moab and destroyed its verdant vineyards. The Old Testament documents the fall of Moab by another prophet. Jeremiah 48:33 says: "Joy and gladness are gone from the orchards and fields of Moab. I have stopped the flow of wine from the presses; no one treads them with shouts of joy. Although there are shouts, they are not shouts of joy."

What a striking word picture. Where once the sound of laughter, hoots, and hollers filled the air, now an eerie silence prevails in the aftermath of destruction. Our culture laughs, hoots, and hollers at too many non-God-honoring things. Crude humor, vulgarity, pornography, and violence are just a few. We've collectively turned from how God would want His world to run and we, collectively, do not want God to do anything about it. Yet, we'll own more joy when we turn from the things that grieve God's heart. Rather than worry about God's judgment, we can hoot our own *hedad* by aligning our desires with our Creator's ways.

Do any non-God-honoring things tempt you? If so, open your heart to owning more joy by repenting and turning back to God's way in that area. If not, humbly thank the Lord for creating a clean heart in you.

Rather than worry about God's judgment, we'll own more joy by turning from the things that grieve God's heart. #joy218ways

—Joy of Trying God First—

Isaiah 22:13

_____

_____

_____

_____

Buckle your seatbelt and let's get up to speed on the oracle of Isaiah 22. The prophet sees a time in Jerusalem when God tries to call His people to repentance and they choose not to pick up the phone. They are under siege and their leaders have run from the battle. The people decide on two courses of action: (1) Let's figure out how to save ourselves by fixing our shattered defenses (vv. 8–11a) and, (2) Let's party! (v. 13). Indulge me; I sense a palm-to-the-forehead tone in v. 11b as God says, "You tried using all these materials to save yourselves but no one thought to look to the One who created them?" Rather than seek God's help, they gave up and decided to have a good time on the way to tomorrow's grave.

I'm guilty of shaking my head at the Israelites. I mean, if I had the attention of the God of the Universe, you'd better bet every time I hit a wall, I'd go to Him before trying to figure out how to fix it myself. Any time I got attacked, I'd certainly get quiet in prayer right away and ask for His guidance over every word and action … Oh, wait. Sigh. I'm more like the Israelites than I care to admit. I'm getting better, but I can still surprise myself with Israelite-idiocy moments. God offers comfort-in-the-storm joy when I go to Him first.

What is your default: Try to fix things yourself or to ask God to handle it? How does going to God first allow you to tap into comfort-in-the-storm joy?

_____

_____

_____

_____

_____

_____

_____

_____

Tweet

Instead of trying to fix problems right away by doing it my way, God offers comfort-in-the-storm joy when I go to Him first. #joy218ways

Joy of Being Counter-Cultural

Chapters 24–27 of Isaiah are known as "Isaiah's Apocalypse." While not as specific as the historical prophecies he speaks concerning particular nations in other chapters, this section of scripture broadly reveals God's intent to deal with sin. It's an equal opportunity kind of apocalypse. Our wealth and social standing will mean nothing (v. 2). In increasing measure, the Lord is aware that human infidelity is shredding the everlasting covenant (v. 5). As the earth begins to bear the consequences of God's judgment, people respond by trying to find joy where they can. However, like the earth, joy is dried up because God, the source of joy, has removed it (vv. 7–13).

I like to think I'm unshaped by our culture. I don't watch television, I never recognize pop songs, and I'm blissfully unaware of who, in Hollywood, is sleeping with whom. However, it would be silly to think any of us can escape being under its influence. Even the most independent among us have a filter of approval through which we screen our decisions. Either God is our "Yes/No" authority or it's culture's "thumbs up/down" that guides our steps. As Christians, we want to say "I look to God," but I imagine many folks in Isaiah 24 fooled themselves with the same thought. Being counter-cultural doesn't mean being weird—that won't attract anyone to Jesus. It simply means that when looking for the joy of approval, we turn to God for the nod.

Being honest, do you know more about your favorite television show (or another cultural trap) than you do about the book of Isaiah? It's simply a window into whether we pursue the true source of joy or the distractions to it.

Being counter-cultural doesn't mean being weird. It simply means when looking for the joy of approval, we turn to God for the nod. #joy218ways

–Joy Response to Tragedy–

_____

_____

_____

Who is doing all this shouting? Referencing Isaiah 24:6, there are two ways to look at their identity. One possibility suggests they're the remaining survivors God will spare from the end-time judgment prophesied in Isaiah 24. They will be the new seed from which the human race rebuilds. If true, this motivates us to consider if we'd make the cut. When God-time reaches Fed Up o'clock and He sends this prophesied gloom to the earth, would He glance our way and say, "Well done. Continue to spread my love and the message of my goodness"?

The other possibility rings a bit more likely to me. In this understanding of Isaiah 24:6, the meaning of the few is that they are the ones who, after facing all the destruction, continue to find joy and comfort in God. Because they soaked in God's joy before it was go-time, they are not devastated by the devastation. Rather than moaning at all the world has lost, they sing for joy that God delivered them. Matthew Henry put it this way: "Those that rejoice in the Lord can rejoice in tribulation, and by faith may be in triumph when all [those] about them are in tears." Seeing God deliver on His promises causes them to worship Him in renewed awe. Is God asking too much for this kind of a joy-response to tragedy? We may not live to be tested in the Tribulation, but we all have the opportunity to worship the Lord in joy when we experience terrible misfortune in our lives.

Chances are you've experienced some degree of tragedy or loss in your life. Were you able to find joy as you navigated the destruction? It certainly doesn't mean you shouldn't mourn. What would a joy-response to tragedy look like?

_____

_____

_____

_____

_____

_____

_____

During tragedy, when we look for how God is at work around us, we can continue to worship Him in joy as we mourn. #joy218ways

— Joy in the Resurrection —

_____

_____

_____

_____

_____

"Have you heard about the guy who was raised from the dead?" One of my friends likes to ask folks that question as a means to start talking about Jesus. Isaiah, too, was excited about resurrection as he prophesied this song of praise in chapter 26. He sees God restoring His people after a time of judgment. Verses 16–18 are a song of humble acknowledgment by God's faithful remnant (described in Isaiah 24:6) that they have no power to save themselves. It is God alone who has the power to raise and save.

Verse 19 also points to the spiritual awakening of the church. The power that raised Jesus' dead body to life is the same power by which all who believe in Him are resurrected from spiritual death to life. 1 Corinthians 15:20–22 makes this case beautifully: "But Christ has indeed been raised from the dead, the first fruits of those who have fallen asleep. For since death came through a man, the resurrection of the dead comes also through a man. For as in Adam all die, so in Christ all will be made alive." Without the resurrection of our Savior, absolutely everything on which Christians base our lives would be a farce. Imagine the overwhelming joy of experiencing the empty tomb (John 19–20). It's good to soak in the joy of Jesus' power over the grave and remember that His resurrection power is active in our lives.

Take a moment to recall the story of Jesus' resurrection (Matthew 28, Mark 16, Luke 24, John 20). Thank Him for the joy of knowing His resurrection power in your life.

_____

_____

_____

_____

_____

_____

It's good to soak in the joy of our resurrected King and remember
that His resurrection power is active in our lives. #joy218ways

— Joy of a Restored Earth —

_____

_____

_____

_____

_____

It strikes me that those who do evil—the ones who purposefully reject God's ways—are unconcerned with the chaos they cause. In fact, that seems to be their goal. On the other hand, those of us who desire to see God's design be the ruling principle of our world are distraught by the work of evil. However, when we lift our eyes from current events and place them squarely in scripture, we find hope. On the heels of the devastation prophesied in Isaiah 34, chapter 35 brings a message of joy as God revitalizes the land and refreshes the redeemed. "As God's day of vengeance is just retribution for the wicked, it introduces the divine repayment of the redeemed for past pain." (The Bible Reader's Companion)[1]

Imagine every wrong in our world being made right. Terrorism eradicated, poverty alleviated, disease obliterated, violence eliminated, and family destruction a thing of the past. This is the feeling of Isaiah 35, and it's the promise to the redeemed of the Lord "on that day." Like a flower bursting into bloom and innocently lifting its face to heaven, those who have hoped in God's Word will have the joy of seeing Him erase all past pain. Do you pray for it to happen? I'm guilty of praying mostly for the praises and pressures of "today." What a powerfully freeing joy to pray this scripture and ask the Lord for His will to be done and for His kingdom to come!

Take some time and tell God the wrongs that you see in our world. Then soak in the freeing joy of praying for the day when He will make all things new.

_____

_____

_____

_____

_____

_____

Rather than only praying the praises and pressures of "today," also pray for the joy of seeing God's will to be done and for His kingdom to come! #joy218ways

---

[1] Richards, Lawrence O.: _The Bible Readers Companion_. electronic ed. Wheaton : Victor Books, 1991; Published in electronic form by Logos Research Systems, 1996

Joy of Healing

_____

_____

_____

_____

Chapter 35 is a refreshing highlight in the first half of the book of Isaiah. Following talk of vengeance, death, and destruction, the prophet turns to seeing a marvelous future when God will give His redeemed a beautiful new earth. One aspect of this restoration is perfect physical healing for those who have been afflicted (vv. 5–6). This will apply universally to all God's people.

What about now? When we—or someone we love—struggle physically, how do we continue to have joy, especially if we've been praying about it for a long time? I do know God is still in the healing business. In my thirties, He did the most surprising healing of a shoulder injury that had rendered me a one-winged wonder for nine months. Yet, I'm currently dealing with and praying through other health issues that, so far, are still a thorn in my flesh (2 Corinthians 12:7–10). The truth is, healing doesn't come from our side—healing is a work of the Lord. So, in full faith I pray for His ability to heal accompanied by full trust that He sees, hears, and answers me—whether yes, no, or not now. I also firmly believe that the most perfect healing God gives is when we leave this world behind and enter heaven. God heals either on this side of heaven or the next. With joy, we can continue to pray for healing and rest in knowing that God hears us and is at work answering us.

Do you need God to work a healing in you or someone you love? Do you know someone at work, church, or school who needs healing? Take this time to pour out what's in your heart.

_____

_____

_____

_____

_____

_____

_____

_____

In full faith we can pray for God's ability to heal accompanied by full trust that He answers—whether yes, no, or not now. #joy218ways

—— Joy of Being Right ——

Isaiah 35:10a

_____

_____

_____

Once upon a time, my husband and I were in a three-day argument. We were fairly new to the marriage thing and the idea of "being one" was bad math in our book. I started this fight in the Valley of Trivial and it quickly escalated to the heights of Mt. Major. Yes, we'd found the hill on which we were willing to die. The end of the battle would only happen when one combatant waved their "Okay, you're right" flag. Can you relate to a time of wanting to be right so badly it overshadowed everything else? Our passion to be right is a strong driver.

Let's channel this passion to be right into the powerful future picture Isaiah paints in chapter 35. After witnessing the devastation of the Lord's judgment on the earth (Isaiah 34), those called the "redeemed" by the Lord will be allowed to walk on His pathway into His promised city (35:8). Others may want to, but their wickedness and unbelief will preclude them from passage. Only those bold enough to live according to Christ's teachings will have the glorious dust from the Way of Holiness on their feet. Witnessing the splendor of all they'd anticipated and believed to be true will be an incredible juxtaposition from walking by faith. Now, they will see all they hoped in. They will have the joy of saying, "I knew it—I knew I was right!"

Are you convinced God's promises in Isaiah 35 are true? If fully convinced, celebrate knowing you're right to believe. If you question whether God will restore His earth in a glorious way, ask the Holy Spirit to lead you to scripture and other resources that will help your understanding so you, too, can own the joy of knowing you're right to believe.

_____

_____

_____

_____

_____

_____

_____

Tweet

When we see God deliver on His promises, it gives us the joy of saying, "I knew it—I was right to believe!" #joy218ways

—Joy to Overtake Sorrow—

Isaiah 35:10b

The great and glorious day of the Millennium has arrived. The righteous people of God have not only survived all the outpouring of God's judgment on the earth (Isaiah 34), they also have the amazing privilege of walking on a holy highway into Zion—the place where God dwells (Isaiah 35:8). Joy overtakes them. They don't have to work to be joyful, they don't have the struggle of keeping away from the world's sinful pleasure-temptations, they don't have to choose right thinking … they literally have reached the place where joy simply is. It's like the best moments of life being lived in endless variations that never lose their blush.

This day will come but in the meantime, sorrow and sighing are part of the human experience. It's true or scripture wouldn't talk of a time they flee away. Understanding this unlocks a new access to joy. To think the purpose of life is the avoidance of sorrow and sighing is like finding out over and over that the Easter Bunny isn't real. We put our eggs in the basket of "If I can just get through this, then everything will be good." Yet, when sorrow comes in its next form, we act devastatingly surprised—like the universe is personally directing its ire at us. The new, unhappy circumstance may be unique to us, but the inevitability of it happening is not. Until the advent of the Millennium, sorrow and sighing are parts of the rhythm of life. Between now and then, we own the joy of being close to the power that, one day, will send these rotten joy-suckers fleeing.

Does knowing sorrow is a part of the rhythm of life help you relax into this "rhythm"? How can the joy of knowing that God will one day remove sorrow help you remember His power when new sorrows hit?

_____

_____

_____

_____

_____

_____

_____

_____

Tweet

Everlasting joy: It's like the best moments of life lived in endless variations that never lose their blush. #joy218ways

— Joy of Diverse Worship —

_____

_____

_____

_____

_____

In Isaiah 42:1–4, the prophet tells of the coming Messiah. This is the first of the "Servant Songs" in Isaiah.[1] Each verse supplies another marker by which the world would recognize Jesus as the Messiah. From his vantage point of prophesying 700 years before Jesus' birth, Isaiah sees the response of praise and joy when the people witness the power and majesty of this Savior (Isaiah 42:9–14).

God wants His people to praise Him. On a recent mission trip to Romania, I stood and listened to my brothers and sisters singing praise in their language, românește. Listening to their songs carried me into the throne room of God. He opened my spiritual eyes to consider the many thousands of languages in which He receives praise every Sunday. God celebrates—and is celebrated by—diversity. In Isaiah 42:11, the townspeople are stationary and they praise God. The settlers are mobile nomads and they praise God. The people of the rock city of Sela and those in the mountains praise God. Whether we're urban or rural, adventuresome or stay-at-home types, we're all united in praising the same God. Our purpose, like God's, should be to celebrate this diversity rather than desire to standardize it to our determined style. Our joy will explode when we respect the beauty of other people's praise.

Do you celebrate diversity or do you desire to primarily be around people who are like you? Can you think of a time when you had the joy to learn something incredible from someone quite different from you? Pray for more of these Godpportunities!

_____

_____

_____

_____

_____

Our joy will explode when we respect the beauty of other people's praise to the one God we all worship. Celebrate diversity. #joy218ways

---

[1]   Isaiah 42:1–4; 49:1–6; 50:4–9; 52:13—53:12

—Joy in a Little Sarcasm—

Isaiah 44:23

_____

_____

_____

_____

Did you know that listening to a sarcastic person on a daily basis may make you more creative? A Harvard Business School study[1] looked into the science behind this fact. Apparently they've solved all the top shelf issues and now are turning to the lower hanging fruit. (Just a little sarcasm to help you feel more creative.) Turns out, sarcasm also has a place in scripture. Isaiah 44:6–20 is an amusing read. It's like sitting around a campfire listening to God roast on crazy cousin Cooter. Grab your s'mores fixings and read it in The Message version. God's sarcasm about idol-making is stingingly delightful.

God hates idols and will use all means to make His point. In Isaiah 44:21, He reminds us that unlike human hands that create powerless idols, His hands made and shaped us. Not only did He form His people, He created all the earth. When we're tuned in to the majestic work of the Creator God—whether by looking in the mirror or looking at nature—we have a song to share. It may find expression in music, gratitude, words of affirmation, fellowship, or the simple joy of being still. The sound of the song isn't the focus, but keeping it inside is not an option. When our God-focus is strong, our life-song hums along with nature's noise purely for the joy of it.

Is there anything you are creating in your own strength that has more of your attention than God does? How is your life-song sounding? Is it silenced by busyness or is it harmonizing with God's creation?

_____

_____

_____

_____

Tweet

A life-song of praise happens when our God-focus is strong. We may even "hum" along with noises in nature for the pure joy of it. #joy218ways

---

[1] Maldarelli, Claire. "Sarcasm May Make You More Creative." _Popular Science_. N.p., 27 July 2015. Web. 05 Aug. 2017. <http://www.popsci.com/research-gives-sarcasm-okay-only-your-friends>.

Joy of Discomfort
in the Pew

_____

_____

_____

_____

_____

Stockholm syndrome is an issue that afflicts some who've been held in captivity. During their trauma they begin to identify with the very ones holding them prisoner. Rather than escaping when they can, they choose to stay. First identified as a syndrome in 1973, the phenomenon has been happening as far back as the 7th century BC. When God sent Cyrus (2 Chronicles 36:23, Ezra 1:1–5) to free the Israelites from their seventy-year-long Babylonian bondage, many wanted to stay. Rather than flee, they sort of yawned and stretched in their comfortable captivity.

Listen to this interesting parallel from Warren Wiersbe: "One would think the Jews would have been eager to leave their 'prison' and return to their land to see God do new and great things for them. They had grown accustomed to the security of bondage and had forgotten the challenges of freedom. The church today can easily grow complacent with its comfort and affluence. God may have to put us into the furnace to remind us that we are here to be servants and not consumers or spectators."[1] If we belong to a church that consistently pushes us outside our comfort zone, it will be our joy to say "Amen" to that statement. If, however, we attend a church where we can come and go without ever feeling the need to serve—both inside and outside the building—beware the quiet, joy-stealing bondage of comfort.

Does your church make it easy for you to settle in with comfort or does it keep you on the edge of your seat? How can we represent God's amazing idea of His church with joy if we are seeking comfort over challenge?

_____

_____

_____

If we belong to a church that pushes us outside our comfort zone, it will be our joy to say "Amen" to being challenged. #joy218ways

---

[1] Wiersbe, Warren W. *Be Comforted: Feeling Secure in the Arms of God.* BE Series Commentary Series. Colorado Springs, CO: David C. Cook, 2009.

———— Joy in our Savior ————

"You're my Savior, Restorer, Rebuilder, Rewarder, My Refuge, Redeemer, Defender, My Healer, Savior." As one of the "Savior Songs" in the book of Isaiah, chapter 49 speaks to every aspect of Christ's attributes expressed in the worship song entitled, "Savior."[1]

Savior (vv. 1, 3, 5, 6, 8, 26)   Refuge (vv. 15–18)
Restorer (vv. 8, 12)   Redeemer (vv. 7, 26)
Rebuilder (v. 9)   Defender (vv. 9, 25–26)
Rewarder (vv. 19–23)   Healer (v. 13)

Jesus is all the above and, as verse 13 compassionately states, He loves the broken. I find encouraging beauty in the word picture of Isaiah 42:3, "A bruised reed He will not break, and a smoldering wick He will not snuff out." A bruised reed represents the weak and depressed in spirit. The smoldering wick symbolizes those who are trying to hang on to faith but are wavering dangerously. Our Savior is tender, gentle, and full of grace toward us when we are weak, depressed, and wavering. He is merciful and compassionate to those around us who are broken and in need of assurance there is hope. May we soak in His tenderness when we are bruised and smoldering. May we extend the same comfort and compassion to others when they're in pain. Even while their struggle continues, when hurting people grasp this love, it changes everything. Joy strengthens as the Savior takes brokenness and rebuilds a life.

Is this a season of brokenness in your life? What would Jesus' comfort and compassion look like to you? Do you need to share that with someone who could help you? If you are not in a broken state, who in your life is in need of receiving the Savior's comfort and compassion? What would the Lord ask you to do to help?

When hurting people grasp God's love, it changes everything. Joy builds as the Savior takes brokenness and rebuilds a life. #joy218ways

---

1   ""Savior" Lyrics." *LetsSingIt*. N.p., n.d. Web. 05 Aug. 2017.
    <https://www.letssingit.com/new-life-worship-lyrics-savior-qs7gwxw#ixzz4owMkMVO3>.

—Joy in Being Lifted Up—

Isaiah 51:3

_____

_____

_____

_____

_____

I imagine walking into a huge banquet hall. People of every sort mill about but I can tell they have something in common. Their radiant happiness shines. It comes from inside—there's not a brittle, surface smile in the room. Their faces … it's almost as though the memories of living wasted seasons outside the comfort of "home" have etched lines of compassion there. Then it hits me: The reason for their joy is God. It's in their song and their inviting warmth. Their thankfulness for Him gathering them together literally feels like an embrace saying, "Come enjoy this vibe with us!"

A group of people who know what it's like to be down and then to have God lift them up is a group that should be marked by inviting joy. This is a beautiful picture of church. God designed it to be the place where His love is on full display. He intended it to be a safe space to lay down the pain of our ruins. It's where real folks receive us as we bring our real selves. I love the tagline of our church, "We're a group of imperfect people, loved by and serving a perfect God."[1] Church isn't about being perfect; it's about the permission to explore growing without being judged. It's where we experience the joy of being lifted up!

Have you found a church that fits the description of this group? If so, are you inviting people like crazy to come enjoy the vibe? If not: Friend, don't give up. Your feet need to keep going until you feel the embrace of real people who enjoy sharing their imperfect journey toward perfection with you.

_____

_____

_____

_____

_____

_____

Tweet

Church: Bringing our real selves and being met by equally real folks whose joy at being rescued by God shines from their inner-being. #joy218ways

---

[1]   "ABOUT US." _Well House North_, wellhousenorth.org

Joy when Shaking with Fear

Isaiah 51:11a

_____

_____

_____

"Jump! I'm not going to drop you!" I remember standing on the side of an indoor pool shivering like a wet mutt forgotten outside in the middle of winter. I wasn't cold; I was scared to death. The idea of rejecting gravity's safe embrace to leap into the depths of Aqualand held no appeal. But the outstretched arms in the pool belonged to the mom I adored. Perhaps I recalled the times she had come through for me, so I jumped. I came up spluttering with joy and with her protective arms around me. Her presence gave me the strength to convert my fear into joy.

The people of Israel often questioned if God would drop them. Years in captivity stoked a desire to cling to their confining surroundings rather than trust God. Isaiah 51:9–10 called them to remember the times God brought His people through hardships. It's as though they stood on the edge of a pool, scared to death, and muttered, "Okay. We're afraid, but for crying out loud, God parted the Red Sea for our people! He's not going to drop us now!" By remembering, they visualized the day God would convert their fear to joy. In our lives, the threats are real. When we're scared and shaking over an awful situation, we can tap into joy by muttering remembrances of God's faithfulness through our chattering teeth. This isn't an easy joy to feel but it's a joy we need. A thread of joy touches our soul when God gives us the strength to keep going.

What/who do you turn to when you are afraid? When facing difficult life challenges, do you take things up [to God] before you take them out [to others]? How does the act of pausing to pray when things are hard allow you to connect to the comforting joy of knowing your God is in control?

_____

_____

_____

_____

_____

_____

Tweet

When we're scared, comforting joy embraces us as we mutter remembrances of God's faithfulness through our chattering teeth. #joy218ways

Sustaining Joy

Isaiah 51:11 is the meat between two pieces of "Whatcha' Scared About" bread. Verses 7–8 instruct Israel not to worry when mere mortals run their mouths. In verses 12–16, God tells them not to fear mortal men. He—the God who can whip up a hurricane— has His eye on those who have oppressed His people (Isaiah 51:15). The Lord calls Israel to look to Him when humans cause them to feel small. He gives His ransomed people gladness and joy as the sorrow and sighing caused by their enemies vanishes from view.

We don't have to wander too far from home to run into people who run their mouths. In fact, they can invade our homes via our devices. These "mortals" can stir fear in our hearts as we listen to their predictions and posturing. More troubling are the co-workers, the bosses, the sports parents, the school activity parents, the church people, our friends, and family who fire us up. It's scary when they begin a campaign against us because we do things differently than they do. We may be at odds philosophically or theologically. Whatever the case, this passage of Isaiah is a sustaining joy during times when we're made to feel small, isolated, and judged. Staying grounded in the power of our God will connect us to joy as we wait for our sorrow and sighing to be a thing of the past.

I don't know about you, but I've personally experienced needing this joy when humans have run their mouths about me. They may have felt justified; I felt judged. Do any situations come to mind when you've needed God to be your defender? How would knowing that sorrow and sighing will eventually vanish help connect you to God's sustaining joy in the face of this kind of trial?

_____

_____

_____

_____

_____

_____

_____

God gives us His gladness and joy as the sorrow and sighing caused by
our enemies vanishes from view. He is our defender. #joy218ways

Joy of Praying
—— for Christian Leaders ——

_____

_____

_____

_____

You know how people tell you something will be hard and you sort of nod like you get it? At some future date when you actually experience it, you nod again but, now, it's really your head jerking as your whole body reels from the "shamwow" of how truly difficult it is. Prior to going into ministry, some friends who were missionaries, pastors, non-profit leaders, and church staff would pull back the curtain and share some of the behind-the-scenes challenges that were an active backdrop to their joy of serving. I listened sympathetically and nodded. However, when God placed me in full-time ministry, I empathized. Ministry is hard, even as it is beautifully so.

In Isaiah 52:7–8, the prophet declares the power of the gospel message and the beauty of those who proclaim it. They look forward to the time the Lord returns, and they actively watch for it. All who share the gospel and believe in the second coming of Christ wait in varying degrees of expectancy. Even more, those whose full-time work is pointing people to the gospel and Jesus' return are like the watchmen in verse 8. The joy they experience now when they see people accept Christ is a foreshadowing of how they'll shout when He returns. Until then, they need our prayers. Ministry is hard so let's pray for those whose feet bring the good news of Jesus. Let's pray and strengthen their joy by letting them know we're praying.

A question I love to ask those in ministry is, "What is the number one way I can be praying for you?" For whom will you pray?

_____

_____

_____

_____

_____

_____

_____

Ministry is hard. Let's pray for those serving and strengthen
their joy by letting them know we're praying. #joy218ways

Joy of a Surprising Rescue

_____

_____

_____

Often, biblical prophecies are vague and require a deep knowledge of history and scripture to interpret them … and that's from our vantage point of looking back at events. I can't imagine how those who heard the prophesies in real-time could've made heads or tails of the imagery. However, when a prophesy specifically names a person, his future role is clear. Cyrus the Great was a Persian king, a Gentile, and a nonbeliever. Approximately 160 years before his birth, Isaiah prophesied that God would use him in surprising ways to free His people (Isaiah 44:28, 45:1).

When the Israelites were in captivity for hundreds of years in the 15th century BC, God went the conventional route and worked through one of their people, Moses, to rescue them from Egypt (Exodus 1–12). Apparently, Israel didn't learn that rebelling against God was a national ticket to captivity. Some 900 years later, they found themselves enslaved in Babylon. This time, God chose to free them through the surprising route of using the nonbeliever named Cyrus the Great (Ezra 1:1–6). Look, we don't have to be a prophecy guru to see how this applies to our lives. When we feel imprisoned by our circumstances, we need to cry out to God. As we do, let's not rule out any of the ways in which He chooses to answer. Like Him choosing to use Cyrus, God's means of rescuing us may very well come in the joy of a surprising form.

It's hard to hang on to hope when we've been waiting for God to move. Can you think of a time God sent you a surprising answer to a need in your life? Is there anything in which you currently need to see God move?

_____

_____

_____

_____

_____

_____

_____

_____

When we cry out to God, His means of rescuing us may very
well come in the joy of a surprising form. #joy218ways

—— Joy in the Impossible ——

_____
_____
_____
_____
_____

Infertility is devastating. I went through a year in which my flame of hope wavered with every passing month. A barren woman in ancient Israel was disgraced, so societal shame was an added layer to the pain of her empty arms. In Isaiah 54, the barren woman (one) is a metaphor for God's people. Like her, they were a nation that had not realized their heart's desire. Yet, in verses 2–3, God speaks abundance into the barrenness. He says that even though she hasn't produced a child, her descendants will be so numerous she'll need to set up bigger tents. How can that be? The people don't feel like they're fulfilling what they were made to do. God would have to do the impossible.

Who, among us, needs God to move in a seemingly impossible situation? We may know God can do anything, but sometimes we need a reminder. Consciously choosing to "shout for joy" in this case can mean we pray boldly in the presence of our pain. When facing an insurmountable challenge, it's joy-altering to remember that God made a virgin pregnant. Gabriel said to Mary, "For nothing is impossible with God" (Luke 1:37 NLT). The God who can do that can handle our impossible. Find a release for your pain by shouting up to God. With joy, remember He can do the impossible.

What looks like an impossible situation in your life? Take a moment and visualize Mary getting the news that, as a virgin, God made her pregnant. That same God is listening to you. "Shout" your impossible question to Him with the joy of hoping in His power to move. He is listening and will answer.

_____
_____
_____
_____
_____
_____

When facing an insurmountable challenge, ask God to do the impossible then rest in the joy that He is at work. #joy218ways

Joy of Taking God
at His Word

_____

_____

_____

"I swear to God." When I hear someone say that, I tend to believe him less. It usually comes tripping over the lips of a person who has, let's say, a track record of not telling the truth. Using the name of the God of absolute truth to cover a lie sounds resoundingly more ironical than factual. My thoughts on it aside, God says not to do it. In Matthew 5:33–37, Jesus taught, "Let your 'Yes' be 'Yes,'"—no swearing to God. Here in Isaiah 55:8–13, God says that not only are His ways higher than we could ever understand, but every word He speaks will come to be. He never breaks His word.

If asked, most of us could name at least one person who has broken his/her word to us. Those human failings cause trust issues in us that spill over to how we view God. We might read a passage in the Bible and wish it could be true while still finding it hard to believe it could happen. Yet, what's the alternative? Give in to letting life wash over us with no hope? Choose the self-exhausting path of relying on ourselves to make everything turn out right? When we trust God at His word, we look forward to seeing how He will work. Adopting the filter that God never breaks His word allows us to live in hope and joy as we trust and wait.

Is it easy for you to trust people? Have you ever had to rebuild trust with someone who broke his/her word to you? How easy is it for you to trust God's promises in His word?

_____

_____

_____

_____

_____

_____

_____

Adopting the filter that God never breaks His word allows us to live in hope and joy as we trust and wait to see what He will restore. #joy218ways

Joy of Inclusion

Isaiah 56:7

_____
_____
_____
_____

"Jesus loves the little children … red and yellow, black and white, they are precious in His sight." This Sunday school song could be the anthem for Isaiah 56. In it, God plainly offers invitation, welcome, and acceptance to all people. Making a point to speak about those whom the religious people consider outcasts, God states that He would include any who "choose to please [Him] and hold fast to [His] covenant." This would have radically exploded the thinking of Jewish traditionalists. They would have rather used the Law of God's Word to exclude people from sharing in His love and grace than to embrace diversity. God's Word, however, teaches the celebration of all those He created.

God knows we are all on a journey; I wonder why we forget that when it comes to loving others as they are on theirs. Loving others doesn't mean accepting their sin; it means separating who they are from what they do. God invites, welcomes, and accepts people as they are and loves them enough to call them to be increasingly more holy by judging what they do. It's important that we let God be God. When we let go of excluding people who are outside our definition of "normal," we experience the joy of creating an environment where they—and we—can explore the joy of growing in God's house of prayer.

I read a quotation, "Hate is unacceptable. Hate of people you believe you righteously should hate is unacceptable." Are there any people groups you hate? Maybe you don't harbor hate but are there people groups you think should not be welcome in church? How does this passage speak to the joy of inclusion?

_____
_____
_____
_____
_____
_____

Tweet

Joy is found in creating an environment where all may grow. Let go of excluding people outside your definition of "normal." #joy218ways

Joy of Fasting

Isaiah 58:14

_____

_____

_____

_____

_____

Isaiah 58 is an instructive chapter about spiritual fasting. Typically, fasting involves going without food for a period of time. However, we can fast from anything if it causes us to be intentional about praying when we want the thing from which we are abstaining. We can set aside coffee, television, social media, devices, et cetera. Fasting can help us get clarity about an issue and it can help us listen for God's will. When we fast according to God's design, we find a joy we can't discover in other ways.

I have fasted multiple times for various reasons during my Christian walk. I think it's interesting that in Isaiah 58, God says fasting is not only about denying ourselves but should also be about serving others (vv. 3–8). If we don't look for ways to pour into others as we fast, we easily can get full of ourselves for how "spiritual" we are. It's hard to stay humble when we're deeply impressed with how holy we are. Out of a heart that is fasting for God's sake, other areas of holiness will flow in our lives (vv. 9–14). When we take intentional steps to get closer to God, such as fasting, we find a new joy in the Lord as He blesses these markers on our journey.

Have you experienced the joy of fasting? If so, what have been the reasons for and outcomes of your fasting? Have you ever gotten prideful about fasting? Are there any areas in which you need to hear from the Lord? Any strongholds that you haven't been able to break? Talk to God about guiding you in fasting and praying for release from those strongholds.

_____

_____

_____

_____

_____

_____

_____

Tweet

When we take intentional steps to get closer to God, such as fasting, we usher in new joy as the Lord blesses these markers on our journey. #joy218ways

Joy in Being a Person of the Light

Isaiah 60:5

_____

_____

_____

_____

Isaiah 60 opens with imagery about the light of Christ's return to earth. Prior to His coming, "darkness covers the earth … and the peoples." When Jesus comes in His glorious light, those who have believed in and have followed Him will bask in the blanket of His favor. However, this will not simply be their reward; their glow will point not-yet believers to the One who can obliterate the dark spaces in their souls.

The foundational joy of a Christian is in knowing that faith in Jesus Christ is all that's needed to be eternally forgiven and adopted by God. The incredible bonus-joy of being a Christian is the ongoing work of the Holy Spirit in our lives. The better we know Him, the more we understand that it's His power shining through us that draws people to Himself. To pursue joy for the sole purpose of making ourselves feel better is to be dulled from experiencing joy in all its dimensions. As we keep our eyes open and keep prayers for not-yet believers on our "praydars," we unlock a facet of joy that we cannot otherwise experience. Roy T. Bennett in _The Light in the Heart_ wrote, "Learn to light a candle in the darkest moments of someone's life. Be the light that helps others see; it is what gives life its deepest significance."[1]

How brightly do you feel the light of Christ shining through you? If you perceive it to be dim, spend time praying for the Holy Spirit to shine through you. If His light is your joy, who is near you that needs this light to shine into their darkest moments?

_____

_____

_____

_____

_____

_____

Tweet

To pursue joy for the sole purpose of making oneself feel better is to be dulled from experiencing all of joy's dimensions. #joy218ways

[1] Bennett, Roy T. _The Light in the Heart_. Roy T. Bennett, 2016.

Restoration of Your Joy
———— Account ————

_____
_____
_____

God is talking to the people of Zion. Acknowledging that they've been through rough times, He now speaks of their restoration when the Messiah returns. He assures them that people will flock to Jerusalem to show their support and belief in their God. Even today, we see glimpses of this future time. Millions, like me, have made the trip to Jerusalem to experience the thrill of being in the Holy Land.

God makes huge deposits into our joy-banks when He does restorative works in our lives. It's important to guard those accounts and not let the past come and rob what we own. If we are still in a season of being down, forsaken, hated, or lonely, we need to hang on to the knowledge that God will restore us. As we wait, we can't let bitterness take root. We are the only ones who lose in that. Instead, going back to the foundational joy of our salvation, we remember we are children of God. No one and no circumstance can take that joy from us. When we stop and focus on what Jesus did for us, we'll know in our souls that we are not alone—a big Somebody loves us. We need to look deeply: Are we blocking any blessings due to hatred, bitterness, or a lack of forgiveness? While it's human to feel those negative feelings, joy comes in knowing we can come to our Heavenly Father, confess them, and prepare to be restoratively cleansed.

Is your "Restoration of Joy" account secured from any past memories that may try to steal from it? If you're going through a season of being down, how does remembering you are a child of God keep the embers of your joy alive?

_____
_____
_____
_____
_____
_____
_____

If we are in a season of being down, forsaken, hated or lonely, the knowledge that God will restore us provides a quiet joy we can hold on to. #joy218ways

-Joy of Contented Waiting-

_____

_____

_____

_____

_____

My Bible heads this chapter, "The Year of the Lord's Favor." It's God's promise to restore His favor to His people after generations of ruin. With the ongoing conflict over land in Israel and Gaza, it's clear this promise is yet to be fully realized. The idea of receiving a double portion of land that will lead to everlasting joy is a future promise with no set delivery date.

Looking more broadly, I know many of us feel that we have not received _our_ double portion yet. Unchecked, this can stir up joy-sucking feelings of discontentment, but check _this_: Many of the heroes of faith in Hebrews 11 died without full receipt of every one of God's promises. However, as God continues to fulfill them, they are able to see and enjoy the blessings from a distance because of their faith. Our joy is not dependent on receiving things or in seeing every promise fulfilled. Everlasting joy is in knowing we're part of the team that God will bless in His time. We all have God-given portions in our lives right now. We're only discontent if we focus on the ones that God hasn't delivered yet. Yes, it's easier to feel joy when we have all we desire. Realistically, until Jesus returns, we'll always be waiting on something. This everlasting joy is consistently available if we don't block it with our discontent.

If you are waiting on God to fulfill a promise, what Scripture covers this promise? It's powerful and joy-giving to pray those verses over your situation. How does knowing you're on the team that God will bless in His time allow you to tap into everlasting joy today?

_____

_____

_____

_____

_____

_____

Joy is easier to feel when we have all we desire. Realistically, however, until Jesus returns, we'll always be waiting on something. #joy218ways

Joy of Being
—— One of His People ——

_____

_____

_____

"Our Father, who art in heaven..." The Lord's Prayer (Matthew 6:9–13) contains praise to God and pleas for His help. Isaiah 63:7–64:12 carries the same vibe from a faithful remnant of God's people. God receives their praise and answers their pleas in Isaiah 65. He not only reveals His deep desire to be in relationship with all people, He also speaks of His intolerance for their sin. In verses 8–16, God recognizes a small band of followers and compares them to those who disregard His ways. Those who choose to reject God will have areas of their lives that cannot be repaired.

When we humbly accept God's offer of forgiveness and love, we are in line for the abundant blessings listed in verses 8–16. We drink [spiritually], we sing for joy, we enjoy God giving us a new character, and we anticipate our inheritance to come. The only way we go thirsty is if we choose to stop going to the source of living water (John 7:38). Our song of joy—whether loud or quiet—is always ours unless we choose to silence it. We know we have a forever place with God that we look forward to with eternal eyes. Being one of God's people is a joy in its own dimension. If we feel like we need more than this to have joy, are we saying God is not enough? I don't think a Christian would say this, but we have to inspect whether our lives reflect this.

How would you answer the question: If you know that you are one of God's people, is that enough for you to feel joy?

_____

_____

_____

_____

_____

_____

_____

Being God's kid is a joy in its own dimension. If we feel like we need more to have joy, are we saying God is not enough? #joy218ways

– Power of a Joy-Filled Life –

_____

_____

_____

God will create new heavens and a new earth. He has plans in motion to restore all that is broken and to extend His blessings on His people. It was refreshing to read in verse 8 that the Lord recognized the good still existing in mankind. When God creates this new heavens and earth, He declares that Jerusalem will be a delight and its people a joy.

Mother Teresa said, "One filled with joy preaches without preaching." In our world today, what kinds of people are a joy? The greatest ambassadors for joy are those who are vessels of it. Joy is a commodity that people want to possess because they always want to have it organically operating in their lives. It's a multi-faceted treasure. Those who reflect the joy they own are magnetic. Too often, we look for joy in order to be a consumer of it; we want joy for what it can bring to our lives. In Isaiah 65, however, we see the facet of joy we can own only when we give it away. The more we understand that living a joy-filled life is a blessing to those around us, the more we understand the power of joy. As we continue on our journey of discovering how to own joy, let's pray to have the unselfish ability to want joy in our lives so that we may be a joy in our world.

Do you see joy as being powerful? Think of people you know who live a joy-filled life. Do they have influence on those around them? Influence is power. Talk to the Lord about how your life can go to the next joy-level.

_____

_____

_____

_____

_____

_____

_____

_____

_____

_____

The more we understand that a joy-filled life is a blessing to those around us, the more we understand the power of joy. #joy218ways

Camp Joy

_____

_____

_____

_____

_____

Depending on the word paired with it, the idea of "camp" elicits a range of feelings: Camp David, campfire, summer camp, and tent camp to name a few. In the final chapter of Isaiah, we see why it's good to be in God's camp. He sees through the fake campers (vv. 3–6), He has a vision for how to run His camp (vv. 7–10), He knows how to show love to His true campers (vv. 11–14), and He knows how to protect His camp (vv. 14–16). In the end, God looks forward to future camps and plans for more people to come (vv. 17–21).

Did you go to any type of camp as a kid? True confession from a Christian-lifer: I never did. Witnessing the church-camp-hangover of joy through the eyes of my kids, I see I missed out. However, we're all invited to be lifetime campers at Camp Joy. It's a place of inclusion to all who want to come. Jesus paid our camp fee, so, no worries on being able to afford it. By saying, "I believe in Jesus," we avoid the scorn God reserves for non-campers and fake campers, but we may receive scoffing from them. They don't reject us though; they're rejecting Him. Prayerfully, our joy will attract them to come.

Have you ever been ridiculed or challenged because of your faith in Jesus? If so, how have you responded? Even on your hardest day, you are surrounded by Camp Joy if you are a believer in Christ. When was the last time you exhibited a sort of church-camp-hangover of joy?

_____

_____

_____

_____

_____

_____

_____

I love to see kids with a church-camp-hangover of joy. I want to live that way—overwhelmed with joy from fresh experiences with God. #joy218ways

End of Joy

Jeremiah 7:34

_____
_____
_____
_____
_____
_____

Through His prophet Jeremiah, God says He will end joy in Jerusalem. This is not the story of a cosmic party pooper. Rather, it's an account of a perfectly patient God allowing His people to ignore every opportunity He's provided. As the true source of joy, God can remove the gift when it's being abused.

Is it possible not to have joy? Don't be too quick to answer "Yes." We can falsely believe that it's natural to not have joy when hard situations hit. However, if we understand that God is present in our high-happy times as well as in the low-valleys of our lives, we'll know that His gift of joy matches the heights and depths of our emotions. He will make a way to reach us with different expressions of joy through the ups and downs. What if we deliberately disobey Him? According to this scripture as well as others like Ezekiel 26:13, joy-removal can be an expected consequence for not following God's ways. If joy feels like a distant dream, we need to examine if we may be causing it due to going our own way. If so, the pathway to joy is repenting. On the other hand, if we know we are staying true to our Lord's ways, then trials are not a punishment. They allow us the privilege of experiencing joy in a quiet, new way as God carries us through them.

When hard times hit, do you pause to examine if you are causing the situation due to going your own way? When life is hard and you know you're in alignment with God, how do you find joy?

_____
_____
_____
_____
_____
_____
_____
_____

Tweet

God will make a way to reach us with different expressions of joy through the heights and depths of our emotions. #joy218ways

–Joy: It's What's for Dinner–

Jeremiah 15:16

_____

_____

_____

_____

The food pyramid is comprised of grains, vegetables, fruits, milk, oils, meat, and beans. According to Jeremiah, they left the super food of God's Word off the grid. Following an unappetizing menu filled with all the ways God would punish the people of the southern kingdom of Judah (vv. 1–9), Jeremiah calls a time out. He wants to register a complaint, lament his position, and remind God of His promises (vv. 10–21). The nugget of verse 16 is a powerful word picture. Jeremiah was not satisfied to simply read God's Word, he ingested it. For him, the words God spoke gave him life-sustaining nourishment.

What's your favorite food? Mine is scalloped pineapple. There might be a dish that is even less healthy, but with its eggs, butter, sugar, pineapple chunks, and three-quarter loaf of white bread, scalloped pineapple is a contender for the title of "Best Food No Nutritionist Ever Endorsed." This little side dish scratches every food itch I have. I can't get enough of it when it's around. Even more than my love for scalloped pineapple, I want to be as crazy over the main dish of God's Word. For me, the Bible scratches every spiritual itch I have. When I spend time in the incredible, edible word of God, I get filled up. God's Word is my joy and my heart's delight. It's challenging and comforting, and it's always worth the time investment.

What is your favorite food? How often do you eat it? Can you connect to the joy of loving God's Word as much as you love your favorite food? If so, spend time thanking the Lord for the gift of the Bible. If not, talk to God about what blocks you from enjoying the incredible, edible Word of God.

_____

_____

_____

_____

_____

_____

_____

Tweet

Spending time in God's Word is challenging and comforting. It's always worth the time investment and it is joy-giving. #joy218ways

"I Do" Joy

_____

_____

_____

_____

_____

_____

A wedding is a joy-filled affair. The love, planning, anticipation, and dreaming bring about the event of the year. On the big day, however, unexpected circumstances pop up. A funky in-law, the mother of the bride who forgets the day is supposed to be about her daughter, bad weather, the ring bearer throws up on the pillow ... it all conspires to burst the romantic vision cast for the wedding. However, the marriage happens and accomplishes the main goal. Walking into the reception, everyone hears laughter, music, and the sounds of joy.

Now, imagine that everything changes. When people arrive at the reception, instead of joy they hear sorrow, weeping, or worse, an eerie silence. This is what it's like to be outside God's favor. The things that should bring us joy simply don't. We plan, work, and dream, but we remain dissatisfied. In this passage, God is done with the Israelites. They have crossed the point of no return by choosing idols and indulgent living over the Lord's ways. The judgment God levels on them will be so harsh as to silence their joy in everything from their day-to-day activities to the special moments in their lives. God's message is clear: Going after the things of this world will cause joy to flee. Instead, say "I do" to God. Love and serve Him, and joy will follow.

What was the best wedding you've ever attended? What made it amazing? Imagine seeing sorrow replace all those details due to the bad choices of the bride and groom. Do your day-to-day choices take you closer to the joy of God or closer to the point of no return?

_____

_____

_____

_____

_____

_____

If we chase the things of this world, joy will flee. As we love and serve God, joy will follow. #joy218ways

—— How to Unbanish Joy ——

_____
_____
_____

If a Judean reporter was covering Jeremiah 25 for the evening news, it might sound something like the following: "In international news, troops in Babylon are on high alert. Following orders from the divine top official, King Nebuchadnezzar is making plans to move into Judah. He's commanded his officers to destroy and conquer the people and the land. Word from a reliable source indicates that at the time of the invasion, all joy and light will cease in the face of the devastation. Local residents are not taking the threat seriously. Life continues normally here as warnings of how to avoid this disaster are largely ignored."

Ignore the threat? I've always been blown away when I read how the Israelites continually turned away from God. Reading about their history, their rescues, and their status, it's hard to fathom why they would turn away from the One who loved them. Of course, we have the benefit of thousands of years and a written record of their journey. For them, it was unfolding one day at a time, one generation at a time. Viewed through that filter, it underscores the necessity of living faithfully every day. One day turns into a week, which turns into a month, and eventually we affect a generation. Every day counts. Looking at our own history, our rescues, and our status as children of God, we have the same choices to make as the Israelites. Will we follow God? Our joy is never at risk and will never be banished when His way is the only way we crave.

Although it's hard to quantify, what percentage of your life would you say that you are living according to God's ways?

_____
_____
_____
_____
_____
_____
_____
_____

Our joy is never at risk and will never be banished when
God's way is the only way we crave. #joy218ways

—— No Matter what Joy ——

_____

_____

_____

_____

_____

Chapter 31 of Jeremiah is refreshing. After punishing Israel for not listening and obeying, God now sends word of a coming time when He will restore His favor. This speaks to the "no matter what" quality of God. Even when His people mess up and break their promises to Him, God continues to love them. He stands ready to bring new levels of joy as He frees them from the pain of their bondage.

I imagine many of the Israelites weren't conscious of how offensively they were living. What God saw as rebellion was simply the accepted way everyone was living. They may have felt as though they were being punished but didn't understand why. We can find ourselves in the same trap. We may be living culturally instead of biblically because it's what everyone around us is doing. Yet, whether intentional or not, breaking God's design for His people leads to pain. We will all be accountable for how we act regardless of what triggers it. God will still love us no matter what but He cannot withhold the consequences. The beauty of our struggle is that with God involved, we know He can restore us after a season of consequences. Like the Israelites, we'll sing for joy when we see how our God turns our mourning into gladness and replaces sorrow with comfort and joy (v. 13).

Do you feel soaked in "no matter what" love and joy from God? Or, do you think it's conditional on you being good enough to merit it? How does this section of scripture demonstrate that God loves you even when you don't perform up to His/your standards?

_____

_____

_____

_____

_____

_____

Even when we mess up and break our promises to Him, God continues to love. He's ready to unlock our pain and release new joy. #joy218ways

——Joy in Jehovah Jireh——

_____
_____
_____
_____
_____

Have you heard the phrase, "Too much month at the end of the money"? The bills are there but the money isn't. In the unfolding story of restoration contained in Jeremiah 31, God promises to give His people a bounty of goodness to reestablish their wealth. Moving forward, they won't have to worry about having enough money at the end of the month!

I've lived through seasons of having very little income, and it is stressful. However, going through them allowed me to experience an aspect of joy I wouldn't otherwise understand—the joy of knowing _Jehovah Jireh_. These Hebrew words mean, "God will provide." It stems from Genesis 22:8 when God asked Abraham to sacrifice his son. Abraham trusted God, even when it made no sense, to provide what was needed in that moment. Going through my times of financial shortfall, I'd pray for _Jehovah Jireh_ to meet my needs. Every time, He answered by either gifting me with contentment so I didn't want "stuff," or He'd connect me with a source of money at the just-right time. It's challenging to live so dependently on God, but, honestly, it's kind of exhilarating. It taught me to trust that when He says He is _Jehovah Jireh_, He truly is the God who provides.

Does the idea of being fully dependent on God to provide for your needs exhilarate you or terrify you? Is it more comfortable to depend on yourself to be sure all your needs are covered? If you trust yourself more than _Jehovah Jireh_ to meet your needs, how might that limit this aspect of joy in your life?

_____
_____
_____
_____
_____
_____
_____
_____

Knowing that if God didn't provide I would sink caused me to deeply appreciate His loving care with joy when I stayed afloat. #joy218ways

Joy in the Spiritual
——— Stock Exchange ———

The stock exchange offers buyers and sellers a virtual meeting space in which they can trade. Regardless of what the sellers bring to the market, their shares become an unwanted burden without a buyer. Jeremiah 31:13 is a picture of a spiritual stock exchange. The sellers are the Israelites returning after years in captivity. They're marked with mourning and sorrow, and these are the commodities they bring. God, the buyer, assesses their offering and decides to exchange their short run pain for the high-yield investment of gladness and joy.

We often see our pain as a worthless waste in our lives. It's tempting to wallow in self-pity rather than assess what we have for trade. Even Jeremiah experienced a personal crash as he called his pain "unending, grievous, and incurable." God sort of snapped back, "If you repent, I will restore you that you may serve Me; if you utter worthy, not worthless, words, you will be My spokesman" (15:18–19). Our pain is not worthless. We have something to exchange but we need a buyer. God offers a sweet deal during tender times. However, the market only works if we, the seller, decide to put our pain in the hands of God, the buyer. If we hide our pain under mattresses or in the coffee cans of our attic, our pain will never realize its full value because we chose not to trade it.

Have you ever considered that your pain has value? You have a commodity to bring to the spiritual stock exchange. What pain do you need to offer up to God in exchange for His gladness, comfort, and joy?

Our pain is not worthless. We have something to exchange. God takes our offering of sorrow and turns it into comfort and joy. #joy218ways

— Joy in Asking Questions —

_____
_____
_____
_____
_____
_____

"Why is the sky blue?" "Why are you so tall?" "Why did Grammy die?" Children have no problem asking honest questions. Sometimes they're being funny but usually they're truly searching for answers. In Jeremiah 32:24–25, the prophet honestly wonders how God could restore a nation doomed to destruction. The Lord replies in Jeremiah 33:3, "Call to Me and I will answer you and tell you great and unsearchable things you do not know." In this case, God says He will bring healing, peace and cleansing to His people to restore them (vv. 6–8). Jeremiah couldn't see how it would happen but He knew to ask the One who had the answers.

How many times do we run into the question of _Why?_ in our lives? We want the answer even knowing that it won't erase whatever situation caused us to ask. When we ask _Why?_ it would be ideal for our human ears to receive an immediate response. However, if needing to know _Why?_ is a stumbling block in our lives, no human voice will have the answer. God invites us to ask Him. If we ask from a place of honestly wanting to know, we open a holy dialog. Usually, it's a journey of discovery more than a one-and-done conversation. Knowing we can ask _Why?_ and that no question is off limits with God leads us toward a soul-deepening joy.

What questions do you have for God? What emotions are tied to that question? Would you be able to ask God your questions from a place of simply and honestly wanting to know the answer?

_____
_____
_____
_____
_____
_____
_____

Knowing we can ask God, "Why?" and that no question is off limits leads to a soul-deepening joy as He reveals new thoughts. #joy218ways

—— Joy of Romans 8:28 ——

_____

_____

_____

_____

_____

_____

As I read Jeremiah 33, I wonder about the people in those days. As they lived through events such as verses 4–5 and 10, did they have any clue that God was disciplining them, or did they think it was just the state of their world? The Lord showed Jeremiah all these things, but he had no mass-media way to get the message out. We know some heard his words because he frequently said, "You heard, but you didn't listen." Those who didn't actually hear, however, still were accountable because their life-choices were not God-honoring ones. The Lord would eventually restore their joy, but the waiting had to be hard.

Restoration is a God-ordained gift. Romans 8:28 says, "And we know that in all things God works for the good of those who love Him, who have been called according to His purpose." God works for the good because that's who He is. He's never at work to ruin us. He is actively bringing new life when we are devastated if we love Him. Those who are called according to His purpose are those who want to live in ways that please and honor Him. When we trust that His Word is His promise, we won't wonder if God will restore us; we look forward to the joy of how He will.

Do you have Romans 8:28 memorized? If not, it's a promise that is joy-giving during hard times, so commit it to memory. If so, when have you tapped into the power this promise contains?

_____

_____

_____

_____

_____

_____

_____

Trusting that Romans 8:28 is God's promise, we won't wonder if God will restore us; we'll look forward in joy to how He will. #joy218ways

When a Nation Needs Joy,
———— Part 1 ————

Jeremiah 48 nestles in a section of scripture known as "The Prophecies Concerning the Nations" (chapters 46–51). God wanted to express His anger and in chapter 48, Moab was on the chopping block. His complaint against them was their worship of a false god (vv. 7, 13, 35), their complacency (v. 11), and their arrogance (v. 29). In response, God destroyed their idols, caused them to move, and forced humility on them by removing all in which they took pride. The people cannot help but notice something is wrong in their land. The orchards and fields that previously rang with joy are now silent because of the destruction. *Yes, something is wrong in their land.*

Looking at culture today, very few would argue that our world is in decline. Political, social, and relational issues cause division, distrust, and discord. Like a ship drifting a few degrees off course, leaving these problems unattended is causing us to steer toward a Moab-like state. *Something is wrong in our land.* If we choose to distract ourselves with the idol of comfort and pleasure, we passively contribute to the issues. *Something is wrong in our land.* If we are complacent and choose to throw words at issues instead of our money, time, and talent, we ignore the pain of others. *Something is wrong in our land.* If we arrogantly believe we are insulated from trouble because we know how to take care of ourselves, we abandon the greater community. *Something is wrong in our land.* Now is the time to stoke our national joy by engaging issues in God-honoring ways.

In your opinion, what political, social or relational issue is the number one problem in your culture? Before the joy is gone, how are you positively—and in a God-honoring way—doing something about it? Pray and ask the Holy Spirit to lead you.

_____

_____

_____

_____

_____

_____

_____

Something is wrong in our land. Before the joy is gone, what can we do in positive and God-honoring ways to effectively change it? #joy218ways

When a Nation Needs Joy, ⸻ Part 2 ⸻

Jeremiah 48:33b

_____

_____

_____

The storm that was forecast is hitting. Winds pick up. Trees don't just sway—they bend. Driving rain, lightning, thunder, and hail pelt windows. Lights flicker, dim, brighten for a moment, and then everything plunges into darkness as the power goes out. Ridiculously conditioned people walk over and flip switches but the result is the same. The flow of electricity has stopped due to an act of God. In Jeremiah 48, the Moabites are feeling the effects of an act of God. It's not difficult to figure out the source of their troubles. God owns it when He says, "I have stopped the flow…" He destroyed their vineyards and rendered their wine presses dry for lack of grapes. He's the cause, and only He is the cure.

Political correctness fractures our ability to fix issues. Protesters, politicians, and pundits are convinced they have the answers; if that were so, why do things continue to decline? _Something is wrong in our land._ This storm has been forecast. Even if people attempt to ignore God's power and holiness, that doesn't negate the fact that ignoring His ways caused our issues and following His ways will be the only cure. It's exhausting to watch leaders bicker over every option except the biblical ones that would advance our nations. When a people decide to go their own way, God not only removes His favor, He dries up corporate joy. For every issue we face, God's ways are the answer. With no human agenda attached, applying His wisdom and principles would lead to unity and healing. _Something is wrong in our land_, and only God is the cure.

How do you pray for your country? Are you able to pray with no agenda except that an act of God would restore national joy?

_____

_____

_____

_____

_____

_____

_____

Tweet

For every issue we face, God's ways are the answer. #joy218ways

When a Nation Needs Joy, Part 3

Jeremiah 48:33c

_____

_____

A high-pitched squeal pierces the air. People nearby turn their heads toward the sound. Was that a laugh or a cry? Unable to see the source, they can't tell whether the person is delighted or in distress. Jumping to their feet, they rush to check. If this scene played out in the year 590 BC in Moab, they would discover those squeals were not shouts of joy. The consequences of God's judgment had devastated the people, and their shouts were of disbelief and shock. Even though their current picture looks bleak, skip down to the end of Jeremiah 48. They can't see it now, but God promises restoration (v. 47).

Assessing our modern-day political, social, and relational climate causes some of us to feel like joy is stuck in our throat. It's good for the grim state of our nation to stir us to grief. _Something is wrong in our land._ Disbelief and shock are the right reactions for much of what we see. Yet, we shouldn't think that God delights in punishing His created beings—His Word says otherwise (vv. 31, 32, 36). It's as though God, the perfect parent, is saying, "This is going to hurt Me more than it hurts you." Where do we find joy in the face of desperate times? We need to draw closer to God now more than ever. We need to take action, but only after receiving instruction and power from the Holy Spirit. Otherwise, our rhetoric will repulse people instead of attracting them to the joy of running our nations God's way.

What is your reaction to our times? When you share opinions, posts, or take action, does it come after a time of prayer? If you have decided to simply remain silent, was that a directive from the Lord?

_____

_____

_____

_____

_____

_____

_____

Tweet

It's good for grim situations to stir us to grief. Any action we take in response should come only after we pray. His ways lead to joy. #joy218ways

Joy in God's
—— Righteous Response ——

_____

_____

_____

Jeremiah concludes his portion of the book of Jeremiah by expounding on how powerfully the Lord would repay Babylon for all the damage they did to others. After the years of devastation, they would now receive a divinely directed pay back. By way of response, the Lord declares that heaven, earth, and all those around would shout for joy to see their enemy destroyed.

It's natural to want our enemies to suffer. It's natural to want justice. It's supernatural to wait on God to work it out. When we've been wronged, our true self emerges. Some handle it by masking their pain and retreating. Others dive into conflict without a sideways—or heavenward—glance. Some actually find a false joy by getting revenge on an enemy. We've all hurt others, and if we think we're better than those who've hurt us, consider this quote from Kahlil Gibran: "An eye for an eye, and the whole world would be blind."[1] Whether actively or passively, if we try to exact retribution on a person who's done us wrong, we often end up in a more complicated mess. We tried to be God, but He won't bless that mess. When conflict fires up, the pathway to joy is in removing our hands and allowing God's hand to represent us. This isn't a passive act. It's powerfully active to intentionally convert ideas of retribution into prayerful watching for God's righteousness. When He moves, we get to shout with joy at the work of His hand.

Do you trust God to be your defender when you are wronged? What if it takes months or years for Him to orchestrate the best answer to your prayers? How easily do you set retribution aside in favor of God's righteous response?

_____

_____

_____

_____

When conflict fires up, the pathway to joy is in removing our hands
and allowing God's hand to represent us. #joy218ways

---

[1] Kannings, Ann. _Kahlil Gibran: Life & Words_ . Vol. 6. CreateSpace Independent Publishing Platform, 2015.

——Joy of True Delight——

Lamentations 2:15

_____

_____

_____

_____

_____

_____

The book of Lamentations is a series of five funeral-type dirges (songs composed to memorialize a dead person). The first four chapters contain twenty-two verses, and each verse starts with a letter of the Hebrew alphabet. Perhaps Jeremiah wrote it this way to underscore to the people that their sin had a sort of "A to Z" complete effect on their lives. In the verses leading up to Lamentations 2:15, the prophet mourns the destruction of the Temple in Jerusalem (vv. 6–7), the annihilation of the siege-held city (vv. 8–9), the lack of leadership (vv. 9–10), and the starvation of kids (vv. 11–12). Their sin destroyed them and it's not funny … except to the people who are happy to see them fall (v. 15).

Would any of us admit to taking secret false-joy in seeing others fail? Perhaps we especially delight in the downfall of those who have done something to offend or hurt us. Look, we would never want to admit to anyone that we have these kinds of joy-stealing thoughts but I'd be a liar if I said I'd never had any. I recognize pretty quickly how off I am and correct course when the Holy Spirit gives the nudge/shove, yet it's in there. Joy is a gift from God and true joy is meant to encourage and build others up, not tear them down. We need to be conscious that we strive to take delight in others rather than take delight in their pain.

So, what about you? Have you ever taken delight when someone trips or falls in his/her life? How can you guard your true joy by developing a filter against this joy-stealing behavior?

_____

_____

_____

_____

_____

_____

_____

Tweet

We need to be conscious that we strive to take delight in others, not take delight in their pain. Build others up with joy! #joy218ways

——Joy of Dying to Self——

Although it ends on a note of hope, imagine the last chapter of Lamentations as a painting. To the left, we see people lined up to buy water and wood. On the streets, men and boys bow under the weight of backbreaking loads. The reds and blues of women's head coverings fly in their faces as they flee lust-blinded soldiers. From stockades and crucifixes, their former leaders hang shamefully in death. I paused as I wrote this and then painted myself, my husband, and my son and daughter into this depiction of devastation. This isn't just a story, It happened to people like you and me as consequences for their sin.

"It's hard to be a Christian." Generally, this is our response when we're confronted with the need to die to something in our lives in order to respond to a situation in a God-honoring way. While it may not be *fun* to choose right thinking, it's not *hard*. Facing the consequences of sin as outlined in Lamentations 5? That's hard. By dying to self daily, we walk in the joy of not having to worry about consequences. This doesn't mean we'll never experience hardships in our lives. What it does mean is that when something difficult comes our way, we have the joy of knowing it's not because we turned our back on God and His ways. Words matter. Instead of saying, "It's hard to be a Christian," we expand our joy by saying, "I'm learning to be more like Christ."

Have you ever thought or said, "It's hard to be a Christian"? It was hard for Jesus to go to the cross; hard is not the right word to describe dying to doing things your way. What areas do you need to stop doing your way so you can become more like Christ?

_____

_____

_____

_____

_____

_____

_____

_____

_____

While it may not be fun to choose right thinking, it's not "hard." The consequences of sin are what's hard. God's ways = joy! #joy218ways

Anti-Joy
—— of Pet Sins and Idols ——

When we were growing up and acting out, my mom had a warning that would stop my three siblings and me in our tracks. Through gritted teeth, she'd say, "I've.had. just.about.enough." When she threw that verbal flag, it was game over. We did not want her to reach DEFCON level *Enough*. Unlike us, the Israelites didn't listen when God said He'd had just about enough. Ezekiel tried to get them to repent through his warnings and crazy stunts (Ezekiel 4–5), but it fell on deaf ears. The people were too busy having fun and living it up with their idols to be concerned about a stuffy old God who wanted to spoil their good time (Ezekiel 6, 8). The moment of no return came; God hit DEFCON *Enough*, and they panicked.

My siblings and I responded to my mom's "just about enough" because at some point, we had experienced The Mother-load of *Enough*. Although well deserved, it wasn't pretty. God has thresholds in place, and He expects us to respect them. If we honor them, we enjoy a loving, consequence-free relationship with Him. If, however, we continue to see how long we can hold on to our pet sins or how long we can ignore the Holy Spirit's leading to lay down anything that is more important to us than God, joy will always be a struggle. God's Word tells us that panic is a byproduct when we disregard His ways. Joy is the gift when we follow them.

A pet sin is anything that causes your relationship with God or others to struggle. Do you have a pet sin you don't want to get rid of? An idol is anything that gets more of your attention than God does. Do you have any idols that need to go?

If we struggle against doing things God's way, we'll
always struggle to feel joy. #joy218ways

Joy of Witnessing
—— without Words ——

_____

_____

_____

On January 15, 588 BC, everything Ezekiel had prophesied over the past four years came true (Chapters 1–24). Israel's hope had been in the strength of Jerusalem, yet, their trust was misplaced. To demonstrate how thoroughly done He was with the people's sin, God asked Ezekiel to respond to a harsh situation in a surprising way (vv. 15–27). Ezekiel's beloved wife would die and God instructed him not to mourn for her. Seeing this, the people asked Ezekiel why he was acting so strangely in the face of tragedy. His answer: In the same way he had loved his wife, God had loved Jerusalem. Yet, because of their sin, God was not mourning the death of Jerusalem and neither should they. Ezekiel caught their attention by his actions, not his words.

This is a challenging story because we don't want God to tell us how to respond to our pain. When it's something that affects everyone (think 9/11), our response will be our witness. In the depths of our shock, joy can sound like a quiet scream. It's quiet in the time and space we take to decide how we'll navigate the situation. Our scream connects us to God as we process losing the "delight" of our lives that was taken. In the face of tragedy, can the way we live still point to the joy of knowing God is near?

It seems like tragedy and joy should not be in the same sentence. While there's no way to enjoy tragic situations, have you experienced the quiet scream of joy when you've faced tragedy? If so, how did people take notice? If not, would you be willing to try it if there is a next-time-tragedy in your life?

_____

_____

_____

_____

_____

_____

_____

In the face of tragedy, people notice our reaction. Can we still point to the joy of knowing God is near? #joy218ways

——Joy of Boundaries——

_____
_____
_____
_____
_____
_____

When you've worked hard for something, you expect it to bring results. You prepare, you put in the hours to launch it, you tend it carefully, and you watch it grow. Just as it reaches the point it will bear fruit, however, it's attacked. This is the scene of Joel 1. As the green stalks of their crops near full height, the people watch with horror as a black cloud of locusts descends on their land. There'll be no harvest this year; they'll only reap the consequences left behind by the destruction.

Joel sees this literal invasion of locusts as a foreshadowing of the day when God will destroy any work that does not honor Him.[1] None of us like to deal with the attribute of God's wrath. Some even try to shove it in the closet of the Old Testament and lock the door. However, we need to embrace it. Unlike ours, God's anger is never irrational. His boundaries are set and will be respected or else. When we struggle to establish healthy parameters in our relationships, this window into God's perfect heart points us to the joy of boundaries. God will not put up with any and all behavior. When we question if we're being treated well, we need to run the person's behavior through the filter of God's Word. His boundaries are our covering and our joy.

It is frustrating when we feel we're being taken advantage of and painful when we're being abused. Are there any situations in your life in which boundaries are being disrespected in a frustrating or painful way? Are you overstepping boundaries with another? How would respecting the joy of God's boundaries bring healing?

_____
_____
_____
_____
_____

When we wonder if we're being treated well, run the person's behavior through the filter of God's Word. God's boundaries are our covering and our joy. #joy218ways

---

[1] Joel 1:15, 2:1, 11, 31, 3:14

•JOY•
——Joy of an Attack Plan——

Joel 1:16

_____
_____
_____
_____

Even though there are ten more books in the Old Testament, this is the last appearance of the word "joy" in it. It's been an interesting journey to inspect joy through the filter of the prophets. Here, Joel presents a pretty joyless setting. A plague of locusts, ministry coming to a stop, a call to repentance, famine, and drought are but a few of the issues troubling the people (Joel 1). As they look over the landscapes of their lives, they may be wondering, "What more can happen?"

Often, our lowest moments come as a result of a series of unfortunate events, and we brace ourselves for, "What more can happen?" If our plan of attack is to slog through taking every crushing blow the minute it hits, it won't take long to come to the end of ourselves. Soldiers know an attack plan is essential to victory, and part of that involves training in the use of weapons. Our God provides us with powerful tools to respond to attacks: prayer and His Word. Even if our current default isn't to turn to prayer and scripture when adversity hits, we can train to do better. Will we be defeated by our circumstances or will we fight back in the power of the Holy Spirit? It will still be a battle, but we'll be armed with an attack plan provided by the Most High God. Our joy is in knowing that our Mighty Warrior God will save us (Zephaniah 3:17).

What is your first response to problems? If it isn't prayer, what can you do to train yourself to grow toward that? Do you know how to search scripture to find verses when you have problems? If not, ask a Christian friend or mentor to teach you.

_____
_____
_____
_____
_____
_____
_____
_____
_____

Tweet

It's better to combat issues with God leading the charge than to engage as a defenseless foot soldier with no plan of attack. #joy218ways

Joy of Embracing
—— a Dirty Truth ——

According to gardenguides.com, plants need seven elements to grow: room, temperature, sunlight, water, air, nutrients, and time.[1] Depending on their application, these seven either help or hinder a seed in becoming a fruit-producing plant. For instance, when received rightly, sunlight will kick-start food producing photosynthesis. If the sunlight is more than the tender shoot can handle, however, the plant will die. In the parable of the sower, four different soils represent how people receive the seed of God's Word. On the rocky ground, the seed sprouts to life immediately. However, when the persecution of following God's Word heats up the environment, it shrivels and falls away. As long as understanding God's Word and His ways is easy, the seed in the rocky soil loves life. As soon as the application of God's Word gets difficult, the little plant gives up and withers away.

The rocky soil provides a look at a dirty truth: Many people want joy in their lives but not if it comes with challenges. I wonder how the gospel got so misrepresented. We can't read the Bible and think the formula for growth is, "Believe in Jesus and presto-change-o, you're a towering plant." When difficulty comes, a seed in good soil knows it needs this transforming power in order to become. Tests and trials move us toward being a plant that will multiply the good around us. Joy is not simply the absence of difficulty. Joy is also found in embracing challenges with arms wide open. It's telling God "Thank You" for believing in us enough to send the transforming power we need to help us become.

Which of the four soils do you connect with the most (Matthew 13:1–9, 18–23)? Do you think there are any drawbacks to being good soil?

Joy is not simply the absence of difficulty. Joy is also found in
embracing challenges with arms wide-open. #joy218ways

---

[1] Van Cecil, Cleveland. "7 Things a Plant Needs to Grow." Garden Guides. September 21, 2017. Accessed October 09, 2017. https://www.gardenguides.com/105738-7-things-plant-needs-grow.html.

First-Love Joy

_____

_____

_____

I love the *first-love* joy illuminated in this parable. If you've ever dated or hung around a special someone, think back to the early days. Her smile, his voice, those eyes … everything was thrilling and you couldn't wait to spend time in that magnetic space. Connection with that person equaled connection to an easy joy. However, as human time advanced, that first-love feeling faded as disappointments appeared. We still loved, but our awestruck wonder became a memory instead of the reality. Our kingdom relationship with Jesus, on the other hand, is designed for our first-love amazement to deepen and intensify with time. When human disappointments hit, our awe and wonder for Him goes to the next level if we are dialed into His presence.

The man in the parable joyfully did what it took to own the most precious treasure he'd ever found. We won't own kingdom joy if our approach is, "Fine. I want joy, so what do I have to do?" Joy is a byproduct of seeking first the kingdom. Our primary goal every day is to seek what God wants us to do (Matthew 6:33). The kingdom of God is now and it is awesome. Before God revealed the kingdom to us, it was a hidden treasure. If we ever lose sight of how valuable the kingdom is in our lives, we'll lose sight of the joy it's designed to bring to our daily lives. Thank God for His invitation to be a part of His kingdom!

How do you view the kingdom of God? Have you considered that it is here and now? Does your morning begin by asking the Lord to use you for His kingdom purpose that day?

_____

_____

_____

_____

_____

_____

_____

_____

_____

If we lose sight of how valuable God's kingdom is, we'll lose sight
of the joy it's designed to bring to our daily lives. #joy218ways

—— Scary to Joy-Filled ——

_____

_____

_____

_____

With every fiber of my being, I hate anything that is scary or suspenseful. When I get scared, I turn into some prehistoric version of myself. My startle reaction is to clap my hands, turn my head, and squawk in terror. If I had been at Jesus' tomb when the ground shook, an angel popped up, and a huge boulder moved on its own, I would have been a clapping, squawking mess. I guess God knew what year to allow me to live … can you imagine how Matthew would have recorded that? For the Marys, God's peace blanketed their initial fear because He had a message He needed them to share.

In our modern context, we won't have the scary-joy of seeing an angel atop Jesus' empty tomb. We are, however, eyewitnesses to what Jesus is doing in our lives. The Marys felt fear and then joy at what they'd seen. I think we flip this sometimes. We experience the joy of God's power moving on our behalf, then we get fearful to tell people about it. What will they think of us? Another look at scary-joy comes when someone in our life delivers a message from God to us. We may feel afraid that we can't let go of the things that are holding us back from loving Jesus more. Yet, God knows that unspeakable joy awaits us if we push past the fear and embrace what we've seen and heard.

Have you ever hesitated to tell people about something God has done in your life? If so, what holds you back? What new joy would happen if the person you told needed to hear your message? How well do you receive a message from God that challenges you to think or act differently?

_____

_____

_____

_____

_____

_____

_____

_____

Afraid to let go of something that holds you back from loving Jesus more?
God knows that unspeakable joy awaits when you do. #joy218ways

Joy in Trusting
—— a Master Gardner——

Mark 4:16

_____

_____

_____

My Gramma Florence had the greenest thumb. Her African violets were my favorite—especially the variety that grew glitter in its petals. When I asked how she got her amazing results, she said, "I just stick things in the dirt and up they come." At times, I watched her take a struggling plant from one pot and transfer it to another. She enjoyed being a part of its growth and was hopeful its new environment would allow it to bloom.

God brings us in contact with people in all types of emotional, spiritual, and relational conditions. It's challenging to be around those who are so full on the circumstances of their lives they have no room for the good seed of God's ways to penetrate (Mark 4: 4, 15). Others listen to Godly advice and seem like they will put it in play, but then quickly lose their drive and fall back to their destructive ways (Mark 4: 5–6, 16–17). Still others want the good things God can give them, but they certainly don't have time to focus on Him; they have "stuff" they need to do and buy (Mark 4: 7, 18–19). How can we help these people? Their soil is in desperate need of the tilling and weeding only a divinely green thumb can give. God, the Master Gardner, may want to use us as part of their soil/soul conditioning. We can help people by praying and listening with joy for how He directs us to love them.

Who, in your life, needs the "help" of you praying, listening and loving them until their "soil" gets better? Will it allow you to feel more joy if you pray, listen and love than to operate in the frustration they currently cause you?

_____

_____

_____

_____

_____

_____

_____

_____

Tweet

We can help people by praying and listening for how God directs us to
love them. We'll own more joy as we trust in His ways. #joy218ways

Joy of Living in Preparation

Luke 1:14

Reading between the lines, I wonder if the scene in the Temple went something like Zechariah saying, "Well shut my mouth," with Gabriel saying, "Great idea." Because Zechariah questioned Gabriel's logistically difficult message, he wasn't allowed to speak until the birth of his son (vv. 11–22). When the day arrived and others began talking about naming the boy, Zechariah wrote out that his name was John (vv. 57–66). That act of obedience released his tongue and returned his voice.

Zechariah and Elizabeth were far enough along in years that no one thought they would have a child. Yet, they chose to trust the Lord rather than blame Him (vv. 6–7). They continued to order their lives in God-honoring ways *before* the blessing came so they were available to receive it when it was time. It's tempting to think they must have had at least a niggle of a notion that God was going to give them their hearts' desire. Yet, the Bible tells us this isn't true. Zechariah got shamwow-silenced when he reacted in surprise. Their story is a great lesson about living in a state of preparation for blessings that are on the way. Even more, Zechariah and Elizabeth's story teaches us to leave the answer to God. They had prayed for a priest to carry on the family line; God gave them a prophet. Every day with God is a new day when an amazing adventure could happen. Breathe out stale living and breathe in the joy of living in a state of preparation.

What, in your life, do you need to breathe out because it is choking your joy? What prayers are you waiting to have answered? Are you living in a state of preparation or in resignation that they will never happen?

_____

_____

_____

_____

_____

_____

_____

_____

_____

_____

Tweet

Every day with God is a new day when amazing adventures could happen.
Breathe in the joy of living in a state of preparation. #joy218ways

Leaping for Joy

_____
_____
_____
_____

I know this guy. He is crazy about Jesus. His life was a mess before he came to a true understanding of how much Jesus wanted to be in a relationship with him. He's giddy about God; I don't know how better to say it. During musical worship, his whole body is an instrument of praise. When he talks about God, the air around you crackles. He embodies what it means to be "sold out" to Jesus. He's a huge extrovert, so he's in the zone when he's around people. When you've been in his space, you know you've been near a vessel filled with the Holy Spirit and your spirit leaps for the joy of it.

Me? I'm an introvert. I love people, as in, I deeply love people. I enjoy knowing their joys and sorrows, and I am grateful to do life with them. In me, however, the joy of Jesus is a quieter joy. God uses both types of people to communicate His joy. I don't picture Mary screeching her donkey to a halt in front of Elizabeth's door, dismounting and yodeling, "Howwwwwwwwdie"! It was the presence of Jesus and her being indwelt by the Holy Spirit that caused John the Baptist to leap for joy in utero. When I block the Holy Spirit, people don't respond to my presence in the same way as they do when I am filled with Him. When we are filled with the love of Christ, people will feel a stirring of joy when they are near us.

Do people typically have a "leap for joy" reaction to the presence of God in you or do they leapfrog away from your sour self? How can you better represent the love God has for you in a way that attracts people to Him?

_____
_____
_____
_____
_____
_____
_____
_____
_____

May we be so filled with the love of Christ that people feel a stirring of joy simply because they were near us. #joy218ways

——— Heart's Desire Joy ———

_____

_____

_____

_____

Years of waiting, nine months in the making, and ushered in with a small cry, Elizabeth's barren-disgrace lifted the moment she cradled her tiny son. Well past normal childbearing age, Elizabeth's baby was special to her neighbors and relatives, too. In the pink face and ten perfect toes, they saw God's ability to do anything.

This is the easy, obvious kind of joy we love—the joy we have when everything is good. When things _aren't_ good, we pray for God to give us a miracle. As we lay the prayers of our hearts in front of God and believe that He is able to make them happen, threads of Elizabeth's story can keep us connected to joy as we wait. First, take strength from knowing our God is the God of the impossible. He brought life from a womb that everyone thought was irrevocably shut. Second, we need to note that God delivered Elizabeth's heart's desire for _His_ purpose. While the Lord granted Elizabeth her personal joy, it was in alignment with what He purposed to do in history—_His_ story. When our desires match with God's purposes, we get to own the easy joy of seeing God fulfill our longings. As we put our petitions in front of Him, we can pray with joy-filled confidence if we begin in a Matthew 6:33 kind of way: Seek first His kingdom and His righteousness, and all these things will be added to you (English Standard Version).

What is your biggest heart's desire right now? When you run it through the filter of Matthew 6:33, is it in alignment with God's kingdom purposes and values? If so, how does this encourage you as you wait? If not, how can you get your heart's desire in alignment with God's?

_____

_____

_____

_____

_____

_____

_____

_____

When our desires match with God's purposes, we get to own
the easy joy of seeing God fulfill our longings. #joy218way

-Joy of Being a Messenger-

_____

_____

_____

_____

It's quiet, dark, and ordinary. Away from the cooking fires and candlelight of town, stars create a twinkling canopy over the small assembly on the hill. The men talk in a low tone. There isn't anything new or interesting to discuss; it's been an ordinary day. Suddenly, a bright glow surrounds a man ... but no, not a man, it's an angel! He brings a message about the long-awaited Messiah. It's hard enough for the shepherds to believe their eyes, but the message? It's too good to be true. The One who would bring great joy to all the people is here! They run because they have to find Him.

Angels are created beings. When we die, we don't/can't become angels. Humans and angels serve different roles in God's kingdom. That said, can you imagine how awesome it would be if God sent _us_ with the message of Jesus into people's worlds as they simply went about their ordinary day? I know, we're not angels, so it isn't like this is going to happen, right? Or ... is this a time when our role parallels the angels' because we are about the same business of showing and telling people about Jesus? What if, as we go about our ordinary day, we are actively praying for awareness of who the Holy Spirit has His eye on? What if, in the middle of an ordinary day, people come face-to-face with the joy of God's message when they encounter us?

Does praying for awareness of who the Holy Spirit has His eye on bring you joy or fear? If fear, is it because of what you might have to say? Read Luke 12:8–12. If joy, pray and look forward to praise reports!

_____

_____

_____

_____

_____

_____

_____

_____

It's a great joy to point people to the love of Christ and to be there when they receive a message from Him. #joy218ways

—— Blessed is Real Joy ——

Luke 6:23

_____

_____

_____

_____

"You've become a Christian? Congratulations! I have all your paperwork here. If I can get your initials in a few spots verifying what you've signed up for, I'll have you on your way in a jiffy. Initial here beside 'Blessed to be poor.' And here, 'Blessed to be hungry.' Yes, and here, 'Blessed to be hated.' Wonderful … wait, wait! Where are you going? What's the matter?" *What's the matter???* Who would sign a contract like this? Who would intentionally sign up to be poor, hungry, and hated? Yet, it's a part of Jesus' teaching, and it's tied to an aspect of joy.

The principle behind this teaching is not that Jesus expects all His followers to be poor, hungry, and hated. Rather, He's poking around to see if we understand what it means to be *blessed*. Our preference is to tangibly hold and relationally feel God's blessings. We want health, wealth, and happiness. Perhaps our mindset is: *If* we own those things, *then* we call ourselves blessed. I see Jesus waving His hand over our definition and it floating up like dandelion fluff. Certainly God gives these kinds of blessings, but if we love the Lord for what He will give us, we are really worshiping ourselves. With the teaching in Luke 6, Jesus challenges us to inspect our attitude toward being blessed. To be blessed is to be one who trusts, hopes in, waits for, fears, and loves the Lord (Psalms 32:1–2, 34:8, 40:4, 84:12, 112:1). If we are rich in trust, hope, patience, awe, and love for God, then no matter what our life circumstances, we will always own the joy of saying, "I am blessed."

Have you felt blessed or have you been holding out to be blessed?

_____

_____

_____

_____

_____

_____

_____

_____

Tweet

If we love God for what He'll give us, our worship is really of ourselves.
Blessed = being rich in trust, awe and love for God. #joy218ways

—— Incremental Joy ——

Luke 8:13

_____

_____

_____

_____

_____

When I was in the Dominican Republic on a mission trip, one of our jobs was to remove rocks from a space that would become a parking lot for the future church. The work left us sweaty, dirty, sore, and bruised. Yet, knowing our labor would lead to a place of worship kept us motivated past our pain and discomfort. When I returned the following year and saw the lined parking spots, it was surreal to recall what it had been like before all the work.

Sometimes, when people's lives are rocky, they seek comfort and answers by turning to God and His power to help them. However, as they continue the journey, they discover that some rocks in their lives need to go so their good soil can be exposed. Hearing what it will take, they say, "I can't do it." It is hard work to get rid of the rocks of addiction, selfishness, pride, gossip, lack of forgiveness … fill in the blank. Doing the programs and counseling necessary to remove them from the landscape of our lives will leave us sweaty, dirty, sore, and bruised. However, the more we keep our eye on the fact that God will use our struggle for His kingdom, the better we cling to joy as we do the work. This is incremental joy. In the face of a life-obstacle, it's saying, "I can't move this thing all at once, but today, I can move it an inch."

Are there any rocks that are covering patches of your good soil? If so, how can you experience joy as you move those rocks an inch today? If not, who needs your prayer as they are doing the hard work of moving their rocks?

_____

_____

_____

_____

_____

_____

Tweet

When facing a life-obstacle, find joy by saying, "I can't move this thing all at once but, today, I can move it an inch." #joy218ways

Joy of "Get To"

_____

_____

_____

_____

In Luke 9 and 10, Jesus gathered first His twelve closest disciples, and then a nameless seventy-two (or seventy depending on your Bible version) to Himself. He sent them out to surrounding areas to share that the kingdom of God was near. He transferred His message, His covering of specific instructions, and His trust to them. Because they were so well empowered, they returned with results that had them in awe. Some of the seventy-two reported, "Lord, even the demons submit to us in Your name." It was as though they were amazed they got to be a part of what Jesus was doing.

Jesus modeled a life of service. He said, "The Son of Man did not come to be served, but to serve..." (Matthew 20:28). We own a significant level of joy when we find places to serve in God's kingdom. It may be inside the church or with outside agencies, but to be a Christian is to be a servant. When we help others, the Lord wants us to keep our eyes on the reason we serve. Jesus reminded the seventy-two that it was not about the numbers or the cool stories of what happened when they ministered. The real joy was the fact that because they followed Jesus, they got to participate in what He was doing (v. 20). "Get to" joy is a powerful antidote to burnout. When anything we do stops being done to honor Jesus, we disconnect it from the joy we get when we serve. Wherever we are, let's strengthen our joy by remembering that Jesus has us there and it's something we "get to" do.

How strong is your "get to" meter in relation to your family? Your friends? Your work/school?

_____

_____

_____

_____

_____

_____

_____

_____

When anything we do stops being done to honor Jesus, we disconnect it from the joy we could have. Do everything as unto Him! #joy218ways

Circle of Joy

_____

_____

_____

_____

_____

_____

Did you ever get called to the principal's office or perhaps summoned to a meeting with a boss? People in positions of authority can be intimidating, and our anxiety in their presence may create barriers to easy communication flow. Jesus wanted His message to spread through the region. With divine wisdom and leadership, He knew that common townsfolk would not receive communication easily from the "wise and learned," so He chose those with childlike trust in Him to be His vessels. These seventy-two (or seventy depending on your Bible version) were amazed at what they were able to do in Jesus' name (v. 17).

As we read God's Word to increase our understanding, it's vital we balance our knowledge with childlike awe at what we're learning. Without that, we risk becoming jaded and so full of scriptural knowledge that we're no earthly good. These seventy-two had the innocent joy of simply believing what Jesus said was true and acting on it. This creates a powerful circle of joy: We step out to serve God by putting our faith in action. He enables us to do more than we thought possible as He works through us with His power. As a result, we bring joy to Him as He sees the work of the Holy Spirit in us (v. 21). Like an electrical circuit, the power of this joy will only flow if we stay connected to its source.

How easy is it for you to trust that what you read in the Bible is true? Do you believe that God can work incredible things through you? Are there ways you could tap into the joy of more childlike faith in God?

_____

_____

_____

_____

_____

_____

If we don't balance Bible study with faith in action, we can be so scripturally knowledgeable that we're no earthly good. #joy218ways

—Too Good to be True Joy—

Luke 24:41

_____

_____

_____

"Yes, of course I remember Him saying He would go to Jerusalem and be handed over to be killed … that He would rise again after three days, but I thought He might have been talking in another of His parables … I didn't really think this was going to happen…" The room is buzzing with conversations like this. It's evening and, out of fear, the group gathers behind a locked door (John 20:19). With a low "Peace be with you," their conversations die and their mouths gape open. Jesus is … here. All-knowing of their confusion, He asks to eat with them so they'll know He's not a ghost. They can't process what they're seeing—this is too good to be true!

Generally, if something is too good to be true, it's probably not true. Yet, I think the adventurous part within us longs to connect to experiences that _are_ too good to be true. We hope to find a priceless treasure in our attic. We want get-rich-quick schemes that are legal and lucrative. With wisdom, we know this isn't how life works, yet we still dream. Earthly too-good-to-be-true schemes do little for us in light of eternity. In Jesus, though, we find the ultimate too-good-to-be-true reality; it's one that actually delivers beyond our understanding. He offers forgiveness and adoption into His kingdom family, and that is truly good truth. Staying connected to our Savior allows this _too good to be true_ joy to abide in us.

Does your relationship with Jesus feel too good to be true, or do you take it for granted? The story of His death, burial, and resurrection is mind-blowing. Thank Him for His joy-giving, amazing love!

_____

_____

_____

_____

_____

_____

_____

Tweet

Earthly too-good-to-be-true schemes do little for us in light of eternity.
Connection to our too-good-to-be-true Savior is our true joy! #joy218ways

——Truly Awesome Joy——

_____

_____

Standing in a park, I've heard moms and dads watch their tiny-tot-blessing swoosh down a slide and exclaim, "That's awesome, buddy!" If the definition of awesome is "extremely impressive or daunting," a child partnering with gravity falls a bit short of the word. Now, standing outside Bethany with Jesus and tracking Him with your eyes as He ascends into heaven? _That_ is awesome! Unfortunately, I think the age of digital movies and special effects may have numbed us to how awesome that history-setting moment was. I've stood in church and been part of a congregation woodenly saying, "I believe in Jesus Christ … who was crucified, died, and was buried; On the third day He rose again; He ascended into heaven, He is seated at the right hand of the Father…" How can we say these words in a Charlie Brown teacher voice? This is _awesome!_

Are we worried about relationships, work, bills, war, social issues, politics, the future, the past, or the catastrophe du jour? In the face of all that, it's one thing to say, "I know God's got this." It's another to say, "The same God who had the power to raise the sinless Jesus Christ from the dead and raise Him to heaven … _that_ God has got this!" The last thing Jesus did was bless His people, and the first thing they did in response was worship. A soul-deep joy bubbles up when we worship Jesus in response to witnessing His awesome power and seeing how He moves.

Take a moment and read about The Ascension in Mark 16:19–20, Luke 24:50–52, and Acts 1:9–12. Imagine yourself there. You are a witness to this awesome scene through reading it in scripture. How does this help you maintain joy when you are facing trials?

_____

_____

_____

_____

_____

_____

_____

_____

_____

_____

A soul-deep joy bubbles up when we worship Jesus in response to witnessing His awesome power and seeing how He moves. #joy218ways

— Joy of Becoming Less —

John 3:29a

_____

_____

_____

In John 3:22–36, we wander into a bit of a grumble-fest. Some of John's followers are disgruntled because they feel Jesus is taking John's glory. John clearly—and instructively—shows kingdom thinking in his response. Like a groomsman, he knows his role is to prepare things for the one ordained to be in the lead role. Rather than this making him feel less than, John says it's his joy to be part of the big event. He doesn't want to compete; he wants to assist in attaining the common goal of saving souls.

John 3:30 is one of my favorite Bible verses, "He [Jesus] must become greater; I must become less." Depending on how we're wired, it can be difficult to let Jesus be greater than ourselves. Believing we can handle what comes our way without consulting Jesus or believing we can provide for our needs purely by our hard work are examples of how we make ourselves greater than Jesus. Yet, that way eventually leads to exhaustion and depletion. John points to a better way. When the goal of our lives is for Jesus to become greater, we dive off the high board into the joy-rush of trusting Him. John declared, "I am not the Christ," and he modeled that when put to the test. All of us would say, "I am not the Christ," but if our joy is lacking due to us blocking His Lordship in our lives, we need to examine who we have on the throne.

Have you thought about how the phrase "I am not the Christ" applies to your life? How well do you give control away to others? How well do you give control over your life to Jesus?

_____

_____

_____

_____

_____

_____

_____

_____

Tweet

When the goal of life is for Jesus to become greater (John 3:30), we dive off the high board into the joy-rush of trusting Him. #joy218ways

Complete Joy

John 3:29b

John the Baptist had a thriving ministry. People listened to his message and responded (Matthew 3:1–3, 5–6). Not only that, he also had a strong sense of self. He knew who he was and that he was chosen by God (Luke 1:76–80). John had a hipster-grunge style and ate a pared-down Paleo diet (Matthew 3:4). Followers of his message surrounded and served him (John 3:23–26). In many regards, John was living with peace, power, and purpose—the marks of a joy-filled life. Yet, it wasn't until he encountered the ministry of Jesus that he declared his joy to be "now complete." Like every human searching for the fullness of joy, John recognized the only answer to complete joy was found in Jesus.

I think, sometimes, we want joy to fill us so completely that it will insulate us from anything bad happening. We mistakenly think we can't connect to feeling any joy until our current trial is in the rear-view mirror. The problem is, while we're checking to see if it's behind us, we drive headlong into the next situation. If we connect our joy to our circumstances, we'll never experience the fullness of joy that is always available. The primary purpose of joy is not to be a shield against bad things; the purpose of joy is to fuel our operating system. Knowing Jesus and being known by Him is joy. This may sound too simple, but it's the fullness of truth. We can either settle for situational joy or we, like John, can own that knowing Jesus is what makes our joy complete.

God is gracious and allows many moments of joy-filled circumstances. How does knowing Jesus allow your joy to be complete during moments that are difficult?

_____

_____

_____

_____

_____

_____

_____

_____

_____

_____

Tweet

The primary purpose of joy is not to be a shield against bad things; the purpose of joy is to fuel our operating system. #joy218ways

—— Joy of the Great I AM ——

Hang with me for a quick, Greek word-study moment. ᾖ (ē) is the Greek word that translates to *may be* in John 15:11.[1] It comes from the root word εἰμί (eimi) that means, "I am, exist." That definition might ring an Old Testament bell. When Moses asked God for His name so he could tell the Israelites who was freeing them, God said, "I AM who I AM. This is what you are to say to the Israelites: *I AM has sent me to you*" (Exodus 3:14). God said His name is "I AM," and Jesus said that His joy *may be* (same verb idea as "I AM") in us. The reason for tying this all together is to help us understand the magnitude of what Jesus communicates in John 15. When we stay close to Jesus by living according to His ways/commands, the joy of The Great I AM is in us.

As we've journeyed through this book, we've seen joy expressed in hundreds of ways. Sometimes it's loud, other times it's silent, but it's always available. If the pressures of life are causing our joy to fade, then it's likely we're focusing more on them than on the power of Jesus. He said that if we remain in Him, His joy *may be* in us. There's no maybe in *that* may be, it's a promise! Especially when things are hard, spending time praising Jesus before asking Him for anything will connect us to Him. We'll be reminded that He is bigger than all we face, and His joy will be in us.

Spend time praising the Lord without asking Him for anything. Write it down, pray it, do it through music ... praise in whatever way you connect to Him. How did you experience joy as you did this?

_____

_____

_____

_____

_____

_____

_____

If pressures of life cause our joy to fade, then it's likely we're focusing more on them than on the power of Jesus. #joy218ways

---

[1] "Strong's Greek: 1510. εἰμί (Eimi)—I exist, I am." *Strong's Greek Interlinear*, Bible Hub, biblehub.com/greek/1510.htm.

—— Joy of Being Pruned ——

"Perfection is achieved not when there is nothing to add, but when there is nothing left to take away," wrote Antoine de Saint-Exupéry.[1] While this quotation was about engineering aircraft, it's an elegant summation of John 15:1–11. Our lives are in constant pruning mode. When we begin our relationship with Jesus, our sinful nature threatens to choke any hope of spiritual perfection. We can see areas that are rotting but since they're all we know, we want to keep them. Yet, if we're brave enough to trust that God knows what He's doing in our lives, we'll listen when He says, "This has to go." It hurts, oh does it hurt when spiritual pruning shears clamp down, but the uncovered beauty is worth the pain.

I heard a sculptor say: "Imagine I want to sculpt the face of Abraham Lincoln from a block of marble. I simply keep removing the marble until it looks like him." This is what God does in our lives when He helps us get rid of things that cause us not to look like Him. Sins like pride, selfishness, addictions, materialism, gossip, and so many more get in the way of our ability to love God and to love others. For our joy to be complete, we need to embrace the loving discipline of our Heavenly Father. When we do, we take our next step toward spiritual perfection. We won't achieve it this side of heaven, but the Lord's perfecting work is evident in those who partner with Him. His joy is in them, and it fills them completely.

Can you identify areas in your life that get in the way of you feeling filled up with God's joy? What keeps you from partnering with God to let them go?

We won't achieve perfection this side of heaven; but, as we partner with God's discipline, His joy is in us and it fills us up. #joy218ways

---

[1] De Saint-Exupéry, Antoine. *Airman's Odyssey*. 1st ed. Boston, MA. Houghton Mifflin Harcourt, 1984.

——— Joy of Taking It Up ———

John 16:20

_____

_____

_____

"Not to be funny, but is Jesus talking about playing Peek-a-boo with us? What does He mean: *In a little while you will see me no more, and then after a little while you will see me?*" Hearing Jesus say He was going away, but then would return made no sense to the disciples (John 16:16–18). And, rather than look up at Jesus and ask Him, they immediately turned to each other to try to figure things out.

I have a saying for times like this: We need to take it up before we take it out. When we're confused, it's tempting—oh so tempting—to reach *out* for human contact before we reach *up* in prayer for God's divine wisdom. We get immediate feedback when we can sit with a friend and process our problems. Sometimes, though, it's not that helpful. We can spend hours chasing answers and we'll end up in the same place we started. When Jesus heard the disciples were confused, He gave them answers. Our God interacts with us the same way. When He hears from us in prayer that we need clarity, He will answer. Yes, it can be challenging to relax into His timing, but God has the answers we need to move forward. Who can turn grieving into joy? Only God. Human answers to this will always fall short. Our joy comes in knowing that we have a God who answers (Psalm 34:17).

How confident are you that God hears you when you pray and that He answers? For more study, pray and read Matthew 7:7–11, 1 John 5:14–15, and Isaiah 30:19, 58:9, 65:24.

_____

_____

_____

_____

_____

_____

_____

_____

Tweet

When Jesus heard the disciples were confused, He answered. It's still the same. When He hears from us in prayer, He answers. #joy218ways

-Joy of Transforming Labor-

_____

_____

_____

_____

_____

I've always equated suffering in our lives to giving birth. If we knew the exact time the pain would end, we could pace ourselves and navigate it well. However, when we're hurting and see no end in sight, it's overwhelming. The final stages of labor in childbirth are the most intense but they are also the most productive. No woman ever asked for her medical team to extend that painful stage. However, she keeps working and pushing because she knows that new life is coming.

Check out this joy-altering truth: The same baby that causes the pain also causes the joy. God brings joy not by substitution but by transformation (Warren Wiersbe).[1] God doesn't see a momma going into labor and decide to replace the cause of her pain with a potato chip. That sounds so ridiculous, yet if we constantly look for ways to distract ourselves from our pain, we put ourselves on the path to that same kind of foolish immaturity. Experiencing our pain and learning from the situation leads to deeper faith, stronger-rooted joy, and spiritual maturity. We can't grow emotionally or spiritually if we're always looking to someone or something to replace what is broken in our lives. The brokenness serves us best if it causes us to lean in to God; when we look to everything but Him, we are actually serving our brokenness. Accepting that pain leads to greater joy is the pathway to maturing in our joy.

Are you comfortable with the statement, "Accepting that pain leads to greater joy is the pathway to maturing in our joy"? If so, what experiences taught you this? If not, how might you be blocking some of God's blessings by resisting this truth?

_____

_____

_____

_____

Accepting that pain leads to greater joy is the pathway to maturing in our joy. Don't try to numb it; go through it. #joy218ways

---

[1] Wiersbe, Warren W. _Be Transformed: Christ's Triumph Means Your Transformation: NT Commentary, John 13-21._ BE Series Commentary Series. Colorado Springs, CO: David C Cook, 2009.

Future Joy

John 16:22

_____

_____

_____

I hate foreshadowing in a book. I mean, I'm reading along, enjoying the story, then like a spooky soundtrack, the author hints of coming devastation. Now I can't relax. I'm worried about the character, and I wish I had her cell number so I could call and warn her. Reading John 16:22, I wonder if there were any foreshadow-haters in the disciples' group because Jesus downloaded a big peek into future events. He also packed tremendous power and promise in the words He spoke to them: "Because of Me, you are going to hurt. In the long run, though, I will restore your joy and it will be untouchable, unbendable, and unbreakable. Hang on through the worst of it; the best is yet to come."

Our world, increasingly, seems to rejoice over Christian values losing influence. Like many of us, I'm amazed at what passes for "acceptable" in culture when it blatantly defies the teaching of scripture. Looking at conditions through our Christian worldview, we live with a degree of grief. Until we are united with Christ—either by our death or by His return—the world's rejection of Him causes us sorrow. This is a holy heartache only those set apart by their faith in Jesus will feel. As eternal people, our experience of joy is not limited to this life. There is a future joy we'll only experience when we see Him face to face. Even more joy will be ours when this life ends.

Do you connect to feelings of grief when you think about people rejecting Jesus? Do you feel the holy heartache at the condition of some aspects of your culture? How does the future joy of seeing Jesus face to face help you maintain your current joy as you wait?

_____

_____

_____

_____

_____

_____

_____

_____

_____

Tweet

As eternal people, our experience of joy is not limited to this life; a future joy will be ours when we see Him face to face. #joy218ways

— Joy is not in the Genie —

John 16:24

Aladdin was lucky. Finding the lamp with the genie inside gave him access to three wishes, but think of the pressure. Only three opportunities to ask for anything he wanted. Only three wishes and then his connection to this power would end. In John 16:24, Jesus introduces us to the exact opposite way of making requests. Whereas Aladdin could ask for anything he wanted, Jesus teaches that we can ask for anything that is in alignment with God's will. The other radical difference between asking Jesus versus asking a genie is that Jesus invites unlimited requests. Jesus removes the pressure of having to carefully screen how often we ask.

The main thing we need to remember is that the words *in My name* are not a magical formula that get God to do our will. We can't ask God for something that is in opposition to what He says in His Word and then say, *I ask all this in Jesus' name*, and expect Him to grant it. Rather, He invites us to see the world through a biblical filter, and pray for Him to move in alignment with His Word. Jesus modeled this when He said, "Your kingdom come, Your will be done" (Matthew 6:10). In our relationship with Jesus, we have the joy of unlimited requests. Additionally, God makes our joy complete by giving us His covering to prevent us from blowing those requests on anything that is not for our good and for His glory.

With all this in mind, if you could have three wishes, what would they be? Thank God for His generous gift of unlimited requests.

A radical difference between asking Jesus versus asking a genie for what we need is that Jesus allows unlimited requests. #joy218ways

Joy of Praying for Others

_____

_____

_____

_____

Those who grew up in church are likely familiar with the Lord's Prayer: Our Father who art in heaven … (Matthew 6:9–13). In those verses, Jesus taught a framework for what to cover when we pray. However, I've often heard John 17 called the real Lord's Prayer. Here, Jesus prays through an ever-widening circle as He moves from talking to God about Himself, then His disciples, and finally, all believers. What makes this prayer even more remarkable is the timing. He knew that betrayal and the cross were the next trials He had to face. Fully knowing what was coming at Him, He still looked outside Himself and prayed for others.

Being able to look beyond our own problems and pray joy into others' lives is the kind of radical teaching Jesus came to model. I think most of us have experienced catching the "self-flu." It's that deteriorating, unhealthy state that afflicts us when we're relentlessly consumed with our issues. Working through difficulties is certainly a part of life, but when they *become* our life, we need a way to get off our sick bed. Looking outside our trials to pray for others is part of a spiritual antibiotic regimen. As challenging as our lives are, none of us will endure death on a cross for all sins for all time. Jesus, when He was about to face that, showed us the power of praying for others. He prayed it so those who followed Him would "have the full measure of [His] joy within them."

Is it easy for you to pray for others when your life's circumstances are heavy? What do you learn most from reading Jesus' prayer in John 17?

_____

_____

_____

_____

_____

_____

_____

_____

Looking outside our own problems and praying for joy in others' lives
is the kind of radical teaching Jesus came to model. #joy218ways

Joy in a Holy Hug

_____

_____

_____

Powerfully nestled in Peter's impassioned sermon of Acts 2:1–40, this verse quotes David's Psalm 16. Nine hundred years before Jesus was born, David prophetically wrote about Him, so Acts 2:25–28 should be read as though Jesus is speaking. In verse 28, Jesus points to the intimate relationship between Himself and the Father when He says, "You have made known to Me the paths of life." He then points us to the fullness of joy we experience when we are close to our holy God.

Nothing can touch the soul-deep peace of being in God's presence. The joy and rightness of that space is an incredible comfort. Often, when I lead group prayer, we begin by saying nothing … we're simply quiet. We allow the silence of His presence to fill the space that human chatter occupied the moment before. We get the sense of, "God, when we're here in Your presence, nothing goes wrong. Being here is safe and the feeling of Your power all around is like a holy hug." No matter the life-storms that swirl and rage, being in His presence is a blessed time-out. We want to stay there and bask in the joy of knowing everything is good and everything is handled. Still, there always comes the time when we feel Him sort of chuckle and gently set us back on our feet. We, then, take this joy and get back to work in our part of the kingdom. This filling joy is available any time we are still enough to seek it.

How do you experience the presence of God? Take time to be still. Consider listening to soaking music if having instrumentation helps you connect to Him.

_____

_____

_____

_____

_____

_____

_____

_____

No matter the life-storms that swirl and rage, being in God's presence is a blessed time-out. There is soul-deep joy in knowing that God is in control. #joy218ways

———— Joy of City Revival ————

Acts 8:8

_____

_____

In Acts 6:8—8:1, we meet Stephen. He was filled with "God's grace and power, and performed great wonders and signs among the people." Some pious Jews, however, didn't appreciate his Spirit-filled message, and they killed him in an effort to silence it. When that happened, persecution of the church broke out in Jerusalem, and people scattered to escape. Philip was one who left and traveled to Samaria. Empowered by the Holy Spirit, he, like Stephen, brought healing and deliverance in Jesus' name. As the people saw the powerful works he performed and heard about Jesus, there was great joy in their city.

The Samaritans felt overwhelming joy when they heard from Philip that Jesus was the answer to all the troubles in their world. It was true then, and it's true now. What would it be like for people to receive God's message of hope, love, and forgiveness in such a way that they got past their opinions and came closer to seeing the truth? God's ways lead to revival and the healing we collectively, desperately crave. In our circles of influence, may we pray to have the kind of effect that Philip had. Think of the impact on our cities if, because we are praying for the Holy Spirit to fill us with His grace and power, we would share His message everywhere we go. Could we dare to believe that the joy of revival starts with each of us praying for the Holy Spirit to move in us and through us?

Do you have a desire to be used like Philip in your city? If not, what holds you back? If so, pray with joy-filled abandon and ask the Holy Spirit to empower you with His grace and power.

_____

_____

_____

_____

_____

_____

_____

_____

_____

Tweet

Could we dare to believe the joy of revival starts with each of us praying for the Holy Spirit to move in us and through us? #joy218ways

— Joy During Persecution —

_____

_____

_____

Are you familiar with the saying, "Been there, done that, got the t-shirt"? It suggests a person has experienced every aspect of a certain topic and has a souvenir to show for the effort. I could envision the apostle Paul saying this around 60 AD as he reflected on his missionary journeys. He certainly had been there and done that (Acts 9:19–30, 13:1—14:28, 15:36—21:16). As far as his souvenirs, he not only witnessed the thrill of seeing thousands believe and receive the message of Christ, he also endured the persecution that accompanied any powerful work for the gospel.

Because Paul was absolutely convinced of the truth of Christ's message, he persevered and the gospel spread. When we decide to take steps to further God's kingdom, we cannot expect it to go unnoticed or unchallenged by enemies of the gospel. It can be anything from resolving to implement daily moments of family prayer to stepping out to serve in Jesus' name. We may, mistakenly, think that if we set out to do something good, it will be easy. However, instead of the family being excited about prayer time, rolled eyes and distractions materialize. Rather than every detail of our serving project falling into line, it requires more effort than we thought. Doing anything for the glory of God is a threat to our enemy. Yet, when we stay faithful to God's leading and His ways, the outcome is joy. He'll even throw in a spiritual t-shirt that says, "Count it all joy" (James 1:2).

Have you ever set out to do something to further your experience with God and had it met with opposition? If so, how did you navigate it? How does knowing you will face spiritual resistance prepare you for future opposition?

_____

_____

_____

_____

_____

_____

_____

_____

_____

Doing anything for the glory of God is a threat to Satan. Yet, when we stay faithful to God's ways, the outcome is joy. #joy218ways

Uneclipsed Joy

_____
_____
_____
_____
_____

Recently, I witnessed a total solar eclipse. The moon's perfect slow dance across the sun is a treasured memory in my visual vault. An added dimension to the day was spending it with a couple of folks I respect—both who don't believe in God. It was interesting to hear them think through, "What are the odds the moon perfectly fits in front of the sun?" What I loved was how easily all of us could share the experience of the eclipse. Regardless of people's worldview, God's works are on display. He hung the moon and the sun; He simply waits for people to discover it was Him.

In Acts 14, we see a mob scene in which the people of Lystra want to honor Paul as a god for the healing he performed. He quickly points them to the fact that it was God's power, not his. Over the roar of the adoring crowd, Paul shouted about God's kindness to them. In forming creation, God not only provided for their physical needs, He also supplied what they needed to experience joy. This joy was designed to point them to the source of creation's beauty as a means to draw them to Himself. When we have the opportunity, we also can share creation-joy moments with not-yet believers. As we respectfully share our belief in God the Creator, we have the added joy of praying for the Spirit to draw them to Himself.

What is the most amazing thing you've experienced in God's creation? Have you had the opportunity to share a creation-joy moment with a not-yet believer?

_____
_____
_____
_____
_____
_____

God's works are on display. He hung the moon and the sun; He
simply waits for people to discover it was Him. #joy218ways

Testimony Joy

_____

_____

_____

"One minute I was about to kill myself—I literally had the knife to my throat. The next, I was on my knees crying out to know God." This is the exciting testimony of the jailer in Acts 16. When it appeared Paul, Silas, and other prisoners had escaped, his world crashed. In that Roman-run prison system, a guard would pay with his life if he allowed a prisoner to escape (Acts 12:19). When he found they were still there, he fell to his knees and asked how to surrender to the One who had the power to save him.

If you're a believer in Jesus Christ, what's your faith story? Some of us celebrate a dramatic intervention from the Lord. For others, we came to a point it simply made sense to start believing. Still others of us have been Christians as long as we can remember and may even feel we don't have a testimony. Can we keep one important filter in place? All believers in Jesus Christ are rescue stories. For those in a pit, Jesus rescued us from a destructive lifestyle. For those who came to faith because it made sense, Jesus rescued us from the remainder of our lives being lived outside His covering. For those who have been Christians all our lives, Jesus rescued us from going through deep pits by keeping us close to Him. Whatever our faith story, we have a testimony. Like the Acts 16 jailer, share it with joy!

What is your faith story? Do you have an "elevator speech" version of your testimony that you can share in less than a minute? If not, take time to pray through that so you're ready to share it when God gives you the opportunity (1 Peter 3:15).

_____

_____

_____

_____

_____

_____

_____

_____

Whatever the circumstances of your faith story, we are all rescued by Christ. You have a testimony; share it with joy! #joy218ways

Joy of Laying Down My Rights

_____
_____
_____
_____

"You can't tell me what to do; you're not the boss of me." This childish statement is the Battle Cry of the Ridiculous: I can do what I want and you can't stop me. Pint-sized kids hurl that statement when authority figures attempt to bend them to their will. Yet, forcing other people to lay down their rights—no matter what their age—is a formula for a dreadful day. It simply works better when individuals _choose_ to set their rights to the side. Romans 14 is the guidebook for those who struggle with hanging on to their rights. God knew His people were bound to come to differing conclusions about the right way to do things. This passage highlights an important joy-releasing truth: We may see things differently than someone else, but that doesn't mean either one of us is wrong.

If we find ourselves in conflict with someone and that person leads us toward anything that is immoral or unbiblical, then it's important to say, "You're wrong." More often, our disagreements are about the way we think things should be done. In Romans 14, Paul exhorts us to withhold judgment, be loving, be peaceful, and build each other up. In other words, we need to lay down our right to be right. We can waste a nuclear payload of energy defending our position, but we'll skate dangerously close to sounding like the stubborn child above. When we lay down our right to be right, we open our ears instead of our mouths. It's amazing the joy that releases.

In what areas of your life do you struggle to lay down your right to be right? How does that affect the people around you? How does it affect your joy?

_____
_____
_____
_____
_____
_____
_____

When we lay down our right to be right, we open our ears instead of our mouths. It's amazing the joy that releases. #joy218ways

184

—— Joy of Being Chosen ——

_____

_____

_____

Imagine standing on a playground when it's time to pick teams for kickball. The first chosen are those with a track record of long kicks, fast legs, and sticky hands that snag fly balls. As the line shortens, the remaining kids become deflated or act like they don't care. In Romans 15, Paul shows how God selected His team. He started with calling the Jews (v. 8) and then the Gentiles (v. 9). However, in that way God has of flipping things upside down, He highlights the second string team more than His first pick. God reached the Jews first so that they would spread His invitation to the Gentiles. He wanted the Gentiles, then, to be instruments of His joy, peace, and hope.

Because the Jewish Christians were faithful to take the Gospel to the Gentiles, you and I know Christ. What if they hadn't? What if they kept it to themselves? Can we imagine our daily lives without Him? If that's not a hard stretch, then there's work to do on our relationship with Jesus. Yet, if we can't picture our lives without Him, then how can we keep it to ourselves? What if the people we see in the office, at school, at the gym, in the store … what if they don't know? Remember that your faith is owed to someone else's faithfulness. Be faithful to share the faith you have.

Because of your faith in God, do you feel chosen or do you feel like it was all your choice? Without God's act of mercy first, no one would be saved (John 15:16). Who, in your life, needs to see or hear about Jesus through you (Isaiah 52:7)?

_____

_____

_____

_____

_____

_____

_____

_____

_____

The Holy Spirit draws us, and we learn by listening to others.
Remember that your faith is owed to someone else's faithfulness.
Be faithful to share the faith you have. #joy218ways

—Joy of Asking for Prayer—

Romans 15:32

_____
_____
_____
_____

At the time Paul wrote the book of Romans, he had not yet been to Rome (Romans 1:13, 15:22). But we see his heart to know them and to help them understand their faith. Paul led them by example. In Romans 15:30–33, he asks those reading his letter to pray for him. Paul wasn't shy about asking for intercessory prayer.[1] He was tremendously giving but he also modeled the power of receiving in the way he graciously accepted help from others (Philippians 4:14–19).

Most of us like to give, but it's challenging for us to embrace the joy of asking and receiving. I heard a message from Dr. Brene Brown that changed how I viewed this. Basically, she proposed that if I don't like to ask for help or prayer then I, on some level, think it's shameful when other people need help. I rejected that right away. "Of course I don't. I have no problem when others need help." However, this settled into some undeveloped spot in my brain, and I had to wrestle with it. The only way I can help others past their feelings of shame at being in need is if I have shared experiences of times when I've needed help. Further, I block God's design for community with my pride. If there are no people to receive, what good are the givers? It's a cycle we need to fully participate in if we want to receive the fullness of joy from it. Let's ask others to lift us up in prayer and give them the joy of helping meet our needs.

Is asking others to pray for you an easy or difficult task? What is your biggest need right now? Who can you ask to pray with/for you about it?

_____
_____
_____
_____
_____
_____
_____
_____

Tweet

The best way I can help others in need past their feelings of shame
is to share experiences of times I've been in need. #joy218ways

---

[1] Ephesians 6:19–20, Colossians 4:3–4, 1 Thessalonians 5:25, 2 Thessalonians 3:1–2, Philemon 22

——Joy of Discernment——

Romans 16:19

_____

_____

_____

_____

The church is God's idea. He designed it to be a body of believers where His love flows and His glory reflects in the lives of those who belong to it. Humans lead churches, so if we expect them to run perfectly, we set ourselves up 100 percent for disappointment. In their purest form, local churches are havens and hospitals for believers and nonbelievers to find healing from their brokenness.

Taking our instruction from Paul's words in Romans 16:17–19, we see that God wants us to be attached to a body that is presenting the gospel clearly and upholding the teaching of His Word. When difficulties occur in local churches, it's easy for the congregation to be swayed by rumors and hearsay. Instead, each of us needs to be diligent in remaining God-honoring as we seek the truth. It requires that we know God's Word in order to hold those around us and those in leadership accountable. Many people don't like conflict, so they'll go along with what they see others doing rather than exercising the joy of discernment to make spiritual decisions. However, reading Romans 16:17, we see we are to be active in guarding our faith walk. When we find a church body being obedient to God's Word—even if it causes corporate discomfort—we know it's a house in which we can grow. The church was one of God's best ideas, and He invites us to steward it with joy.

Do you belong to a local church? If so, what joy are you experiencing there? If any issues, how are you handling them? If you are not attending a local church, would you pray again for the Holy Spirit's leading?

_____

_____

_____

_____

_____

_____

_____

_____

Tweet

God knew church would be a place where we could experience the joy of community. Its creation was one of His best ideas! #joy218ways

Joy during
—— Misunderstandings ——

_____

_____

_____

Will Rogers said, "Plans get you into things, but you have to work your way out." In 2 Corinthians 1:12–24, Paul writes to the believers in Corinth to explain why he hasn't been able to visit again. He had planned to return, but due to circumstances and, more importantly, being obedient to God's leading, he wasn't able to come. It wasn't that he was haphazard about making plans; he simply wasn't always sure what God wanted him to do (Acts 16:6–10). Some in the church were causing problems, and they leaped on Paul's apparent waffling as a sign he wasn't fit to lead. It's exhausting to have your every move examined under a microscope by a critic's imperfect eye.

We've heard it said, "You can't please everyone." Probably most would intellectually agree with that. However, when we deal with people who believe the worst of us, it's difficult to weather it with joy. Even Paul, the towering giant of faith, admitted to feeling "under great pressure ... and despair" (2 Corinthians 1:8). No one is immune to these attacks. In fact, the more successful a person is, the farther he has to fall. What can we do? We know we can't get others to think correctly—chasing after that is guaranteed to pour gas on their tongues of fire. Like Paul, we have to lean in to God as our unceasing and unwavering source of real joy. "If we live to please people, misunderstandings will depress us; if we live to please God, we can face misunderstandings with faith and courage [and joy]" (Warren Wiersbe).[1]

How well do you handle it when people talk badly about you? When misunderstandings interrupt your joy, how can you turn it over to God so He can restore it?

_____

_____

_____

_____

_____

If we live to please people, misunderstandings will depress us; if we live to please God, we'll face them in faith and courage. #joy218ways

---

[1] Wiersbe, Warren W. _Be Encouraged: God Can Turn Your Trials into Triumphs: NT Commentary, 2 Corinthians._ BE Series Commentary Series. Colorado Springs, CO: David C. Cook, 2010.

Joy in Godly
—— Conflict Resolution ——

2 Corinthians 2:3

_____

_____

_____

Paul planted the Corinthian church around 52 AD. After he left, reports of church members gone wild and false teaching reached his ears. Initially, he sent Timothy to deal with the issues and followed up with the letter we call 1 Corinthians (1 Corinthians 4:17). Unfortunately, that didn't stop the decline. Paul then wrote a "severe letter" (of which we have no record), and it seems to have brought the necessary repentance. Paul took a risk when he wrote that letter. Truth hurts. Actually, truth in love hurts; truth without love harms. Paul knew his words would hurt, but he knew that "sometimes those who love us must hurt us in order to keep us from harming ourselves" (Warren Wiersbe).[1]

Even if some pain is involved, love will confront an issue rather than try to go around it. David Garland wrote, "Sometimes confrontation is the clearest proof of love. One needs wisdom, however, to know (1) what is worth a showdown, and (2) when airing the differences will yield the most fruitful resolution … because [loving conflict] costs enormous emotional energy."[2] We need to prayerfully—not spontaneously—decide which issues need resolution and which are simply differences in style. Additionally, we cannot indulge ourselves by mouthing off the moment our emotions threaten to trigger a verbal volcano. As in the case with Paul and the Corinthians, we want conflict to lead to the joy of deeper relationships that reflect God's love and His ways.

Are there issues in your relationships that cause your joy to suffer? If not, give God praise for His peace. If so, have you tried to address them in love? If you aren't able to resolve them, have you considered seeking Godly counsel so you can enjoy these relationships?

_____

_____

_____

Tweet

We can't mouth off the moment emotions threaten to trigger
a verbal volcano. Conflict should lead to the joy of deeper
relationships that reflect God's love and His ways. #joy218ways

1 Wiersbe, Warren W. *Be Encouraged: God Can Turn Your Trials into Triumphs: NT Commentary, 2 Corinthians*. BE Series Commentary Series. Colorado Springs, CO: David C. Cook, 2010.
2 Garland, David E. 2 Corinthians. electronic ed. Logos Library System; The New American Commentary. Nashville: Broadman & Holman Publishers, 2001, c1999.

Joy of Vision

_____

_____

_____

_____

Paul had no internet, GPS, or Siri to guide his missionary journeys; he only had the Lord. When God sent directions, they weren't simply coordinates for the next church plant; He also provided vision for what those churches should be like. During the first eighteen months Paul was with the church in Corinth, he gave them spiritual blueprints and parameters that would set their spiritual foundation. After he left, that foundation began to crack due to immorality and false teaching. In response, Paul fired off a strong letter calling them back to the original vision. He held to God's revealed plan and fiercely engaged against those who tried to derail it.

Eventually, the church members repented when they viewed their behaviors in the mirror of Paul's letter. Hearing this, Paul wrote 2 Corinthians to commend them and to further encourage them (2 Corinthians 7: 2–16). He provided a powerful leadership model throughout this situation. When we are in a position of authority, we must lead with vision. It begins with how we lead our families and, from there, branches out to any organization in which we have influence. A leader may have to make unpopular decisions and use words that make some members unhappy. However, if it's done for the greater good, the group takes ground when its members know the parameters of what prospers it and what harms it. We bring joy to those we lead when we provide the covering of vision.

Do you have a vision for what is acceptable and not acceptable in your family? Your work/school? Organizations you lead? If not, pray for vision and for the Holy Spirit's power to lead well. If so, pray for continued strength to hold to the vision God gave you.

_____

_____

_____

_____

_____

_____

_____

A group takes ground when its members know the parameters
of what prospers it and what harms it. Lead those entrusted
to your care with vision and joy. #joy218ways

—— Joy of Caring Friends ——

_____

_____

_____

_____

_____

"If instead of a gem, or even a flower, we should cast the gift of a loving thought into the heart of a friend, that would be giving as the angels give" (George MacDonald)[1]. After planting the Corinthian church, Paul left to continue his missionary journey. Since leaving, he had endured "beatings, imprisonments and riots; hard work, sleepless nights and hunger" (2 Corinthians 6:5). To top it off, he'd had to get harsh with the Corinthians, and he felt emotionally wrecked (2 Corinthians 2:4, 7:8–13). Finally, Titus returned to Paul after visiting the Corinthians. He brought Paul a "loving thought" from the Corinthians, and their tenderness fell like rain in the desert of his hurting soul (2 Corinthians 7:6–7).

It's a tremendous joy to have friends who are there for us. These are the people who long to be with us, who share our triumphs and our sorrows. They care about what goes on in our lives, and we are every bit as interested in theirs. Deep friendships survive storms. Sometimes, though, our storm winds blow at each other. Tracking the story of Paul and the Corinthians shows the deep love they had for each other—a love that could withstand hard truths being spoken. They model what we want in our relationships: joy and relief at having navigated rough waters and surfacing with love still intact. Caring friends bring joy to our lives and are worth every bit of the time and emotional energy we invest.

Do you have caring friends like this in your life? Send them a message to tell them how much joy they bring to you. If not, what do you think is causing the barrier to these friendships?

_____

_____

_____

_____

_____

Caring friends bring joy to our lives and are worth every bit
of time and emotional energy we invest. #joy218ways

------

[1] "71 George Macdonald Quotes." ChristianQuotes.info. 2017. Accessed October 09, 2017. http://www.christianquotes.info/quotes-by-author/george-macdonald-quotes/#axzz53M1wSzrU.

—— Joy of Generosity ——

2 Corinthians 8:2

_____

_____

_____

_____

Talking about spiritual growth, Mike Baker, a favorite pastor of mine, said this to the congregation: "If I told you that in order to grow you need to read your Bible more, you'd say, *Yes, yes. Teach me how.* If I told you that in order to grow you need to pray more, you'd say, *Yes, yes. Teach me to pray.* If I told you that in order to grow you need to give more money, you'd say, *Get out of my wallet.*"[1] Money, possessions, wealth, greed, and contentment are topics of over two thousand verses in the Bible, yet it's hard for us to handle our money biblically. Somehow, many of us have bought the lie that the money we make is "ours"; unfortunately, we forget that God provides it all.

In this passage, Paul highlights the importance of generous giving. Even though the churches in Macedonia faced poverty, they gave unselfishly. Giving to God—especially through giving to a local church—runs counter to our selfish human nature. It also involves giving up control of our money by trusting those in leadership to use it well. Consider this: If we regularly attend a church, this indicates we trust their spiritual leadership in our lives. If we trust them with the care of our discipleship, it's only logical to trust their integrity with the care of our dollars. There is joy in giving. Given that God inserted money talk thousands of times into His Word, it spiritually and intellectually makes sense that if we withhold "our" money, we are blocking blessings He wants to give. We'll own more joy if we'll share what we own.

Are you generous with your money? Do you connect to joy when you give? Are you willing to pray for the Lord to reveal if He wants you to be more generous?

_____

_____

_____

_____

_____

_____

Tweet

God wrote money talk thousands of times into His Word, and He teaches generosity. We'll own more joy when we share what we own. #joy218ways

---

1   Baker, Mike. Eastview Church. Accessed Sept. & Oct. 2017. http://eastview.church/.

——— Joy of Guidance ———

_____

_____

_____

_____

In this letter to the Galatians, Paul is frustrated by how they're listening to teachers tell them they must add Jewish rituals to the gospel of Jesus Christ. He argues that the Old Testament law does not have the power to save, so he encourages them to stay true to the teaching they received from him. When he says, "What happened to all your joy?," he refers to how joy-filled they were when they first received freedom through faith in Jesus—so much so they would've done anything to prove their love. His letter is a call back to remembering the truth of a gospel free from ritualistic Jewish additives.

New believers are typically ill-prepared for the Christian life. Like newborn babes, they need nurturing, protection, and care. New Christians are likely to die away from faith unless someone is there to assist their growth. They can easily turn back to their former ways and begin pursuing happiness (temporary highs) instead of joy (soul-deep satisfaction). Mature Christians have a responsibility to walk alongside them. We need to take up the slack when those who are younger in the faith lag. With compassion, we need to lovingly challenge them by asking, "What has happened to all your joy?" There's no need to judge; simply let them know that while their feelings are normal, we won't let them fall. Assure them that putting their faith in Jesus was the best, first-decision. From there, it's our joy to walk with them on their journey.

Are you a newer Christian? If so, do you have a mature Christian guiding you and walking on this journey of life with you? Are you a mature believer? If so, are you walking alongside a younger Christian to offer guidance when he/she needs it?

_____

_____

_____

_____

_____

_____

_____

_____

Without guidance, it's easy to turn back to former ways (temporary highs) instead of pursuing joy (soul-deep satisfaction). #joy218ways

Joy of All Nine, ——— All the Time ———

Galatians 5:22

_____

_____

_____

Growing up, I thought the nine characteristics of a Spirit-filled Christian were sort of a fruit basket. It made sense to me that no one could be good in all the fruity areas of love, joy, peace, patience, kindness, goodness, faithfulness, gentleness, and self-control. I was pretty decent in a few of them, so I figured my job was to use those and let the others stay in the basket. Much later, I heard Alistair Begg teach the text. As he unpacked the Greek word study on "fruit," he obliterated my basket-case thinking. The apostle Paul wrote the word Καρπός *karpos* as a singular noun, not a plural.[1] So, rightly understood, the fruit of the Spirit is not a smorgasbord from which I can choose the ones I want; the fruit of the Spirit in me is to be all nine, all the time.

A fruit tree doesn't intentionally set out to "make" fruit; it's simply what it does. Yet, if the conditions around it aren't conducive to growth, the tree cannot bear fruit. In the same way, we won't produce more love, joy, peace, patience, kindness, goodness, faithfulness, gentleness, or self-control by tightly squeezing our eyes and concentrating until they pop out of our souls. Instead, intentionally tending our connection to God is what causes the fruit in us to become stronger. This book is all about joy, but it is only 1/9 of the fruity equation. The closer we are to God, the more the fruit of the Spirit expands and grows in us—all nine, all the time.

Which aspects of the fruit of the Spirit show up more easily in your life? Which parts are the most difficult? Ask the Holy Spirit to pour into you as you stay more connected to Him.

_____

_____

_____

_____

Tweet

The fruit of the Spirit won't come by concentrating until it pops out of our souls. It's a byproduct of our connection to God. #joy218ways

---

[1] Begg, Alistair. "Life By the Spirit - What's Normal? - Truth For Life." Archive - Truth For Life. July 23, 1989. Accessed July 05, 2008. https://truthforlife.org/resources/sermon/life-by-the-spirit-pt-3/.

Overflow Joy

_____

_____

"I've got the joy, joy, joy, joy down in my heart. Where? Everybody sing!" Ok, I doubt Paul knew this camp song, but reading the book of Philippians, it's not a stretch to imagine Paul singing some 1st century equivalent. He is "in chains," but the way he is living while awaiting sentencing is drawing those around him to Christ (Philippians 1:13–14). Rather than thinking about all the bad things that happened when he was in Philippi (Acts 16), his mind is trained on the good that came as a result of his time there. With smile-crinkles forming at the corners of his eyes, he writes to tell them that simply the thought of them brings him joy.

The tone at the opening of Paul's letter to the Philippians almost begs the question, "Am I the kind of person who, at simply the thought of me, brings joy to others?" When we consider joy, often it's through the filter of how we can acquire more so our lives will be better. However, stockpiling joy for our solitary gain runs counter to everything Jesus taught. The purpose of acquiring anything—money, possessions, love, wisdom, joy—is to have the overflow cause an increase of these things in the lives of others. The Philippians caused Paul's joy to swell as he benefited from the intentional way they showed him they cared (Philippians 4:10–19). It isn't always convenient to connect with a person who needs what we have in abundance. Many times, we have to move from our place of comfort so that we can experience the joy of giving our overflow away.

What do you have in abundance? Is it material possessions or do you have an abundance of joy, wisdom, or compassion? Are you experiencing the joy of giving your overflow away?

_____

_____

_____

_____

_____

_____

_____

Stockpiling joy for our solitary gain runs counter to everything Jesus taught. The more we have, the more we should share. #joy218ways

Joy in the Faith

Philippians 1:25

_____

_____

_____

_____

With all Paul's gone through—shipwrecks, beatings, imprisonment, slander, poverty—the idea of leaving this world behind is tempting (Philippians 1:20–26). However, he sets his desires to the side and knows it's best he remains alive. In verse 25, he tells the Philippians he looks for them to make spiritual progress and to have "joy in the faith." I love that last phrase. For many Christians, it's more about the "rules of the faith" than about their "joy in the faith." Jesus Christ came for freedom, not to place bondage on His people (John 8:32). This doesn't give us license to abuse our Christ-given freedom,[1] but it does mean we're not to become so enslaved by religious rules that nonbelievers want nothing to do with Jesus.

Thinking about our experiences in local churches, how would we describe them to a person who is not a believer? Beyond the uniting truth that he would find forgiveness for his sins, what would he have to do to belong? What kinds of things would cause him to get disapproving glances? How would he be received if he royally messed up even after coming to faith? We may have built an accepted immunity to the hidden do's and don'ts of being a church member, but hope-filled seekers run before they get crushed when they sense the nonsense of legalism closing in. We need to throw off the shackles of religion. Those who live in the joy of their faith are spiritually attractive; their lives reflect the drawing, invitational power of the Holy Spirit.

Does the idea of the "rules of religion" seem like a burden to you or are they your comfort zone? Do you feel you live with joy in your faith? Does the way you live it out attract others to Jesus?

_____

_____

_____

_____

_____

_____

Tweet

> We need to throw off the shackles of religion. Sensing the nonsense of it, hope-filled seekers run before they get crushed. #joy218ways

---

[1] Romans 14:14, 1 Corinthians 6:12, 10:23

Carriers of Joy

Philippians 1:26

_____

_____

_____

_____

Seventh grade social studies: Mr. Luster. Piano: Helma Koslofski. High school Sunday school: Ruthie Wilson. College professors: Rick Champ and Bob Monts. Pastor: Mike Baker. These teachers impacted my life. Over the years when I've thanked them for their contribution to my journey, they've made it apparent that it's their joy to use their gifts to help others unlock theirs. Great teachers who daily pursue Christ exude a joy that's contagious to new people they meet and a deep comfort to old friends. The apostle Paul had this kind of influence on the Philippians. When he was near them, he multiplied the good work Christ was doing in their lives by his words of affirmation and in the way he served them.

The whole reason I initially embarked on this project of studying joy was to grow in being more like this. I want to be full of joy at all times. This doesn't mean I desire to be giddy and bouncing with it 24/7; I simply seek to be full of the countenance of joy. When I meet new people, my hope is that the joy of the Lord is so apparent they feel they've had an encounter with … something. I pray for opportunities to convert that feeling into a conversation about the source of my joy. As I spend time with my family and friends, I want the joy of the Lord to guide my interactions. I want to be a person who humbly recognizes that when people have been with me, their joy in Christ Jesus overflows because we've spent time together. I know I'm not alone in desiring this. If we ask for it with these God-honoring reasons, He will increase our joy.

Do you think people feel that the joy of Christ overflows when they've spent time with you?

_____

_____

_____

_____

_____

_____

_____

Tweet

The joy of the Lord: Those who carry it are contagious to new people they meet and a deep comfort to their old friends. #joy218ways

197

•218•

Joy of Unity

Philippians 2:2

Unity: A thing forming a complex whole. Christian unity certainly fits under that umbrella because it's complicated at times. People can be united and be wrong. John Piper gives an example of "bad unity" by citing the time—more than fifty years ago—his church voted *with unity* to forbid blacks from attending services.[1] There was unity, but it was wrong. For it to be God-ordained unity, it must pass through the filter of God's truth. In Ephesians 4:13, Paul wrote that unity in the faith can only be attained when it's based on "the knowledge of the Son of God."

God obviously knew we'd need holy help. One way He teaches about unity is in His directive of how *not* to do it. "Do nothing out of selfish ambition or vain conceit. Rather, in humility value others above yourselves ..." (Philippians 2:3). To be in a Christian environment and see things not being done biblically requires that we speak when the truth is threatened. However, the delivery and receipt of that intervention are the marks of whether the Christians involved are working for the joy of God's unity or the ambition of being right. If a group is allowed to go off track and we remain silent, we're accountable to God. If we speak and it becomes harsh, we're accountable to God. Look, I've done it wrong and I've done it right. When it goes wrong, it's deeply painful: how could God bless what He has not ordained? When it's done well, it is a magnificent joy to see His people working through challenges to form a complex whole.

Have you ever been part of a church split or deep issues in a church? If so, how did you see these principles applied? If not, thank the Lord and pray for the continued unity that surrounds you.

Tweet

When Christian unity is done well, it's a magnificent joy to see God's people work through challenges to form a complex whole. #joy218ways

[1] Piper, John. "John Piper: I Was Racist." ChristianityToday.com. September 21, 2011. Accessed September 14, 2017. http://www.christianitytoday.com/ct/2011/septemberweb-only/john-piper-racism-bloodlines-excerpt.html?start=1.

—Joy of Welcoming a Hero —

Epaphroditus was a "brother, fellow worker and fellow soldier" to the apostle Paul (Philippians 2:25). His efforts to obey God and serve alongside Paul almost cost him his life (2:26–27, 30). At that point, Paul commissioned Epaphroditus' return to his home church. The Philippians originally had sent him as their representative, so Paul wrote to assure them that he was pleased with all Epaphroditus had accomplished for the sake of the gospel. Further, he asked the Philippians to give Epaphroditus a hero's welcome. He had set aside his comfort and risked his life to further the gospel and they should be proud of him.

This brings two groups of people to mind: missionaries and the military. Both are driven by their desire to serve a greater good. They train and intentionally engage in activities that stretch their physical, emotional, and mental abilities in order to benefit others. The sacrifices they make allow for life change to happen in those they affect, but it comes at a cost. At the least, they leave behind comfort, family, convenience, and stability in favor of taking part in an adventure that, while grand, may put their lives at risk. Independent of how well-acquainted we are with—or even if we agree with—their mission, this biblical example guides how we should receive them when they come home. Whether they have returned for good or are on furlough, we are to welcome them with great joy and provide a hero's homecoming. As we do, we get to share in their joy of a mission accomplished.

Do you support any missionaries or sponsor any children to whom missionaries give care? Do you know any military families to whom you can show support? Pray for opportunities for your life to increase the joy in theirs.

The sacrifices missionaries and the military make allow for life-change to happen in those they serve. It's our joy to honor them. #joy218ways

– Crowning Joy of a Mentor–

_____

_____

_____

When the best athletes in the world stand on the Olympic podium, they receive a medal, and the crowd goes wild. As gifted and disciplined as they are, they didn't get there by themselves. A coach watched over their development and is sharing their win from the sidelines. This is the heart of Philippians 4:1. Paul planted, nurtured, and prayed over the growth of the church in Philippi. Knowing them made his life better; they were his joy and crown. The Greek word for crown that Paul uses is Στέφανος (stephanos). He understood it as a wreath or garland awarded to a victor in ancient athletic games such as the Greek Olympics.[1] In effect, Paul told the Philippians that their faith in Christ was his medal of victory.

Paul was proud of them. When the Philippians heard their mentor's words of praise, their hearts had to burst with joy. If you've ever had that one special Christian in your life who motivated you to grow, who challenged you, or who spurred you to be more like Christ, then you know how special it feels for him/her to recognize your progress. Having someone you trust and admire speak words of affirmation helps you see how far you've come. That support also encourages you to stay on track and "press on toward the goal to win the prize for which God has called [you] heavenward in Christ Jesus" (Philippians 3:14). As we become more like Jesus, our mentors stand on the sidelines cheering our wins. Joy multiplies when we share these crowning moments of victory.

Do you have a mentor in your life? If so, thank God again for him/her pouring into your life. If not, ask the Lord to send one so you can receive his/her covering and encouragement.

_____

_____

_____

_____

_____

_____

Having someone you trust and admire speak words of affirmation helps you see how far you've come. With joy, you can keep going! #joy218ways

---

[1] Hill, Dr. Gary. "4735. stephanos." The Discovery Bible with HELPS. 2016. Accessed September 15, 2017. http://biblehub.com/greek/4735.htm.

Joy Given by the Holy Spirit

Most humans don't like change. This dynamic led to suffering for the new believers in Thessalonica. Those Christians who formerly followed Jewish doctrine found themselves shunned by the Jews who continued to cling to the old ways. And for the Gentile Christians, the pagans in town heaped scorn on them rather than accept the invitation to life-change contained in the gospel. In spite of the cost, the believers in Thessalonica pressed on because the Holy Spirit within gave them joy.

God often leads Christians to do things that don't seem to make worldly sense. With "the joy given by the Holy Spirit," we serve, give, and love in ways that defy human logic. At times, we even find ourselves going against the expectations of those close to us. Yet, in the face of great hardships, the more convinced we are that Jesus is who He says He is, the more our joy will shine—sometimes through our tears. "It is interesting that Christians who have tribulations in their daily walks often seem to have greater joy in the Lord than those who live in more comfortable spiritual climates. A Christian's joy should be determined not by his [her] circumstances but by his [her] relationship with Christ" (Walvoord, Zuck).[1] People around us will notice the changes in us and how we react to suffering. Our lives will be a testimony to God's supernatural, sustaining joy as we draw on the joy the Holy Spirit gives.

How convinced are you that the Holy Spirit indwells you? Have you ever been ridiculed for your faith in Jesus? Do you connect to the idea that those "who have tribulation in their daily lives seem to have greater joy in the Lord"?

Even in the face of hardships, the more convinced we are that Jesus is who He says He is, the more our joy will shine. #joy218ways

[1] Walvoord, John F., Roy B. Zuck and Dallas Theological Seminary. *The Bible Knowledge Commentary: An Exposition of the Scriptures.* Wheaton, IL: Victor Books, 1983-1985.

—— Joy of a Holy Huddle ——

1 Thessalonians 2:19

_____
_____
_____
_____

Think back to the clubs, organizations, churches, or groups to which you have belonged. What drew you to join them? Whatever brought you there, you found a community with whom you could share laughter and ideas. In 1 Thessalonians 2, Paul celebrates the joy he has in his community of believing friends. He knows he is free to tell them his deepest hopes and to share about his faith in Christ.

There is a powerful joy in being around other Christians who share our love for the Lord and our desire to live according to His ways. In a culture increasingly less tolerant of Christian values, it's a delight to talk freely with other Christians about what God is doing in our lives with no apologies. With love, however, we need to keep in mind the reason not-yet believers have no tolerance for the things of the Lord. In 1 Corinthians 2:14, Paul wrote that without the Holy Spirit, what Christians talk about sounds like foolishness to them. I think it's this lack of understanding that causes us to seek out the company of those who _do_ get it. Being a part of a holy huddle on a regular basis strengthens our faith as we recall moments of spiritual challenges and victories together. It renews our conviction that our joy in Jesus is real. Always keeping in mind that Jesus said, "Go and make disciples" (Matthew 28:19), spending time with like-minded believers shores up our faith to be more ready to "Go."

Do you have any "holy huddles" in your life? If not, ask the Lord to guide you to one. We need community. If so, thank the Lord for these people and ask Him to take all of you to your next level together.

_____
_____
_____
_____
_____
_____
_____

Tweet

Being a part of a holy huddle on a regular basis brings joy. It strengthens
our faith to recall moments with the faithful. #joy218ways

Being Someone's
—— Glory and Joy ——

1 Thessalonians 2:20

Paul's joy radiates in these words to the Thessalonians. Sneaking a peek at 1 Thessalonians 3:6–9, we see that the faith and love of the Thessalonians inspired Paul to declare they are his "glory and joy." Not only that, but he cannot wait to be in their space again. Being separated from them actually causes him grief (1 Thessalonians 2:17–18). When Paul shared the gospel with the Thessalonians, he was convinced it would produce the same radical life change in them that it had in him. Seeing it playing out in their lives made him overflow with joy.

Whose faith inspires you? Who makes you want to be more like Jesus because of how you see this person living out his/her faith? Ultimately, this is our unifying purpose in life. We are to accept God's invitation to believe in Jesus, be filled with the Holy Spirit, get baptized, and embark on the life-long journey of sanctification (becoming more like Jesus). When we have the opportunity to observe the faith walk of another strong Christian, it allows us to see the truth of the gospel in action. When we're able to be the stronger Christian in the lives of others, watching them put *their* new faith in action is a joy that is hard to contain or explain. It's all about encouraging each other to keep pressing on toward the prize (Philippians 3:14). I can't think of a more powerful blessing than for someone who poured into us to say, "You are my glory and joy" as they observe how we live out the teachings of Christ. Glory Up!

Whose faith inspires you? Who is your "glory and crown" as you think about his/her faithfulness? Who makes you want to be more like Jesus because of how you see this person living out his/her faith?

Tweet

Watching someone take a new understanding of his/her faith and put it into action is a joy that is hard to contain or explain. #joy218ways

— Joy of Unfulfilled Doom —

_____

_____

_____

_____

A widely quoted study on worry done by Dr. Walter Cavert showed that only 8 percent of our worries are actually about legitimate troubles. The apostle Paul had a worry on his mind in 1 Thessalonians 3. He was "afraid that in some way the tempter" might have pulled the Thessalonians away from their faith in Christ. He was worried, but I think we'd agree this issue would fall into that 8 percent of legitimate concerns category.

Another of those 8 percent of legitimate worries is when we have loved ones headed toward a dark hole and we're unsure if they'll choose to back away before they're swallowed. We visualize all the ways they could mess up, and we live under an umbrella of doom. By God's grace, when they somehow begin taking healthy steps, we breathe easier and say, "How can I thank God enough for you …" In seasons where lives are out of control, we anchor to joy by remembering that _God is always in control_. A powerful window into understanding our joy is to answer this: Is our faith wide enough to speak 1 Thessalonians 3:9 over our loved ones while they are still in the pit? We can't get so scared of the outcome of life's situations that we lose joy in the presence of our God. Connect to joy by speaking words of life over troubled people and situations instead of words of worry.

Are you currently a worrier? If so, begin by changing your label. Instead of speaking the curse of, "I am a worrier" over yourself, speak words of life like, "I am learning not to worry." Read Matthew 6:25–34 and memorize the powerful truth of Matthew 6:27. If you're not a worrier, give God praise for how He wired you.

_____

_____

_____

_____

_____

_____

_____

_____

_____

We can't be so scared of a situation's outcome that we lose joy in the presence of our God. Speak words of life, not worry. #joy218ways

—Junk-Drawer-Friend Joy—

Who knows all (or most) of the stuff you have shoved in the junk drawer of your life? It's possible this person was along for the ride helping to make some of those memories! With whom can you be the most authentic? Knowing there is a person with whom you don't have to explain yourself is a gift from God. You don't have to apologize for who you are, you can just be. You and your person are on the same page; he/she knows a whole bunch about you and still loves you.

When Paul originally wrote the verse above, he was imprisoned in Rome and longed for his great friend, Timothy. Timothy knew about the junk in Paul's drawer. Prior to his conversion, Paul (then known as Saul) had delighted in persecuting Christians. It's interesting that in 2 Timothy 1:3, Paul said he had a "clear conscience." Obviously, he hadn't forgotten all his previous sins, nor did he think his friend had either. Rather, he knew God would use everything that happened before he became a believer as preparation for how he would serve Him the rest of his life. Since putting his faith in Christ, Paul's conscience was clear because he was convinced God had forgiven his tremendous sin. Our deepest friends don't hold our past sins against us, but neither do they glorify them by trying to drag us back toward the "good old days." A true friend "doubles our joy and divides our grief" (Swedish proverb). Here's to friends who double our joy!

As you read this, whose name came to mind as the person who knows the most about you and still loves you? Reach out and share how grateful you are for him/her. Maybe you haven't met this person yet and you are longing for him/her. Take this opportunity to ask God to send that person to you.

A true friend "doubles our joy and divides our grief" (Swedish proverb). Here's to friends who double our joy! #joy218ways

– Drawing on Joy Deposits –

_____

_____

_____

Even though I feel this reads a bit like a soap opera, here's what's going on around this verse. Philemon led or hosted a house church in Colosse. He had a slave named Onesimus who, evidently, stole from him and then ran away (v. 18). Eventually, Onesimus crossed paths with Paul and gave his life to Christ. They became close and, when Tychicus left Rome carrying Paul's letter to the Colossians in 62 AD, Paul sent Onesimus along to return to Philemon (Colossians 4:7–9). Paul hoped Philemon would forgive Onesimus and receive him as a "brother" rather than a slave (Philemon 9–16). Paul recognized the love in Philemon and credited him with joy, encouragement, and a refreshing spirit. Stay tuned for next week's episode …

What's remarkable to me is that Paul orchestrated all this while imprisoned in Rome. If we were "in chains" (vv. 10, 13), would our lives be preoccupied with the well-being of so many others? I think the next, obvious question is: How preoccupied are we with the well-being of others as we walk around freely? It would've been natural for Paul to have a pity party, but he chose to focus on the joy he had in others during a time when making new deposits into his joy account was difficult. Prayer is vital in these settings. It's counter to our human nature to feel joy during hard times, but we can pray and ask God for it. If we're willing to get off the pity-party train, the Holy Spirit will minister to us by helping us focus on the people and events that bring us joy.

What is draining your joy account right now? Have you been tapping into your joy-deposits to give you strength as you navigate it? Who or what brings you joy?

_____

_____

_____

_____

_____

_____

_____

_____

During hard times, we get the perspective we need to face our current situations by drawing on thoughts of what brings us joy. #joy218ways

——— Joy in the Trinity ———

Hebrews 1:9

_____

_____

_____

The opening chapter of the book of Hebrews is packed with powerful, doctrinal statements about Jesus. As Christians, we believe that Jesus was fully human and fully God. As the Son of God, He is the third part of the Trinity: the Father, the Son, and the Holy Spirit. Jesus is the full expression of who God is, and His Word contains the fullness of truth. As our Savior, His sacrifice on the cross and triumph over death cleanses our sins when we put our faith in Him (v. 3). Angels are His companions in accomplishing the work of the kingdom, but Jesus is above them. It is the joy of the angels to worship Him (vv. 4–8, 13).

I wonder how often we consider the joyous occasion of Jesus Christ taking His seat at the right hand of God after completing His earthly mission. I can't imagine the glory of that kingdom moment. How can we comprehend the majesty of the Creator Father welcoming the Savior Son as the Holy Spirit anoints Him with the oil of joy? And, amazing as our best Spirit-filled worship time on earth has been, the holy hallelujah that broke forth as the angels witnessed the glory of Jesus being seated on His throne transcends anything we have yet to experience. This happened. This God—the Father, the Son, and the Holy Spirit—is the God who loves us. This is the God we worship. This is the source of our joy.

Set everything aside and allow yourself to visualize being in the throne room with God. Play Christian-soaking music (Google it if you're not familiar with this). Give yourself the joy of simply worshiping the One who is the source of true joy. How do you feel after experiencing this time with Him?

_____

_____

_____

_____

_____

_____

_____

_____

Tweet

I believe in the Trinity God: The Father, The Son and The Holy Spirit. Worshiping my God brings me joy! #joy218ways

——Joy of a Trust Walk——

_____
_____
_____
_____
_____

Let's say you're standing at the edge of a steep, narrow canyon. On the other side of the divide—perhaps ten feet away—sits that thing you've been praying for recently. You look down, but you can't see the bottom. You might be able to descend the jagged wall and then scale the other side to reach your heart's desire, but you know the odds are not in your favor. In desperation, you pray. A thin cord suddenly appears to connect you to the other side. Following the line with your eyes, you look up and there's Jesus. Smiling, He encourages you to step onto that tightrope of faith. Looking in His eyes, you sense His wisdom guiding you. Step by step, you walk toward Him by faith.

To be honest, we all want Jesus to put our heart's desire on His back and walk it across to us. That's much less scary, but it doesn't require much faith. When we struggle to hang on to hope, we need to fix our eyes on Jesus and His example of how to do hard things. He walked through situations more desperate than ours. He will show us the way to walk forward if we keep our eyes fixed on Him in prayer. Trusting He's heard our heart's desire assures us that He is guiding us toward the answer that will bring us joy (Jeremiah 29:11).

Would you rather have Jesus walk your heart's desire over to you or would you want to walk across with Him showing you every step? Picture the joy you'd have when you made it to the other side. Not only would you have your heart's desire, you'd be that much closer to Jesus.

_____
_____
_____
_____
_____
_____

Trusting that God has heard our heart's desire assures us that He is guiding us toward the answer that will bring us joy. #joy218ways

—Joy of Persuaded Trust—

Hebrews 13:17

_____
_____
_____
_____
_____

A number of years ago, I was the co-director of VBS at our church of 5,000. During that week, the halls teemed with a thousand kids, 500 volunteers, and enough Goldfish to feed a village. It was awesome! About a month later, the children's pastor called the directors in for a meeting. "Great job this year. Now the hard news: The leadership has decided this was the last year for VBS." We were shocked. He told us their reasoning (which was valid), and that this was a final decision. For a minute—or more—I tried to think of loopholes, but there was no wiggle room. Through not a few tears, we bowed our heads and prayed together. In the quiet, we thanked God for the leaders He had given us.

A right application of this verse is needed in our churches. The word that translates as either "obey" or "have confidence" in our leaders is πειθω (peíthō). It means to be persuaded of what is trustworthy. If we choose to attend a church and sit under its leaders, it means we are persuaded they are worthy of our trust. There will inevitably come a time when the leaders make a decision we don't like. If we trust them, then we need to bless them by submitting to their leadership. We want—and need—them to enjoy their life's work. The next time we have the opportunity, let's find a way to bring joy to our leaders we trust.

Have you ever run into a church leadership decision with which you did not agree? If so, how did you handle it? Which church leaders can you bless this week?

_____
_____
_____
_____
_____
_____

Tweet

None of us want to be a church member who causes a church leader to lose joy. Find ways to bring joy to the leaders you trust. #joy218ways

——Trials to Trails of Joy——

_____

_____

_____

It is a deep and personal joy to arrive at this verse in _218 Ways to Own Joy_. During one of the darkest times in my life, I "happened" across James 1:2–4. I could barely find my footing during that painful season, and I remember latching onto these words as an anchor to hope.

Most of us resist trials. We want things to be easy, and when they become hard, we lose our ability to maintain perspective. We can mistakenly believe that we'll never recover from what we're facing. We cry out, "God could fix this, but He isn't." Whispers start murmuring in our isolation. _No one else has ever had it this bad._ We buy the lies and, if we're not careful, we can end up wasting our suffering. We have to go through whatever we're facing, we might as well get something from it. With that as our filter, the Lord will open our eyes to how He can work good through the pain (Romans 8:28). We get caught up in the trial and forget that we're on a _trail_. This trail leads to growth, to spiritual maturity, and to being "complete, not lacking anything." We have a choice. We can be marked as people who want to be graceful and grace-filled through our suffering, or we can allow our trials to trample us. God gives us a way to stay encouraged when we suffer: consider it pure joy, because it's leading somewhere. With joy, we can trust that our trials are trails leading to something greater.

Have you had a trial that became a trail to something good? This doesn't minimize the pain or the fallout, but were you able to see God working through it? How well do you "consider it pure joy" when you face trials?

_____

_____

_____

_____

_____

_____

We can either be graceful and grace-filled through suffering or we can let our trials trample us. Trials can be trails to joy. #joy218ways

-Turn Worldly Joy to Gloom-

If we only read James 4:9, our eyebrows might shoot up; we might even wonder if our Bible has some typos. Why would James tell us to turn our joy into gloom? Hello? Doesn't he know how hard we're working to maintain our joy? Of course, reading the verse in context reveals that James is taking a spiritual baseball bat to counterfeit joy. In verses 1–6, James boldly states that if we find our joy in the things of the world, then that joy needs to die. Joy that only comes when we get the toys we think we want is a breeding ground for our enemy. He will capitalize on our desire for *more* which draws us away from the true joy of *enough*.

This doesn't mean we can't have nice things. But, if we're honest, the overwhelming majority of us spend the greater part of our time on things other than our relationship with God. We fill our days with things to feed and entertain us and tell ourselves, "This is joy." The call here in James is to holiness. Instead of pursuing all the worldly joy we think we want, would we be willing to set some of it aside in favor of seriously grieving over a sin-issue in our community? Out of that call to action, would we pursue solutions to these problems with our time and talent instead of using the bulk of our resources making sure we get the things we desire? Worldly joy versus Godly joy: only one leads to life and life change. Which joy do you choose?

If James looked into your life, do you think he would say you are a friend of the world or a friend of God (James 4:4)? What brings you joy? How does that line up with this passage?

_____

_____

_____

_____

_____

_____

_____

_____

_____

_____

Worldly joy comes when we get the toys we think we want. Godly joy is inner and constant: Only one leads to life and life-change. #joy218ways

Hose-Full of Joy

_____

_____

_____

"Can you see me?" My pint-sized, tow-headed cutie stood in the middle of the kitchen with his chubby hands over his eyes. Because he couldn't see me, his toddler deduction led him to believe I couldn't see him. I played along. When he popped his hands away and saw me standing there, "glorious joy" filled his face. Even though he couldn't see me, he had known I was there. Our experience with Jesus is similar. We can't physically see Him, yet we know He's there. There are times, though, when it's more difficult to sense Him. If we can't see our troubles resolving in front of our eyes, we may struggle to believe the spiritual reality that He is working on our behalf.

Peter describes the trials in our lives as a refining fire that will help us more purely reflect God's glory (vv. 6–7). Reflect His glory? Sign me up. I want to be refined— right up until it's "Go Time." But God provides a way to navigate these trials with joy. Warren Wiersbe said it like this: "When a trial hits, immediately lifting our heart to Christ in true love and worship will take the poison out of the experience and will make space for His healing medicine. Satan wants to use our trials to bring out the worst in us; God wants to use them to bring out our best."[1] In the face of a fiery trial, we need to aim a hose-full of faith at the issue or else it will burn us, not purify us. We may not see it, but that hose is filling with faith from its joy-connection to Jesus

What would a "hose-full of faith" look like?

_____

_____

_____

_____

_____

_____

_____

_____

In the face of a fiery trial, we need to aim a hose-full of faith at
the issue or else it will burn us, not purify us. #joy218ways

---

[1]   Wiersbe, Warren W. *Be Hopeful: How to Make the Best of Times Out of Your Worst of Times.* BE Series Commentary Series. Colorado Springs, CO: David C. Cook, 2009.

——— Lie Detector Joy ———

1 John 1:4

_____

_____

Do you swear to tell the truth, the whole truth, and nothing but the truth? I've never had to put my hand on a Bible and say those words, but just typing them made me a little sweaty. What if, in another setting, the questions went something like: *Do you swear to walk in the light, the full light, and nothing but the light? Do you swear to be honest about your sin, all your sin, and nothing but your sin?* Lord help me, I might pass out.

What's on trial here is fellowship with God. In 1 John 1:4–10, the apostle John wants to know if we could pass a lie detector test to determine if our fellowship with the Lord is real or counterfeit. Here's what we'll be asked to answer: (1) Are we walking in the light? If we prefer to dally in darkness, we'll fail this section of the test. A requirement of fellowship with God is stepping away from the dark things of the world so His light can shine in us. (2) Are we honest about our sin? Another requirement of fellowship with God is honestly putting our sin in front of God so He can forgive us. If we try to hide our junk, the polygraph will go ballistic, so it's better to 'fess up so we can clear our mess up. Walking in the light and being honest before God will not only give us fellowship with Him, it will make our joy complete.

Are you walking in the light, the full light, and nothing but the light? Are you being honest about your sin, all your sin, and nothing but your sin? How will confessing help connect you to the true joy of fellowship with God?

_____

_____

_____

_____

_____

_____

_____

_____

_____

_____

Tweet

It's useless to try to hide our junk from God; He already knows. It's better to 'fess up so He can help us clear our mess up. #joy218ways

213

Joy of Walking in the Truth

_____

_____

_____

According to the Guinness Book of World Records, the farthest distance walked balancing a lawn mower on the chin (not powered, weighing 18 lbs) is 403.28 ft (122.92 m). Ashrita Furman (USA) performed this stunt on June 29, 2015.[1] Why would he do this? Obviously, he didn't simply wander across a lawn mower one sunny afternoon and think, "Hey, I'll pop that on my chin and see what happens." No, he set a goal, and as he took intentional steps, people noticed his record-breaking walk. In 2 John, the apostle commends some folks for how they were walking. In their case, John expressed his appreciation that these "children" were walking in the truth of God's ways.

Most likely, the children mentioned by John were adult offspring of the "chosen lady" in verse 1. Regardless of their age, the way they conducted themselves demonstrated they were Christ followers. Their language, the way they treated others, the care they gave to those in need, and the way they used their resources brought glory to God as they did things His way. Their example shines through the ages to inspire us. When people are watching us, do they see us walking in the truth? In 1 John 2:3–6, John got powerfully direct. He said that we either do what God commands or we are a "liar and the truth is not in [us] … Whoever claims to live in Him must walk as Jesus did." When people watch our lives, may we bring joy to them as they see us walking in obedience to God's truth.

Will you pray to increase your joy by asking the Holy Spirit to show you areas in which you are not walking in the truth?

_____

_____

_____

_____

_____

_____

When people watch our lives, may we bring joy to them as they
see us walking in obedience to God's truth. #joy218ways

---

[1]   "Farthest Distance Walked Balancing a Lawnmower on the Chin (not powered)." _Guinness World Records_, www.guinnessworldrecords.com/. Accessed 27 Sept. 2017.

Face-to-Face Joy

2 John 1:12

_____

_____

_____

If the apostle John lived in today's world, I wonder if his social media handle would be @frompatmoswithlove (a little Revelation 1:1 humor). Would he even put his toe in the water of digital communication? His ability to communicate was limited to snail mail delivered by messengers, not DMs, IMs or PMs.[1] In 2 John, he writes to "the chosen lady" to share his joy in her family (vv. 4–6) and to warn her about false teachers (vv. 7–11). But in verse 12, I think John transmits a guiding and timeless principle from across the ages: Make time for face time (and no, not FaceTime).

Unless we deal with the very real disorder of social anxiety, most of us are deficient at being in the physical presence of others we enjoy due to busyness. 'Joy' would like to interrupt our regular life-program to ask these important questions: How is our pace working out for us? Do we feel relaxed and energized? If our primary interaction with our friends and family is digital, do we feel 'known' on authentic levels? Society claims women want face time more than men, but I think that's a lie men are taught to believe. All of us lean in to the comfort of a listening ear and someone to laugh with as a counterbalance to the pressures of life. Let's take a cue from John and complete our joy by making time to be in the presence of those who bring joy to us.

Who comes to mind as you read this? Who will you schedule lunch, coffee, dinner, or a night out with so you can increase your joy by being in his/her presence?

_____

_____

_____

_____

_____

_____

_____

_____

Tweet

Increase your joy by scheduling time to be in the physical—not digital—presence of someone who brings you joy. #joy218ways

---

[1]   (DM) Direct Message, (IM) Instant Message, (PM) Private Message on social media

Joy in Healthy People Pleasing

I recently came across the saying, "I'm a recovering people pleaser. Is that ok?" While I'm not much of a people pleaser, with compassion, I know it's an exhausting cycle when it's your nature to be one. However, there are beautiful elements in people pleasers. My friends who have this personality trait are loving and outward-centered. In part, it's because their antennas are up reading how they are being perceived, but this characteristic also causes them to look around for ways they can show God's love to others. Like everything, it's about a healthy balance. Non-people pleasers have a strong sense of self, but they can become self-centered if they are left unchecked. Any strength we have becomes a weakness when it gets out of control.

Sometimes our motivation for doing things that are pleasing is to bring joy to our elders, teachers, parents, pastors, or mentors. When we make good choices and order our lives in a God-honoring way, we don't have to look left or right or over our shoulder because we have nothing to hide. As John wrote this letter to Gaius (v. 1), he must've had a light feeling at the thought of him because Gaius was doing the right things on a regular basis. His life choices caused others to notice, and they good-gossiped about him to John. While this probably wasn't the reason Gaius chose his actions, it was a byproduct. When we're tired of making good choices, dying to self, and purposefully living for God, let's keep in mind that people are noticing, and our lives are bringing them joy.

In your life, who brings you joy when he/she notices your spiritual progress? Send that person a note or make time to be together to celebrate your relationship.

Don't grow weary in doing well (Galatians 6:9). Someone is noticing the good you do and you are bringing joy to him/her. #joy218ways

— Joy of a Good Example —

My mom often said she wished she'd had more children. I, on the other hand, always wanted to be an only child. I wouldn't trade my brother and sisters for anything; it's only that I sort of wanted mom all to myself—but enough about me. My mom was a multiplier before that term was a thing. She instinctively brought out the best in people through her unconditional love. Her absolute belief that the person in front of her could be anything he/she wanted to be caused that person to stretch toward believing it, too. If you didn't have faith in yourself, she'd let you borrow hers until you got your own and began to wear it like a skin. She loved Jesus, and it was her joy to give people the eternal-hug of pointing them to His love. Nothing made her happier than seeing those she poured into taking strides toward their emotional and spiritual success.

I hear this same joy-filled pride in John's words to Gaius (v. 1). John modeled the Christian life to him, and Gaius wanted to emulate it. This God-designed model continues today. Other Christians—especially those younger in the faith—are always watching us and learning from us. Humbled by that knowledge, we need to pray we would never be a stumbling block in their faith walk. Like Paul, we want to be able to say, "Follow my example, as I follow the example of Christ" (1 Corinthians 11:1). Seeing the joy others have in Christ sets a good example for us—not only to follow, but also to multiply.

Who all would look at your life and say that your walk is bringing them great joy? Who, younger than you in the faith, brings you great joy as you watch him/her walking in the truth?

_____

_____

_____

_____

_____

_____

_____

_____

_____

_____

Other Christians (especially ones younger in the faith) watch us and learn. It's a joy to celebrate the faith walk of others! #joy218ways

Ensure You Are Secure —————— in Your Joy ——

Jude 1:24

—————————————————————————
—————————————————————————
—————————————————————————

We have a God who is able. He can handle anything we throw at Him, and He provides everything we need. He sent Jesus Christ to be the perfect, humanly understandable representation of Himself. The work that Jesus did on the cross is the sustaining joy of our lives. He keeps us from staying down when we stumble. Through the Holy Spirit, He picks us up and reminds us of who we can be. Our God is glorious, majestic, and powerful. He holds all authority in heaven and on earth. He is the Alpha and the Omega—the beginning and the end. Nothing was created except by His design, and nothing escapes the filter of His plan. He cares only to prosper us and is at work bringing good for those who love Him and are called according to His purpose. He equips us with everything we need to not only survive, but to thrive.

Our God wants to ensure that we are secure in our joy. The enemy whispers lies; the Lord proclaims the truth through His Word. The enemy accuses; Jesus defends. The enemy seeks to steal, kill, and destroy; the Holy Spirit equips with peace, power and prayer. We are a target to the enemy, but we are the beloved of our King. God is more than able to secure our joy if we're willing to keep ourselves in His love. Joy anchored to our identity as a child of this God is unstoppable. It cannot be shaken and it cannot be taken. This joy is pure and powerful, and for this we say, "Glory Up!"

Life will continue to happen, but as you stubbornly stay near your God, do you connect to the truth that nothing can take your joy?

—————————————————————————
—————————————————————————
—————————————————————————
—————————————————————————
—————————————————————————
—————————————————————————

Joy anchored to our identity as a child of God is unstoppable. This pure and powerful joy cannot be shaken and it cannot be taken. #joy218ways

—————— Joy Inventory ——————

Congratulations on finishing the project! I hope your study of joy has unlocked the understanding that joy is always yours. Take this quick inventory, then compare to the questions you answered on page ix. Celebrate your growth!

How would you define joy? _____

_____

_____

_____

_____

Circle the answer that best describes your current feeling for each statement. Don't overthink it; go with your gut.

1. I don't think too much about joy.
Strongly Agree   *Agree*   *Not Sure*   *Disagree*   *Strongly Disagree*

2. I feel joy only when everything is going well.
Strongly Agree   *Agree*   *Not Sure*   *Disagree*   *Strongly Disagree*

3. Joy is hard to come by.
Strongly Agree   *Agree*   *Not Sure*   *Disagree*   *Strongly Disagree*

4. Joy comes and goes.
Strongly Agree   *Agree*   *Not Sure*   *Disagree*   *Strongly Disagree*

5. I've tried to find joy through many means, but I feel overwhelmed, exhausted, and sometimes defeated because I still don't have it.
Strongly Agree   *Agree*   *Not Sure*   *Disagree*   *Strongly Disagree*

6. I feel like I'm seeing the world in more dimensions than I did at the beginning of this project.
Strongly Agree   *Agree*   *Not Sure*   *Disagree*   *Strongly Disagree*

7. I believe in God but He's not always where I go to find joy.
Strongly Agree   *Agree*   *Not Sure*   *Disagree*   *Strongly Disagree*

8. I am walking in joy more consistently now than when I started this project.
Strongly Agree   *Agree*   *Not Sure*   *Disagree*   *Strongly Disagree*

9. Joy is a choice.
Strongly Agree   *Agree*   *Not Sure*   *Disagree*   *Strongly Disagree*

10. I feel changed from having spent this time in God's Word.
Strongly Agree   *Agree*   *Not Sure*   *Disagree*   *Strongly Disagree*

Let's explore joy together! Join our Facebook group "218 Ways to Own Joy."

Index

C

Challenge to Joy
1, 3, 4, 6, 9, 23, 27, 28, 43, 53, 59, 77, 85, 86, 91, 97, 112, 120, 123, 124, 126, 127, 137, 139, 142, 144, 145, 146, 147, 148, 150, 152, 154, 155, 156

Christian Leaders
83, 125, 187, 190, 192, 193, 196, 198, 200, 209

Christ's Return
68, 117, 125, 131, 133, 176

Church
6, 13, 45, 49, 50, 65, 83, 84, 118, 120, 122, 125, 129, 187, 188, 190, 192, 196, 198, 209

Comfort/Discomfort
28, 44, 58, 120, 129, 142, 151, 156, 158, 164, 165, 171, 175, 181, 184, 188, 195, 199, 201, 211, 212, 213

Community
6, 146, 148, 180, 186, 187, 193, 200, 202, 203, 205

Comparing
32, 51, 72, 97, 118, 133, 164, 170

Condemnation
16, 17, 86, 97, 124, 129, 152, 154, 214

Confession
17, 54, 55, 76, 158, 165, 173, 213

Confidence
44, 51, 60, 72, 116, 154, 161, 162, 164, 169, 174, 177, 179, 180, 182, 183, 186, 188, 190, 209, 216, 217, 218

Conflict
1, 3, 4, 22, 25, 46, 74, 77, 85, 90, 110, 114, 147, 148, 149, 150, 158, 169, 175, 176, 178, 181, 184, 186, 187, 188, 189, 190, 191, 198, 201, 204, 210, 213

Consequences for Sin
1, 4, 12, 55, 58, 102, 109, 137, 139, 140, 141, 147, 148, 150, 151, 152, 153, 154, 173, 213, 214

Contentment
29, 35, 41, 43, 64, 80, 103, 133, 134, 136, 142, 157, 164, 197, 218

Control
13, 18, 22, 53, 77, 80, 89, 95, 96, 99, 139, 140, 151, 152, 154, 158, 159, 162, 170, 173, 175, 184, 189, 194, 198, 204, 208, 209, 214, 217

Corporate Joy
2, 5, 13, 15, 19, 20, 58, 59, 71, 83, 101, 114, 147, 153, 176, 180, 187, 190, 198

Surprising Joy
15, 22, 62, 87, 92, 103, 115, 125, 126, 137, 138, 142, 153, 158, 160, 161, 162, 163, 166, 167, 168, 183, 197, 215

T
Temptation
54, 55, 89, 90, 94, 102, 109, 111, 139, 141, 150, 152, 156, 162, 165, 170, 171, 172, 173, 174, 175, 181, 192, 193, 204, 210, 211, 213

Tests/Trials
12, 20, 22, 25, 28, 31, 33, 34, 36, 39, 42, 43, 46, 47, 48, 60, 63, 66, 67, 73, 74, 75, 79, 85, 86, 98, 112, 114, 115, 121, 124, 127, 132, 137, 143, 144, 145, 151, 155, 156, 157, 160, 162, 165, 169, 171, 172, 174, 175, 178, 181, 186, 188, 189, 198, 201, 204, 206, 208, 210, 212

Thankfulness
20, 29, 41, 44, 53, 64, 70, 76, 80, 103, 113, 122, 134, 158, 164, 166, 199

Time with God
3, 36, 37, 38, 41, 42, 45, 48, 65, 67, 78, 83, 92, 99, 107, 130, 138, 144, 171, 172, 174, 175, 177, 179, 194, 207, 211

Tiredness
42, 96, 165, 179, 188, 210

Trinity
167, 207, 218

Trusting God
1, 5, 6, 8, 9, 13, 15, 20, 22, 25, 28, 31, 33, 39, 40, 42, 43, 46, 47, 54, 58, 59, 60, 62, 63, 69, 73, 74, 75, 79, 82, 90, 91, 97, 98, 110, 111, 114, 115, 116, 117, 123, 126, 127, 128, 132, 133, 137, 142, 143, 144, 145, 147, 149, 153, 155, 158, 160, 162, 164, 167, 170, 172, 173, 174, 177, 180, 181, 190, 192, 201, 204, 208, 210, 212, 218

Truth
32, 52, 55, 95, 108, 128, 129, 134, 138, 147, 156, 159, 168, 176, 180, 182, 189, 193, 196, 198, 202, 211, 213, 214, 217, 218

U
Uniqueness
72, 100, 101, 111, 118, 129, 161, 168, 170, 202

Unselfishness
5, 23, 26, 87, 96, 120, 121, 131, 135, 146, 170, 181, 184, 185, 186, 192, 195, 197, 198, 199, 206, 216

V
Victories
12, 19, 20, 22, 39, 102, 114, 126, 155, 165, 166, 181, 200, 218

Vision
2, 15, 80, 176, 180, 187, 190, 204, 207, 214

W
Waiting
13, 14, 15, 22, 25, 28, 40, 43, 47, 48, 60, 63, 74, 75, 80, 90, 92, 95, 98, 104, 115, 124, 126, 127, 128, 132, 133, 145, 149, 160, 162, 174, 175, 176, 189, 204, 208, 210

Wickedness
4, 22, 54, 55, 89, 91, 94, 109, 114, 116, 137, 139, 151, 152, 153, 159, 173, 213

Wisdom
2, 11, 39, 61, 69, 88, 94, 95, 102, 108, 131, 144, 147, 148, 155, 159, 167, 171, 174, 177, 184, 187, 190, 193, 200, 208

Witnessing
8, 19, 21, 24, 26, 49, 56, 71, 84, 96, 99, 100, 107, 108, 111, 112, 119, 120, 121, 131, 135, 147, 148, 153, 158, 159, 161, 163, 166, 167, 169, 176, 180, 181, 182, 183, 185, 196, 197, 199, 200, 201, 202, 203, 214, 216, 217, 218

Work
103, 104, 142, 163, 166, 169, 190, 211, 216

Worry
9, 25, 28, 34, 36, 39, 48, 60, 63, 66, 74, 88, 105, 106, 110, 117, 121, 123, 142, 155, 160, 162, 165, 169, 171, 174, 175, 176, 179, 186, 188, 204, 206, 208, 210, 212

Worship
6, 7, 38, 45, 50, 65, 67, 68, 70, 71, 83, 112, 113, 118, 119, 164, 169, 196, 207, 212, 218

Y
Young People
2, 88, 97, 99, 104, 136, 193, 204, 217